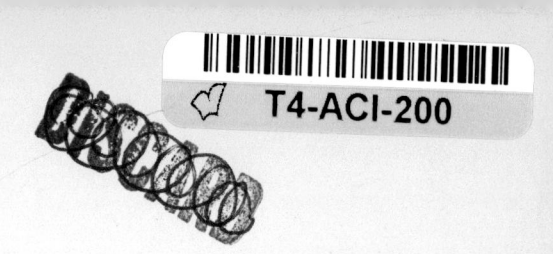

SEEING PENNSYLVANIA
THIRD IMPRESSION

By JOHN T. FARIS

SEEING THE MIDDLE WEST
Colored frontispiece and 90 illustrations in doubletone.

A fascinating journey through that great inland empire of amazing cities and thriving farm lands.

SEEING THE EASTERN STATES
Colored frontispiece and 90 illustrations in halftone.

Tells of and pictures the historic states from Maine to Delaware. Replete with scenic interest, story and legend.

SEEING THE SUNNY SOUTH
115 illustrations. Frontispiece in color.

It covers everything of interest in houses, roads, traditions, sports, entertaining stories and historical anecdotes about the different places.

SEEING THE FAR WEST
113 illustrations and 2 maps. Octavo.

A wonderful panorama in text and illustrations of the scenic glories from the Rockies to the Pacific.

SEEING PENNSYLVANIA
Frontispiece in color, 113 illustrations in doubletone and 2 maps. Octavo.

A rare and fascinating guide to an American wonderland which all Americans should know.

THE ROMANCE OF OLD PHILADELPHIA
Frontispiece in color and 101 illustrations in doubletone. Decorated cloth. Octavo.

OLD ROADS OUT OF PHILADELPHIA
117 illustrations and a map. Decorated cloth. Octavo.

By THEODOOR De BOOY and JOHN T. FARIS

THE VIRGIN ISLANDS
OUR NEW POSSESSIONS AND
THE BRITISH ISLANDS
97 illustrations and five maps especially prepared for this work. Octavo.

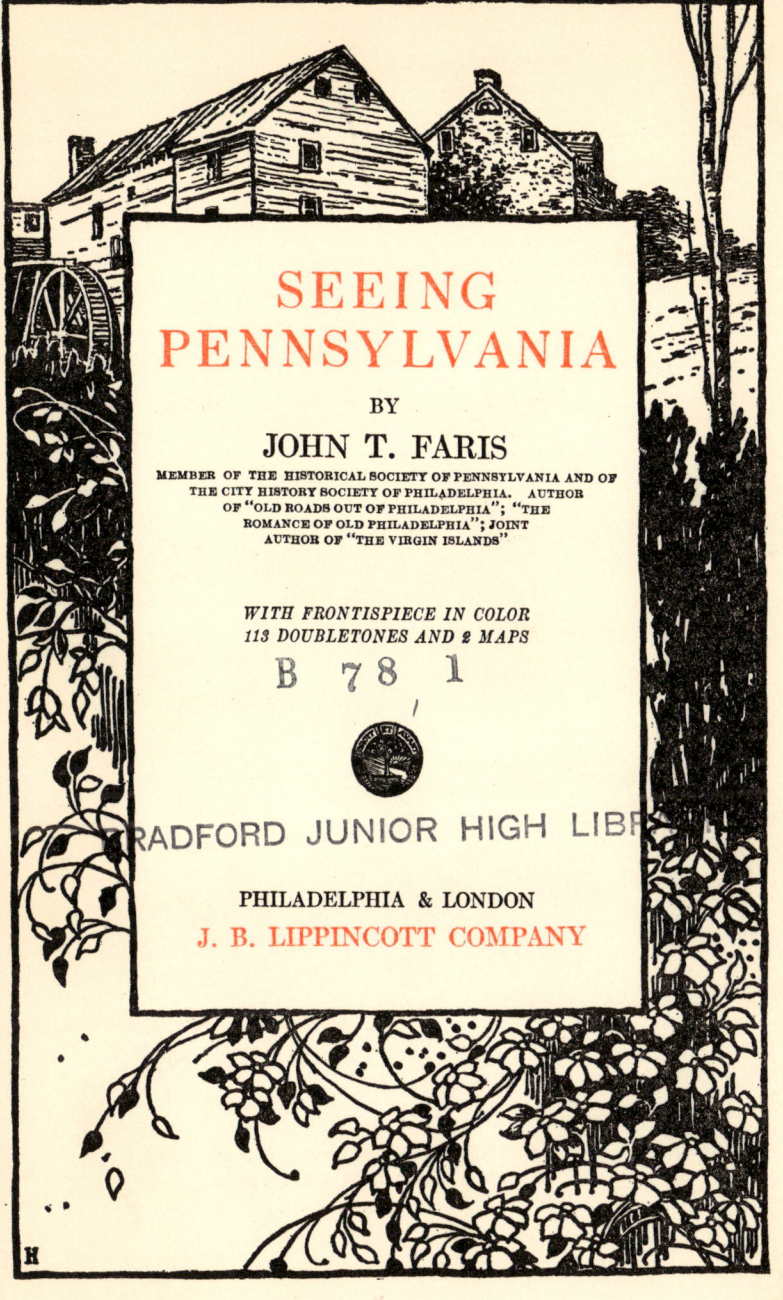

SEEING PENNSYLVANIA

BY

JOHN T. FARIS

MEMBER OF THE HISTORICAL SOCIETY OF PENNSYLVANIA AND OF THE CITY HISTORY SOCIETY OF PHILADELPHIA. AUTHOR OF "OLD ROADS OUT OF PHILADELPHIA"; "THE ROMANCE OF OLD PHILADELPHIA"; JOINT AUTHOR OF "THE VIRGIN ISLANDS"

WITH FRONTISPIECE IN COLOR
113 DOUBLETONES AND 2 MAPS

PHILADELPHIA & LONDON
J. B. LIPPINCOTT COMPANY

COPYRIGHT, 1919, BY J. B. LIPPINCOTT COMPANY

PRINTED BY J. B. LIPPINCOTT COMPANY
AT THE WASHINGTON SQUARE PRESS
PHILADELPHIA, U. S. A.

TO
A LOVER OF NATURE
MY WIFE

Let me view thee once again,
Fair, though rugged, Land of Penn.
Fondly now my mem'ry clings
To thy cool and limpid springs,
Forest glades and babbling brooks,
Sunny spots and shady nooks,
Rocky glens and mountains green,
Glistening in their summer sheen,
Miles of multi-colored trees
Bending to the autumn breeze,
Mountain ridges wreathed in snow
With the sunshine all aglow,
Till my spirit breaks control
And stirs the longings of my soul.
Land that soothed the savage breast—
Bent its will to love's behest,
Trusting in the powers above,
Preaching peace and God is love.
Land where monarch power was shorn,
Land where Liberty was born.

—William Bauchop Wilson.

PREFACE

It seems strange that the wonderful scenic features of Pennsylvania, like its remarkable historic interests, have received so little attention from those who write of the beautiful world and of the things that happen in it. Apart from a few well-known scenes, like the Horseshoe Curve, the Delaware Water Gap, and the lake at Eaglesmere, comparatively little is known of the revelations in store for the traveler who goes up and down and to and fro in the state. Just so most of those whose theme is the picturesque or the remarkable in local history have passed by the state in their search for subjects, with the exception, of course, of some outstanding events with which nearly everybody is familiar. An examination of the files of the magazines for many years past, as well as the more recent numbers of the travel periodicals and the journals devoted to history, shows that Pennsylvania has not yet come into its own; for some reason greater recognition is given to other sections of the country, including states near by. These states are altogether worthy of the attention paid to them. But why is so little said of Pennsylvania?

Many even of those who live in the state have scant idea of the wonders there are off the beaten track of travel, and of the riches of historic lore waiting to be uncovered. In the spirit of the traveler who longs to share with someone else a new beauty he has found, or of the reader who is not content until he has asked a friend to enjoy with him a treasure discovered in a book, the author of "Seeing

SEEING PENNSYLVANIA

Pennsylvania" covets the privilege of sharing the joys Pennsylvania has been giving him, an adopted son, with others not natives of the state, as well as with those who have spent a lifetime within its borders.

For the pleasure of readers, as well as for the convenience of those who may wish to take the trips outlined herein, the state has been described in connection with eight distinct routes which may be traced on the map in this volume. Every county in the state is entered by one of the routes, a few counties by several routes. Each route is practicable for the automobile or for the foot traveler. Those who use the railroad will be able approximately to cover the ground described.

The map of Pennsylvania printed in this volume is based on the road map of the National Highways Association. Additions have been made to it from the map of the State Highway Department. The relief map is copied (by courtesy of the Philadelphia Commercial Museum) from the volume, "Pennsylvania and its Manifold Activities," by Guy C. Whidden and Wilfred H. Schoff.

Portions of the routes described can be covered in a delightful manner, on foot or by trolley or by railroad. Among the many trips of varying length the following are suggested:

From Washington to Waynesburg.

From Altoona to Bedford, and from Bedford to Huntingdon.

From Tyrone to Clearfield and Curwensville.

From Jersey Shore up Pine Creek.

From Wellsboro to Antrim.

Along the various railroad lines of north-central Pennsylvania. These are designed as coal carriers,

PREFACE

little provision being made for passenger traffic; yet they lead through some of the most delightful sections of the state.

From Wilmington to Reading.

From Montrose to Scranton and Wilkes-Barre by trolley.

By trolley through parts of Berks, Lebanon, Dauphin and Lancaster Counties.

From Wilkes-Barre down the Susquehanna to Sunbury, Harrisburg, Columbia, and Perryville, Maryland.

Up the Delaware from Philadelphia to Stroudsburg, by highway to Port Jervis, New York, along the Delaware to Binghamton and back to Philadelphia by rail, or on to Sayre, New York, and thence to Philadelphia.

Along the West Branch of the Susquehanna from Harrisburg to Williamsport, Lock Haven and beyond.

From Scranton to Hawley direct and return by way of Honesdale.

The trips for vacation days are numberless. An examination of trolley guides and of the time cards of "feeders" of the Reading, the Pennsylvania, the Lehigh Valley, the Lackawanna, the Erie, and the New York Central will provide suggestions for years.

Without the assistance of many lovers of Pennsylvania it would have been impossible to write this volume or to gather the photographs from which the illustrations have been made. Acknowledgment of indebtedness is made to the volumes named in the Bibliography, as well as to scores of histories of sections, counties, cities, towns, and boroughs. Access has been given to these at the library of the Historical Society of Pennsylvania, made available by the unfailing courtesy of Mr. Ernest H. Spofford, the assistant librarian.

The author's grateful acknowledgments are due to Henry van Dyke, Hamlin Garland, Bliss Carman, and to George H. Doran & Co., publishers for Joyce Kilmer, who gave his life in France in July, 1918, for hearty permission to use poems quoted in this volume; also to Katherine Mayo, author of "The Standard Bearers," and to Houghton, Mifflin & Co., for permission to tell the story of "John G," as well as for additional facts supplied by her.

Special mention should be made of the delightful books by Col. Henry W. Shoemaker, who has written so appreciatively of his native central Pennsylvania highlands. Quotations have been made from these in many instances; again they have furnished inspiration for paragraphs that may perhaps give more than a surface hint of the original source. This is true also of some of the local histories consulted. Whenever it has been possible to tell of indebtedness, this has been done.

Generous assistance in securing photographs and information has been given by Mr. George H. Biles and Mr. George G. Hatter of the State Highway Department; by Mr. Robert S. Conklin and Mr. George H. Wirt of the State Department of Forestry; by Mr. Guy E. Mitchell of the United States Geological Survey; by Mrs. Julia Mifflin Donnelly of the State Museum at Harrisburg; by Rev. William F. Klein of Reading, and by many others whose courteous interest and coöperation have made a pleasant task yet more pleasant.

JOHN T. FARIS

PHILADELPHIA, AUGUST, 1919

CONTENTS

		PAGE
	PREFACE.................................	3
	LOOK AT THE MAP!......................	15
ROUTE I	ALONG THE LINCOLN HIGHWAY,...........	22
	FROM PHILADELPHIA TO PITTSBURGH	
ROUTE II	BY THE NATIONAL ROAD,................	77
	FROM PHILADELPHIA TO WHEELING AND PITTSBURGH	
ROUTE III	FROM PHILADELPHIA TO PITTSBURGH,....	124
	BY WAY OF READING, HARRISBURG AND THE WILLIAM PENN HIGHWAY	
ROUTE IV	THROUGH THE PENNSYLVANIA HIGHLANDS,	166
	FROM HARRISBURG TO OLEAN AND ELMIRA, NEW YORK, AND BACK TO HARRISBURG, BY WAY OF WILKES-BARRE	
ROUTE V	ALONG EASTERN WATERWAYS.............	212
	THE ANTHRACITE COUNTRY AND THE POCONO PLATEAU	
ROUTE VI	FROM PITTSBURGH TO LAKE ERIE AND BACK..................................	268
ROUTE VII	THROUGH THE OIL REGION AND SKIRTING THE FOREST COUNTRY.................	287
	A ROUND TRIP FROM PITTSBURGH.............	
ROUTE VIII	THROUGH THE HEART OF THE BLACK FOREST.................................	135
	A ROUND TRIP TO THE NORTH OF ALTOONA	
	BIBLIOGRAPHY...........................	336

ILLUSTRATIONS

	PAGE
SEPTEMBER SUNSHINE, NEAR READING................*Frontispiece*	
From the Painting by Edward Stratton Holloway	
ON BELMONT PLATEAU, FAIRMOUNT PARK. SCHUYLKILL RIVER AND BUSINESS SECTION OF PHILADELPHIA IN DISTANCE..............	24
Photo by Bell & Fischer	
VALLEY GREEN BRIDGE, WISSAHICKON DRIVE....................	24
Photo by J. Horace McFarland Company	
ON THE WISSAHICKON...	25
Photo by Frank Sjostrom	
IN VALLEY FORGE PARK.......................................	28
Photo from Philadelphia & Reading Railroad	
A LANCASTER COUNTY LANDSCAPE, NEAR GAP.....................	29
Photo by Miss L. A. Sampson	
ICE CAKES ON THE SHORE AT MCCALL'S FERRY, SUSQUEHANNA RIVER	29
Photo by United States Geological Survey	
LOOKING UP THE SUSQUEHANNA RIVER TOWARD PENNSYLVANIA, FROM BALTIMORE & OHIO RAILROAD BRIDGE, PERRYVILLE, MARYLAND.	50
Photo by United States Geological Survey	
A PENNSYLVANIA SUGAR MAPLE TREE............................	51
Photo by State Department of Forestry	
VIEW FROM LITTLE ROUND TOP, GETTYSBURG BATTLEFIELD. (WARREN STATUE ON ROCK)..	51
Photo from Philadelphia & Reading Railroad	
MONUMENT ON THE SITE OF THE BIRTHPLACE OF PRESIDENT JAMES BUCHANAN, FULTON COUNTY...............................	64
Photo by Lloyd M. Smith	
WEBSTER MILLS BRIDGE, FULTON COUNTY........................	64
Photo by State Highway Department	
ALONG THE RAYSTOWN JUNIATA, NEAR EVERETT...................	65
Photo by Lloyd M. Smith	
BUTTERMILK FALLS, LIGONIER..................................	72
Photo by W. T. Brown	
SUSPENSION BRIDGE ON FOUR MILE RUN, NEAR LIGONIER.	72
Photo by W. T. Brown	
OHIO, ALLEGHENY AND MONONGAHELA RIVERS, PITTSBURGH, FROM SOUTH SIDE	73
Photo by John C. Bragdon	
IN THE HEART OF PHILADELPHIA, FROM RITTENHOUSE SQUARE	78
Photo by Bell & Fischer	
SYCAMORE MILLS, NEAR MEDIA.................................	79
Photo by J. E. Green	

ILLUSTRATIONS

On Ridley Creek at Irving's Mills, Chester.................. 79
    Photo by J. E. Green
Stone Bridge crossing the Cocalico, near Ephrata. (Built in
    1800).. 86
    Photo from Philadelphia & Reading Railroad
Along Swatara Creek... 87
    Photo by J. Horace McFarland Company
Susquehanna River at Harrisburg............................ 96
    Photo by State Department of Forestry
A Peep into the Valley, Cumberland County................. 96
    Photo by State Department of Forestry
The only Stone Tollhouse on the National Highway still
    standing in Pennsylvania, at Addison..................... 97
    Photo by State Highway Department
Old Viaduct across Toms Creek on Tapeworm Railroad...... 97
    Photo by State Department of Forestry
The Great Meadows, with Fort Necessity outlined in Center 106
    Photo by James Hudden
Washington's Mill, owned by Washington at the time of his
    Death, Built 1776. (Still standing, twelve miles north
    of Uniontown)... 106
    Photo supplied by Dr. F. C. Robinson
Turkey's Nest Bridge, Fayette County...................... 107
    Photo supplied by Robert Bruce
In Washington County.. 107
    Photo by State Highway Department
Waterfall on Ravine Tributary to Meigs Creek, Washington
    County... 120
    Photo by State Highway Department
Over the Greene County Hills............................... 120
    Photo by State Highway Department
In Jenkintown.. 124
    Photo from Philadelphia & Reading Railroad
On the Perkiomen at Collegeville........................... 125
    Photo from Philadelphia & Reading Railroad
Valley Creek, near Valley Forge............................ 130
    Photo by Miss L. A. Sampson
On the Road to Valley Forge................................ 130
    Photo by Miss L. A. Sampson
The Golf Club at Wernersville.............................. 131
    Photo by J. Horace McFarland Company
Old Cornwall Furnace.. 131
    Photo from Philadelphia & Reading Railroad
Near Rutherford.. 134
    Photo by J. Horace McFarland Company
Rockville Bridge over the Susquehanna, near Harrisburg 134
    Photo by J. Horace McFarland Company

ILLUSTRATIONS

The Ravine, Cove Forge, near the Mouth of the Juniata.... 135
    Photo by J. Horace McFarland Company
The Road to Mifflintown................................... 140
    Photo by State Highway Department
Along the Juniata... 140
    Photo by State Highway Department
Jack's Narrows, from Mount Union Bridge................... 141
    Photo by State Department of Forestry
Juniata River, Mifflin County.............................. 141
    Photo by State Department of Forestry
Arch Spring, near Birmingham.............................. 148
    Photo supplied by Dr. Alvin R. Grier, Birmingham School
Old Stone Arch, Plane Number Ten, Portage Railroad, near
    Duncansville 148
    Photo by Stouffer
Stone Sleepers, Fourteen Mile Level, Old Portage Railroad
    Looking toward Mineral Point........................... 149
    Photo by Stouffer
At Saltsburg on the Kiskiminetas........................... 149
    Photo supplied by Dr. A. W. Wilson, Kiskiminetas School
In the Hemlock Forest....................................... 192
    Photo by State Department of Forestry
Valley View toward Tivoli................................... 192
    Photo by J. Horace McFarland Company
Ruins of Ole Bull's Castle, Oleona........................ 193
    Photo by State Department of Forestry
Asaph Nursery... 193
    Photo by State Department of Forestry
Lumbering in Potter County................................. 198
    Photo supplied by Boyd S. Rothrock, Curator Pennsylvania State Museum
The Chemung River, near Athens............................ 199
    Photo from Lehigh Valley Railroad
Homet's Ferry, near Wyalusing.............................. 204
    Photo from Lehigh Valley Railroad
On the Susquehanna, West of Falls......................... 205
    Photo from Lehigh Valley Railroad
On the Way to Eaglesmere, Columbia County................ 210
    Photo by J. Horace McFarland Company
On the Susquehanna, near Danville......................... 211
    Photo copyrighted by Detroit Publishing Co.
Looking toward Mount Penn, Reading........................ 214
    Photo by State Department of Forestry
Near Berne, Berks County................................... 215
    Photo from Philadelphia & Reading Railroad
A Bend in the Schuylkill River............................. 218
    Photo from Philadelphia & Reading Railroad
Near Pottsville... 218
    Photo from Philadelphia & Reading Railroad

ILLUSTRATIONS

Along the Schuylkill Canal.................................... 219
    Photo from Philadelphia & Reading Railroad
Ringtown, from Shenandoah Mountain....................... 226
    Photo from Philadelphia & Reading Railroad
Mountain Stream above Buck Hill Falls..................... 227
    Photo from Lehigh Valley Railroad
Within Delaware Water Gap, Looking from the right bank 232
    Photo by the Kirkton Studios
Delaware Water Gap from the Southeast (Delaware River near Manunka Chunk in the foreground)................. 233
    Photo by United States Geological Survey
Looking up the River, Delaware Water Gap................. 236
Sugar Maple Avenue on State Road, near Echo Lake........ 236
    Photo by State Department of Forestry
Peck's Dam, Pike County...................................... 237
    Photo by State Department of Forestry
Falls on Dingman's Creek in Childs' Park.................. 237
    Photo by State Highway Department
Valley View North of Honesdale............................. 244
    Photo by State Highway Department
Abingdon Hills, Lackawanna County......................... 245
    Photo by Horgan
Near Montrose.. 248
    Photo by Horgan
Nicholson Viaduct, Wyoming County......................... 249
    Photo by State Highway Department
Salt Lick on Wharton Creek, Lackawanna County........... 249
    Photo by State Highway Department
Horseshoe Curve, Nay Aug Valley........................... 250
    Photo by Horgan
Wilkes-Barre Colliery, Pittston............................ 251
    Photo from Lehigh Valley Railroad Company
Glen Summit Springs... 252
    Photo from Lehigh Valley Railroad Company
View from Flagstaff Mountain, Mauch Chunk................ 253
    Photo from Philadelphia & Reading Railway Company
Glen Onoko... 256
    Photo from Lehigh Valley Railroad Company
Along the Lehigh, near Allentown........................... 257
    Photo by The Kirkton Studios
Delaware River and Canal.................................... 262
    Photo from Philadelphia & Reading Railroad
Delaware River, near Easton................................ 263
    Photo from Philadelphia & Reading Railroad
Six Miles East of Doylestown............................... 266
    Photo by the Clay Studio
Neshaminy Falls.. 266
    Photo from Philadelphia & Reading Railroad

ILLUSTRATIONS

BEAVER... 274
    Photo by John C. Bragdon
JORDAN RUN, ERIE COUNTY.................................... 275
    Photo by State Department of Forestry
PENETRATION ROAD IN MERCER COUNTY.......................... 275
    Photo by State Highway Department
ON THE ROAD IN CRAWFORD COUNTY............................ 276
    Photo by State Highway Department
AFTER A FRESHET IN LAWRENCE COUNTY........................ 276
    Photo by State Highway Department
OVER THE HILLS AND FAR AWAY............................... 277
    Photo by J. Horace McFarland Company
IN THE RAVINE, NEAR PITTSBURGH............................ 277
    Photo by State Highway Department
ON THE SHENANGO, NEAR GREENVILLE.......................... 286
    Photo by State Highway Department
THE CONOQUONESSING, NEAR FRISCO, BEAVER COUNTY............ 287
    Photo copyrighted by Detroit Publishing Company
IN VENANGO COUNTY... 290
    Photo by State Highway Department
UNLOADING LOGS FOR THE MILL, FOREST COUNTY................ 290
    Photo by State Department of Forestry
LITTLE BROKENSTRAW CREEK, WARREN COUNTY................... 291
    Photo by State Highway Department
ALLEGHENY RIVER, WARREN................................... 291
    Photo by State Department of Forestry
THE START OF A FOREST FIRE................................ 298
    Photo by State Department of Forestry
PINE ROCKS, BETWEEN BEECH CREEK AND RENOVO................ 298
    Photo by State Department of Forestry
TWO MILES SOUTHEAST OF CLEARFIELD......................... 299
    Photo by C. W. Howard
ON THE ROAD FROM TIONESTA TO CLARION...................... 304
    Photo by State Department of Forestry
ON THE PLATEAU BETWEEN CLEARFIELD AND PENFIELD............ 305
    Photo by State Department of Forestry
GAP IN BALD EAGLE MOUNTAIN, LOOKING NORTH FROM BELLEFONTE 316
    Photo by the Mallory Studio
WHERE CLEARFIELD GETS HER DRINKING WATER. (MONTGOMERY
    DAM, FIVE MILES UP ON THE MOUNTAIN).................... 317
    Photo by C. W. Howard
HIGHWAY BRIDGE ACROSS ELK CREEK, NEAR RIDGWAY............. 320
    Photo by State Highway Department
OLD HIGHWAY BRIDGE, NEAR BRADFORD......................... 320
    Photo by State Highway Department
FIRST FORK OF SINNEMAHONING, NEAR COSTELLO................ 321
    Photo by State Department of Forestry
BEECH CREEK, CLINTON COUNTY............................... 328
    Photo by State Department of Forestry

ILLUSTRATIONS

On the Black Moshannon, Center County.................... 328
    Photo by State Department of Forestry
On the Road to Brush Valley Narrows, Center County..... 329
    Photo by State Highway Department
Penn's Valley, looking toward Boalsburg.................... 329
    Photo by State Department of Forestry
Along the Juniata, Huntingdon County....................... 332
    Photo from Birmingham School

MAPS

Relief Map of Pennsylvania................................. 16
Map of Routes Suggested in this Volume....................End

The Cover Design is a view of the Allegheny River from
Kinzua Hill, Warren County.

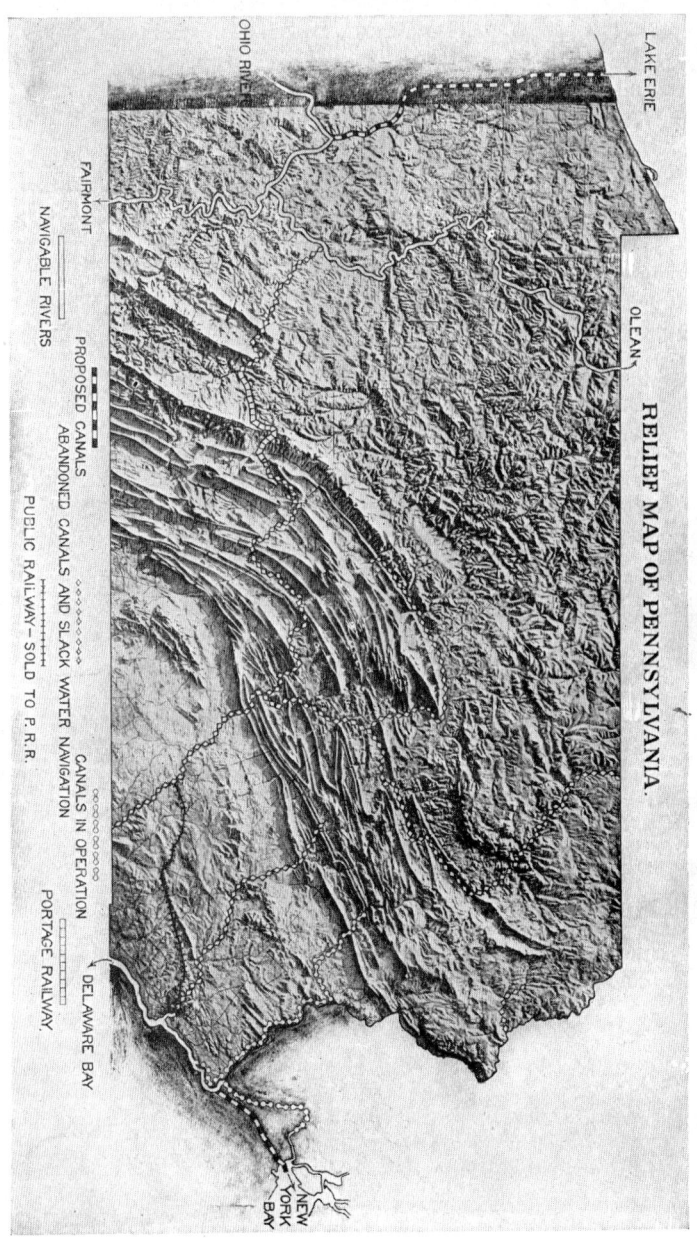

RELIEF MAP OF PENNSYLVANIA
By Courtesy of the Pennsylvania Commercial Museum

SEEING PENNSYLVANIA

LOOK AT THE MAP!

ONCE upon a time there was a successful teacher in the South who won local fame because he taught geography without maps. He did this because maps were scarce and money with which to buy them was even scarcer. He was quite successful, too. But he would have been the first to own that success would have been far greater if he had been able to place maps in the hands of his pupils.

Now it is still possible to learn something of geography without map study. But when maps are so cheap and so good, why make the attempt? To be sure, there are some maps which can have little interest for those who are not making a specialty of work in geography, and it may not be such a loss to pass these by. There are maps, however, that are as interesting as a romance, and it is a pity to deprive oneself of the pleasure of reading these.

For instance, there is the map of Pennsylvania, one of the most eloquent of maps. It has a delightful message for Americans, not only because Pennsylvania has had a wonderful part in the history of the nation (think of the Declaration of Independence, of Valley Forge, of Washington's crossing of the Delaware, of Gettysburg, the decisive battle of the Civil War, and of scores of other events of national significance), but also because it carries on its face the heartiest sort of invitation to explore majestic mountains, fascinating river valleys, and deep, dark forests where once the Indian hunted the buffalo and the elk.

Two maps are needed. One of these should present clearly the counties, the rivers, the highways, and the railways. It is good to refer to such a map now and then, but it is far better to make it a daily companion, a familiar friend—to take it from the pocket when reading the newspaper, or to keep it before the eye for study in connection with the railway time-table or the automobile route-book. One reason sight-seeing from the railway train becomes wearisome is because the traveler seldom has a map at hand which tells of the region through which the road leads; or, at best, he has nothing but the distorted, unreliable map in the time-table, which is content to show the particular railroad in use at the moment as the shortest line between two points. But what a difference when there is at hand a folding map such as can be bought readily for twenty-five cents!

The best way to convince the reader of the attractiveness and suggestiveness of the map of Pennsylvania is to show it right here, that those who see it may revel in what J. P. Lesley has called its "symmetrical, compound, and complicated curves." In the boundaries of the state there is just enough departure from the straight line to show the truth of the words quoted. There is, for instance, the Circle Line at the southeast corner, which forms the northern boundary of Delaware. There is a story behind that circle. Then one notes the Triangle in the northwest corner. Another story! We look at the southwest corner, and wonder why there was not at this point a third departure from the rectilinear, so as to include West Virginia's famous Panhandle and reach out to the Ohio River, which would seem the natural boundary. Story number three!

The eye is attracted by the sweeping curves and sharp turns of the Delaware River, which forms the eastern boundary, and the observer is startled to note the almost exact correspondence of the North Branch of the Susquehanna River in its course from the northern line of the state to Northumberland, where it helps to form the main Susquehanna; and the further fact that the two rivers, though close together in the north, keep far apart across the state, while they are once more within a few miles of each other when they cross the southern boundary.

For the explanation of this striking parallel in direction of flow it is necessary only to study the relief map of Pennsylvania, with its story of the Susquehanna's search for a passage through the mountains that again and again bar its passage to the sea. This map also should be a companion during the study of a state that can equal or surpass the best scenery in England, in Ireland, in Scotland, or in France, with many added beauties to which nothing in those countries can be compared.

The relief map shows further that the only navigable streams in the state are in western Pennsylvania; that the railway engineers faced most difficult problems as they sought passage from the east to the west; and that three-fourths of the surface is highland territory of such attractive contour that it is no wonder the Indians from the North made it their vacation ground, as so many of those who have displaced them are taking vacations there to-day. The attraction which the valleys of the Delaware and the Susquehanna had for the native American is appreciated by Agnes Repplier; she says that if ever Americans—blotted out in their turn, as they have blotted out the Red men—are destined to live on reservations as the Indians live now, "may Pennsylvania be the allotted territory!"

Another glance at the relief map shows that Pennsylvania is divided naturally into three parts. There is the southeastern district of valleys and hills; a central mountain belt of symmetrical sweep whose parallel ranges enclose numberless narrow valleys; and a rolling table land which becomes a plain as it approaches Lake Erie. The combination of these three sections presents, as one scientist has pointed out, a variety hardly equaled in any other state.

The mountain region has, ready to disclose to the sympathetic traveler, a series of surprises that will keep his gaze transfixed, all the way from Somerset County in the southwest to the border of Wayne County in the northeast. The rocky, tree-covered mountains are, in general, about two thousand feet high, though many ridges are higher. They extend for 270 miles, if they are followed along their sinuous course. For one hundred and fifty miles the traveler is within their portals if he seeks to cross them by the Pennsylvania Railroad. Yet the thirteen principal ridges which traverse the state might be crossed in less than fifty miles from Tyrone to Carlisle—that is, if there were a road that way. But the traveler must follow the example of the Indian and the engineer, and choose a path that leads through one of the marvelous water gaps, as, for instance, the Delaware Gap, or that in Sharp Mountain, or through Blue

LOOK AT THE MAP

Mountain, or through Jack's Mountain; or he may go by one of the less pronounced wind gaps to and from which so many routes of travel converge.

However the mountains may forbid passage in some directions, they invite it in others. The ravines made by the North Branch, the Muncy Creek, the Lycoming, Pine Creek, the West Branch, and Beech Creek, are used both by railways and by highways, and this is one explanation of the attraction of travel in Pennsylvania. Such passages, it has been said, "offer the only avenues of connection with the northwest part of the state and between central Pennsylvania and New York state."

Still other river valleys present unrivaled opportunities for studying the state—the Delaware, the Schuylkill, the Lehigh, the Youghiogheny, the Juniata, the Conemaugh, the Allegheny. Who follows these streams with eyes open has presented to him a series of pictures of such rare beauty that he would not find it difficult to enter into the feelings of the nature-lover who declared that, if he knew he must soon lose his sight, he would not ask better preparation for the days of darkness than a series of tours through the valleys and mountains, the fields and forests of Pennsylvania.

It is remarkable that territory so broken by mountains is so well covered by transportation routes. There are, indeed, large tracts in the bituminous coal regions where railroads have not yet been built, as there are still entire townships and even large sections of counties through which there are no roads fit for the traveler. Yet it is possible to indicate a series of eight routes that enter or traverse every county in a state which is, in the words of an enthusiastic traveler, "so wildly and nobly beautiful that in Europe it would attract the tourists of the world."

Even the names of the towns and streams encountered in taking these attractive tours through the state awaken interest. Canoe Camp, Snow Shoe, Warrior's Mark, Standing Stone, Cornplanter, Young Woman's Creek, Elk City, Pitch Pine, Buffalo Creek —each of these has a story to tell to sympathetic ears. The names of the counties repay study; they tell of settlers who remembered England and Wales, of the Indian tribes who held on to the country until they could hold on no longer, of Revolutionary leaders and early statesmen who helped to win the state for later generations or strengthened the hands of those who sought to preserve the boon of liberty.

Then note the music of the names of some of the streams. There is the Shenango, the Conoquenessing, the Moshannon; the Wallenpaupack, the Swatara, and the Conococheague (pronounce it!); the Octoraro, the Conestoga, and the Sinnemahoning; the Kiskiminetas, the Pequea, and the Nescopeck. And they are all as attractive as their names!

Some of the romantic tales connected with these localities are well known; the stories of Bethlehem and the Moravians, and of Harmony and Economy and their peculiar people may be familiar friends, yet a reference to them in connection with these towns and cities is not unwelcome. But comparatively few remember about Prince Demetrius Gallitzin's town in Cambria County and Horace Greeley's colony in Pike County, or know of Ole Bull's tragic experiences in the wilds of Potter County, of the settlement of the French refugees at Asylum in Bradford County, of the dream of Samuel Taylor Coleridge and his

LOOK AT THE MAP

friends to found a community with wonderful laws somewhere on the banks of the Susquehanna, or of the way Williamson the colonist cut a road through the wilds of central Pennsylvania that he might reach the site of his settlement farther north.

The trips outlined in later chapters will lead to points made famous by these and other events, and will show the road to some of the marvels of Pennsylvania, all the way from the Delaware Water Gap to the forks of the Ohio, from Kinzua Viaduct to Great Meadows, from the Brandywine to the Youghiogheny, from Milford on the Delaware to Presque Isle on Lake Erie.

ROUTE I
ALONG THE LINCOLN HIGHWAY
FROM PHILADELPHIA TO PITTSBURGH
296 MILES

"WHO has not heard of Philadelphia? And to whom should not this preëminent city be known?"

This sentiment of an early visitor from Europe has been echoed by millions since the words were written in 1788.

"That pleasant city, Philadelphia," wrote another visitor who debated whether to wonder more at the checker-board plan of the city of Penn or at its superb seat between the two rivers and the wonderful country tributary to it. Those who have followed him in more modern days have felt that the characterization was as apt as it was brief.

The best possible preparation for a trip along the Lincoln Highway from Philadelphia to Pittsburgh will be found in a few days spent in a survey of Philadelphia. In this survey the first step may well be an ascent to the foot of the statue of William Penn. This rises above the City Hall to a height of 549 feet—but six feet less than the Washington monument. From the circular balcony it is possible to see on a clear day a rare panorama. To the east and south, beyond Camden, lie the rolling lands of New Jersey. To the southwest is the Delaware, ever widening as it reaches out toward the sea. Great ships float on the tide-swollen stream, and shipyards —among them the greatest establishment of the kind in the world—tell of other ships that soon will be ready to take the water. Across the romantic Schuylkill, and for miles beyond the teeming wards of West Philadelphia, lie, like a bit of rural England, the suburban districts of Philadelphia and the rich farmlands of Chester County. The completion of the circle brings into view the northwestward sweep of the Schuylkill, with Fairmount Park near at hand, while in the far distance glorious Valley Forge appears on the left bank, and Audubon's Perkiomen Creek meanders among the hills on the right. Then Chestnut Hill, Germantown, and Jenkintown lie at the portals of the glories of Montgomery County, where Washington and Lafayette led the heroes of the Revolution along roads consecrated by their steps, all the way from Coryell's Ferry to the Neshaminy, and from Whitemarsh on to Valley Forge.

Next, perhaps, will come a pilgrimage to the shrines of a city that belongs in a peculiar sense to all America; in fact to all the world that loves democracy—shrines so identified with those heroic days from Penn to Washington that their history means more than their architecture. Their glory, in the words of John Ruskin, is "in that deep sense of voicefulness, of stern watching, of mysterious sympathy, nay, even of approval or condemnation, which we feel in walls that have long been washed by the passing waves of humanity."

Rambles about the streets between the rivers will give an appetite for a day on the Delaware. First should come a steamer trip to the north, past Cramp's famous shipyard, and by Torresdale's pleasing shore —along that portion of the stream where John Fitch in 1787 made regular trips with the first successful

SEEING PENNSYLVANIA

steamboat. Then let there be a ride to the south, past League Island Navy Yard and Hog Island Shipbuilding Plant, whose erection was one of the wonders of a world accustomed to marvels; then on past Chester, where William Penn's ship *Welcome* sought the land.

The inviting reaches of the Schuylkill are best seen during a ride through Fairmount Park, whose thousands of acres abound in forest and meadow, in crag and glen, in beckoning pathway and roads that urge the wayfarer to seek new delights. In Fairmount it is always difficult to realize that one is in the playground of a great city; at every turn there is the feeling that the noise of the multitude is far away—until perhaps the noble vista from George's Hill opens out, or the slopes of Belmont Mansion or Lemon Hill disclose the gleaming Schuylkill and the city beyond. No wonder Richard Peters and John Penn, Samuel Breck and John McPherson, David Rittenhouse and Robert Morris gleefully turned from their labors in the city to their country homes on these hills, where they spent their hours of leisure in houses that are to-day among the treasures of Fairmount.

The glimpses of the river from the heights give a foretaste of what is in store for those who motor—or, better, walk—along the famous East River Drive and the enticing West Drive up to the spot where the remarkable Wissahickon enters the Schuylkill. Instead, however, of ascending the lower portion of this stream by the road that leads along the left bank, it is wise to go to Chestnut Hill and there take the street that ends in the leafy road whose abrupt descent shows the way to the dark upper glen through which

ON THE WISSAHICKON
Photo by Frank Sjostrom

ON BELMONT PLATEAU, FAIRMOUNT PARK
Schuylkill River and Business Section of Philadelphia in Distance
Photo by Bell & Fischer

VALLEY GREEN BRIDGE, WISSAHICKON DRIVE
Photo by J. Horace McFarland Company

the Wissahickon seeks the Schuylkill. Here, indeed, it seems impossible to credit the fact that the heart of bustling Philadelphia is only a few miles distant. Not a sound breaks the stillness but the gurgle of the rapidly descending water over the stones, or the voice of the birds in the trees whose branches arch the pathway. The steep ridge on either side of the stream is tree-clad to the summit. Now and again the ridges are broken by a gap, and through the little valley a tributary trickles into the waters of the creek by which mysterious hermits lived and daring patriots stole upon their enemies. Along this leafy path motors do not interfere with the pleasure of the pedestrian; those who use a machine must rest content with the ride along the lower miles of the Wissahickon's course—miles where is beauty abounding, though the beauty there is as nothing compared to that to be enjoyed by those who are willing to take a slower method of travel through what tourists who know their Europe say excels anything enthusiastic guides can show.

The ten miles by Wissahickon's side are ten miles of marvel and surprise. Every turn—and the glen is a succession of unexpected turns—discloses fresh charms: ledges that jut into the stream, trees that bend over the waters, shadows in the depths that repeat the beauties of the heights, bridges of varied design, from the great Walnut Lane viaduct to the stone arch at Valley Green, falls and cascades and pools that add glory to a prospect already so glorious that the observer holds his breath in wonder.

The only difficulty is that to see this crowning beauty of Fairmount is to long to see it again and yet again. But let it be seen ever so often, it cannot disappoint. And the visit may be paid at any hour, with results that add to cherished memories. The dewy morning, when the trees drop with moisture even while the sun shines serenely, seems to be the best time for the walk; until it is taken at noonday when the sun pierces the overshadowing trees, or in the late afternoon, when there is the gloom of twilight long before the sun sets, or during the full of the moon, when the soft lights and the deepened shadows give an air of mystery to a spot that could tell such strange tales of romance and adventure.

From out the glen a pleasing route leads across the Schuylkill, past Memorial Hall, memento of the Centennial Exposition, to Fifty-second Street, and then along a forgotten section of the Gulph road on which—almost within the city limits—are the ruins of one of the paper mills of colonial days and, by its side, a ford across the stream which supplied power to the mill. The way beyond the ford is up hill and down, and is, for a space, almost as primitive as it was in the days when Philadelphia was a colony. Soon, however, the better road is reached that leads through one after another of the garden-like suburbs until there appears what some appreciative travelers have called the "panorama road," because of the view afforded of the wide and varied stretch of country toward the Schuylkill and Norristown beyond.

There is little opportunity to regret the passage of the panorama, for almost at once the way leads to the boulder bearing the plate that tells of the passage of Washington and his little army to Valley Forge, then past Gulph Rock which stretches protectingly above the traveler to-day as it did at the time of the army's march—though it is true that one soldier wrote of this very rock as though it spoke of menace instead of protection.

After a few miles of travel through a charming countryside Valley Forge Park is spread out, with its miles of driveways along the old entrenchments, traces of which can still be seen, its many memorials erected by a grateful country, and its heights from which Valley Creek and the Schuylkill delight the eye.

Valley Forge Park is some distance to the north of the Lincoln Highway, but the Lancaster Pike may be reached at Paoli by a short ride over a pleasing road. Then come many miles of what was the first turnpike road in America, successor to the old Lancaster road, and the still earlier Conestoga road, whose beginning dates back to 1683. Every little while something speaks of the days of the wagoner and the stage driver—the milestones, restored to the places where they greeted the weary travelers of long ago, the taverns where entertainment was provided for man and beast, the hills (some of them steep enough to-day) whose slopes must have been a trial to the driver of the wagon laden with goods from Pittsburgh or the emigrant who toiled on foot toward the West that promised to make life worth while.

Warren Hill, beyond Malvern, leads into the Great Valley, one of the noteworthy landscapes of Chester County, and one of the most attractive features of a state presenting a long succession of views that reveal the futility of adjectives to describe and define. The valley is from two to three miles wide, and it crosses a section of the county from southeast to northwest. It is bounded by parallel hills whose slopes, now cultivated, now wooded, are a fitting frame to a region filled with tilled fields and luxuriant groves. This valley, with its encircling rim of hills, its villages and farm buildings, and its general air of prosperity, presents one of the most satisfying pictures to be seen in this or any land.

It is not difficult to understand how the residents of Downingtown in early days were so contented with this peaceful valley and their homes on the east branch of the historic Brandywine that they would not have the county seat, when this was to be moved from Chester, and other settlements were clamoring for what, perhaps, the Downingtowners might have had for the asking. No one in the town would sell a lot for the courthouse, and the seat of Chester County passed on to West Chester.

The rich lands of the county—which originally included Delaware County—were bought from the Indians in 1685. The red men, who had all confidence in William Penn, agreed to let him have the lands from Duck Creek to Chester Creek, "backwards as far as a man can ride in two days with a horse." The moderate territory later claimed under the terms of this loose agreement compares favorably with later purchases elsewhere, when similar indefinite provisions were made.

The historic two days' ride which fixed the western boundary of Chester County led past one more stream, the west branch of the Brandywine. Though the road crosses this creek at Coatesville, six miles from Downingtown and the crossing of the east branch, the two streams are but half a mile apart at their source in the Welsh Mountains, a few miles

A LANCASTER COUNTY LANDSCAPE, NEAR GAP
Photo by Miss L. A. Sampson

ICE CAKES ON THE SHORE AT MCCALL'S FERRY, SUSQUEHANNA RIVER
Photo by United States Geological Survey

IN VALLEY FORGE PARK
Photo from Philadelphia & Reading Railroad

north of Coatesville. The two creeks continue to be widely separated through their winding courses, until they meet five miles from Chadd's Ford, and not many miles from the site of the battle of the Brandywine, one of the noteworthy struggles of the Revolution.

Coatesville-on-the-Brandywine has for more than a century been famous for its iron and steel mills. It also clams distinction as the birthplace of Thomas Buchanan Read, the poet whose "Sheridan's Ride" has been spoken by schoolboys for half a century (though, as a matter of fact, the birthplace is located between Downingtown and Coatesville, at a point several miles north of the Lancaster road). Furthermore, Coatesville rejoices in surroundings so pleasant that one of its citizens is said to have remarked, in a spirit of utter satisfaction with his lot, "In the world to come, if Providence can give me a place as comfortable as Coatesville, I shall be content."

This steel town on the Brandywine has a setting that is a delight. It is partly in the valley of the stream, which is seen to advantage from either the highway bridge or the railway bridge, and it rises on the ridge that reaches away toward South Mountain. In the region south of the town Rokeby Furnace was built in 1793, the first rolling mill in America. The founder was the grandfather of A. F. Huston, whose great steel mills are to-day a dominating feature in the Coatesville landscape.

The glorious Chester Valley ends at Gap, where there is a natural portal through Mine Hill. On either side of the gap the hills rise some seven hundred feet. The tourist who looks back into the Chester Valley, then forward into the valley of Pequea Creek, will not find it difficult to understand why this is the central section of what was once known as the "Granary of America"—Chester, Lancaster, and York counties.

William Penn's interest in this country brought him this way more than once, and there is a witness to his presence on the roof of the frame structure that protects the William Penn Spring. The inscription records the fact and the date of one of his visits. No record is kept, however, of the presence in this region of the band of counterfeiters and outlaws known as the Gap Gang, who, in early days, terrorized the community as well as the adventurous travelers who sought the western country.

William Penn was not the only notable of colonial days who made his way from Philadelphia to the Gap. James Logan of Stenton once formed a company to work the Gap copper mine, two miles from the railway station. This was discovered in 1720, and was later developed during nearly a century and a half. It was a spring that led to the discovery of the vein, and at this spring the settlers marveled, because, as several of them testified in writing, "We have very often, when at the mines, put the blades of our knives into the water, which, in a few minutes, would be covered with copper."

With real modern spirit a company, formed in 1798 for the improvement of the mine, issued a prospectus in which the estimate was made that by the expenditure of $51,712 the property could be developed so as to make a profit of $81,288 the first year and $256,726 the second year. The fair promises were not fulfilled, as might have been expected.

For many years the Gap was famous as the possessor of the only nickel mine in the United States.

The first ore was marketed in 1863, and seven years later the product was worth $66,000.

The outlaws and the promoters who made headquarters at Gap had a worthy successor, so far as interest is concerned, in Reuben Chambers, who taught school in 1829 or 1830 at a place he called Bethania, south of the highway, toward Strasburg. His peculiarity was shown when he was beginning to think about getting married. Whenever he saw a young woman he thought would be suitable as a wife he would enter her name in a memorandum book. At length, when he had about twenty names, he began to get acquainted with them. And this was his method:

"I did not call upon the girls in the evening... I called in the daytime when they were at work or should be, .. I could generally make up my mind in one or two visits whether they would suit me or not."

As candidates proved unavailable he would cross off their names, at the same time adding others. Ultimately the book contained sixty names, all of them being erased in turn until but one was left. "I was then ready to marry," he wrote. "So I went to see her and told her I wanted to marry her and believed her the most suitable girl for me that I was acquainted with."

She married him!

Fifty years before this strange courtship Thomas Ambury passed this way and noted a striking feature of the landscape that has long been spoken of as a characteristic of Lancaster County rural life:

"The farmer pays more attention to the construction of the barn than the dwelling-house. The building is nearly as large as a country church ... and at the gable end of the building there are gates, so that a horse and cart can go straight through."

Another English visitor of the eighteenth century had an eye for the landscape rather than the buildings. To him the approach to Lancaster was marvelously pleasing, and he wrote:

"You can conceive nothing more beautifully romantic than the appearance of the country. The hills, bold, rounding, and lofty, are covered with wood to the very summit."

Lancaster is proud of its situation on the Conestoga, a stream called by a local historian "one of the most beautiful in the world." It is not necessary to make too much allowance for local pride, for the creek is rarely beautiful, especially south of the city, where it winds about as if eager to keep away from the Susquehanna as long as possible.

Lancaster County was organized in 1729, and Lancaster city is nearly as old. At first the county seat was at a tavern much farther south, but the canny Hamiltons of Philadelphia, seeing a chance to make money, bought a tract of land on the Conestoga, and used their influence to have the county seat moved. In 1730 the town was laid out when there was no road to the spot and there were few people in the neighborhood. But the place grew rapidly, and long before the Revolution it was famous as the largest inland town in the Colonies. The residents groaned under the necessity of paying ground rents to the Hamiltons, but new residents continued to come, attracted by the reputation of the town where treaties were made with the Indians and where manufacturing industries were developed at an early date. One of the chief occupations was the making of pack-saddles for use on the roads which soon led from the town in several directions, and the fashioning of locks, latches, and rifles.

Because of Lancaster's location, as well as its manufactures, Benjamin Franklin, at the time of Braddock's expedition against Fort Du Quesne, decided that here was the best place to outfit a huge train of wagons and pack-horses to carry supplies to the West.

Philadelphia patriots like Franklin turned anxious eyes to Lancaster during the Revolution, when the barracks, built in 1758 for use in protecting the region from Indian raiders, were occupied by British prisoners. In some unexplained manner many of these prisoners made their escape and found their way back to Philadelphia. All efforts to discover the traitors who were aiding in the escapes were vain until an American captain, disguised, consorted with a company of fleeing prisoners. His daring bore fruit in the arrest of fifteen men, and after that the Lancaster barracks were a safe prison.

For one day this city on the Conestoga had the distinction of being the capital of the United States. Just after the battle of Brandywine, which foreshadowed the capture of Philadelphia, the members of Congress reached Lancaster on horseback, coming from Bethlehem. Next day the body met in the court house, but before evening it was decided that caution dictated a further removal to York. The reasons given were that Lancaster was but sixty-eight miles from Philadelphia, and that many of the members of the State Legislature, then in session at Lancaster, were not friendly to the cause of the patriots. So York was chosen instead, and Lancaster was compelled to be content with the distinction of being the capital of Pennsylvania, a privilege continued until 1812.

Twelve years after the removal to York, when Congress had long been seated quietly in Philadelphia, the citizens, learning that a permanent capital was to be chosen by the lawmakers, forwarded an appeal "humbly presuming to offer" Lancaster as a candidate. In this it was argued:

"As an Inland Town we do not perceive ourselves inferior to any within the Dominion of the United States.... We venture to assert that there is not a part of the United States which can boast within the Compass of ten miles the same number of Waggons and good Teams... We are thoroughfare to the 4 Cardinal Points of the Compass... Labor is to be had at the rate of 2 shillings per day... Our Centrical Situation..."

Lancaster lost the capital, and it came near losing some of the advantages of its "centrical situation" when the first surveys of the Philadelphia and Columbia Railway left the town to one side. The danger of being passed by was all the greater because many residents felt that the intrusion of traffic would be a nuisance. Others led in an appeal to the state for a change of route. To this request objection was made by those in charge of the public works that to build the road through Lancaster would increase the expense $91,000. Fortunately the re-routing was ordered, provided the town would see to it that the expense was not greater than $60,000, and that the community would pay the bills. The conditions were met, and Lancaster secured the railroad.

A few years later Lancaster had the further distinction of being an important point in the first telegraph line in the country after the experimental line between Baltimore and Washington. There was great excitement and curiosity as the poles were planted and the wires were strung on the line, which was to extend from Harrisburg to New York, by way of York, Columbia, Lancaster, and Philadelphia. Wherever the laborers were busy there was a crowd watching them and listening to them as they sang:

"Sink the poles, boys, firm and strong,
   Short and close together;
Solder the joints of the mystic thong,
   And let it stand forever."

The line did not stand forever; it stood only a few weeks. The first day's receipts at Lancaster were only six cents, while at Harrisburg the amount was ten cents.

At Lancaster the Lincoln Highway leaves the main line of the Pennsylvania Railroad, following in a general way the route of the original road to Columbia on the Susquehanna, through a pleasing country that becomes more rugged as the river is approached.

The story of Columbia goes far back of the laying out of the town in 1787 by Samuel Wright. For many years there was a settlement here known as Wright's Ferry, a name fortunately preserved by the town of Wrightsville, across the river in York County.

At the time when Lancaster was having its first struggles with the Philadelphia proprietors, the neighborhood of Wright's Ferry was facing troubles of a more serious nature, for it was frequently a central point of Maryland's efforts to make good her claim to that part of Pennsylvania west of the Susquehanna. This difficulty dated from 1684. In 1717 the two colonies agreed on the present boundary, but in 1718 Maryland sent surveyors to take up lands below what is now Columbia, while seven years later settlers were sent to a point on the east bank still farther north. The coming of Thomas Cresap to the west side of the river, not far below what is now Wrightsville, brought matters to a head. When he began to operate a ferry across the river, and was asked for his license, he said he had a license from Maryland. His defiance was the signal for the beginning of Cresap's War. Cresap was captured by the Pennsylvanians. Many conflicts followed. In 1735 there was a pitched battle near Wrightsville, while in 1736 three hundred Marylanders gathered there to face the Lancaster County military force. Discretion proved the better part of valor, however, for they disbanded and went home. Fortunately, in 1738, the king of England put a period to the inter-colonial strife.

Again, one September day in 1777, Wright's Ferry was the center of attraction. Then the members of Congress arrived, in flight from Lancaster to York. They crossed the river on flat boats; then they continued the journey on horseback, all except John Hancock, who had a chaise, while Joseph Jones rode in Washington's private carriage, borrowed for the occasion. Two days after this, from York, he wrote to the general a letter which told of some of the consequences of the rough journey:

"I have your phaeton here ... The bolt that fastens the pole part of the long reins was lost, some brass nails also gone, and the lining much dirtied and in some places torn. I will have these little matters repaired and the carriage and harness kept clean and in as good order as I can, which is the least I can do for the use, though I would rather buy it . . ."

Twelve years later it looked very much as if members of Congress would make Wright's Ferry the terminus of their journeys. For when the question was before Congress as to the permanent location of the capital, this famous place was long the most prominent candidate. Once it was within one vote of victory. A commission was appointed by a vote of 28 to 21 to select a spot on the banks of the Susquehanna. Harrisburg was spoken of as a possibility, while Peach Bottom, not far from the state line, was mentioned. Washington favored Wright's Ferry because of "beauty, security, and other natural advantages." Members of Congress from New England declared that Wright had put his ferry at a spot which must be "the center of population for years to come"; that when the center moved it would be "to the eastward, not to the south; to the manufacturing, not to the agricultural states." Someone spoke of the possibility that the settlement of the Ohio country would change calculations, but the reply was made, "When the Ohio will be settled, or how it will be possible to govern it, is past calculation."

The prophecy concerning the future of Wright's Ferry for many years seemed to be on the way to fulfillment. Soon after Columbia, the Lancaster County terminus, replaced Wright's Ferry, the town began to boom by reason of the large river traffic from the north. Because the keel boats could not descend farther, the town became a sort of port. It is recorded that often as many as 1500 or 2000 arks and rafts and a large number of keel boats would come on a single freshet.

In 1805 Robert Sutcliffe visited the town. "I saw a number of large flat-bottomed boats in the river," he wrote, "some of which had come upward of three hundred miles, and could carry one thousand bushels of wheat. The largest of these are more than seventy feet in length, and calculated for one voyage only, and for floating down the river with the stream, over shallows and falls; for when they arrive at their destination, they are taken to pieces, and the timber is used for other purposes."

The growing importance of the town made necessary the building across the river in 1812 of what was said to be the longest bridge in the world, at a cost of $233,000. For a structure a mile and a quarter long this sum certainly does not seem excessive. This bridge and its successors had a history of disaster. In 1832 ice destroyed it. The rebuilt bridge was burned in July, 1863, to prevent the crossing of the invaders from the South, who had reached Wrightsville. In 1868 a new bridge was built on the old piers and with the old abutments. This, said to be "the longest covered bridge in the world," was thrown into the river by a tremendous storm in 1896.

The coming of the railroad from Philadelphia gave the booming town a fresh impetus. The opening of the Pennsylvania Canal up the Susquehanna, and the Tidewater Canal to Maryland, the development of deposits of iron ore, the building of smelting furnaces—one of them the first furnace in Lancaster County to use anthracite coal—helped to make Columbia a busy place.

The atmosphere of these early railroad days is most acceptably conveyed by the perusal of the account of a journey from Philadelphia to Columbia, written in 1836:

"We had chosen a unilocular car of oval shape with a seat running around the entire inside, so that the nose of each passenger inclined toward some point in a straight line drawn between the two foci of an ellipse. There were in the car about twenty people ... one, an old woman, amused the company with dreadful accidents supposed to have happened on the self-same road; an old gentleman was fully occupied in parrying from his ignitable proboscis the dangerous sparks emitted by the engine, which continually flitted like fireflies in every direction through the car....

"Two cars filled with passengers and covered with baggage are drawn by four fine horses for about four miles to the foot of the inclined plane, which is on the western bank of the Schuylkill, and is approached by a spacious viaduct ... At the foot of the inclined plane the horses were loosed from the cars, several of which were tied to an endless rope, moved by a steam engine placed on the top of the plane, and finally began to mount the acclivity with the speed of five miles an hour ... when the cars had all arrived at the top of the plane, some twelve or fourteen were strung together like beads, and fastened to the latter end of a steam tug ... The inclined plane is more than nine hundred yards in length and has a perpendicular rise of about one hundred and seventy feet....

"The Columbia Rail Road is made of the best materials, and has cost the State a great sum; but it has some great faults. The curves are too numerous, and their radii generally too short, in consequence of which the journey to Columbia (eighty miles) consumes seven or eight hours, instead of four or five. The viaducts are built of wood instead of stone, and the engineer, doubting their ability to bear the weight of two trains at once, has brought the two tracks on them so close together, as to prevent two trains passing at the same time ... The roofs are so low as to prevent the locomotives from having chimneys of a sufficient height to keep the cinders out of the eyes of the passengers, and to prevent the sparks from setting fire to the carts and baggage. The chimneys of the steam-tugs are jointed, and in passing a viaduct the upper part is turned down, which allows the smoke to rush out at so small a height as to envelop the whole train in a dense and noisome cloud of smoke and cinders . . . We soon found that the smoking ordeals could be passed without damage, by shutting our mouths and eyes, and holding our noses and tongues. . . .

"We left Lancaster . . . in a Rail Road Car drawn by two horses, tandem; arrived at Columbia in an hour and a half . . . Here is the western termination of the Rail Road, and goods from the seaboard intended for the great West are here transhipped into canal-boats. . . .

"The State does not afford the public as good a commodity of traveling, as the public ought to have for the money paid. For locomotive power each passenger car pays two cents per mile, and half a cent per mile for each passenger: for toll each passenger car pays two cents per mile, and one cent per mile for each passenger: burthen cars pay half the above rate. The estimated cost of working a locomotive, including interest and repairs, is sixteen dollars per diem; and the daily sum earned is twenty-eight dollars; affording a daily profit to the state of twelve dollars on each locomotive. Empty cars pay the same toll and power-hire as full ones. . . ."

To-day the main line of travel passes Columbia to the north, river traffic has ceased, the canals are a memory, some of the furnaces are abandoned, but Columbia is still a thriving town. Closed buildings on the street facing the river bear mute witness to the activity of days gone by, but better buildings on the other streets tell of present activity and a measure of prosperity.

One of the glories of the early days cannot be taken away—the striking scenery about the town which led Sutcliffe to call this "one of the most beautiful and romantic parts of America."

The best way to see the beauty of which the early visitor told is to go two miles up the river, to the top of Chickies Rock. From this eminence, two hundred feet above the river, which stretches away to the southeast and sweeps in a stately curve almost directly west, is spread out before the eyes what a traveler of fifty years ago called "one of the loveliest landscapes on which my eyes have fallen." Then he declared, "The whole region round about is a miracle of God's handiwork, not mountainous, but hilly, as if, in Mrs. Browning's phrase, 'His fingers touched, but did not press, in making it.'"

It is difficult to turn from the sparkling river to a panorama vastly different, the Chickies Valley and the Donegal Valley—mile on mile of cultivated fields, green forest, gently sloping hills, and houses nestling in the midst. And it is just as difficult to turn back to the river from this alluring prospect.

The present location of the road from Columbia to Marietta is better adapted to sightseeing than the original road built in 1826, which follows the river most of the distance. From a point back of the rock, and still higher, it is possible on a clear day to look on and on to the Lebanon hills.

Chickies Rock was originally called Chikiswalungo, "the place of crawfish." But the long, though musical, name was in time broken up. Half was given to the rock and the creek from which it has its name, while half was given to the village Salunga, between Lancaster and Elizabethtown.

Marietta, the delightful town located just above Chickies, is a monument to a double union, rather than a division. Once there were two towns near by, Waterford and New Haven. Instead of the two names one was given, Marietta, made up from the names Mary and Henrietta, who were the wives of the founders.

From the summit of Round Top, opposite Marietta

in York County, there awaits the visitor who chooses a clear day a view forty miles in extent. While this is in many respects the same as the backward view from Chickies, it is different enough to make the climb worth while. The Susquehannocks, at least, thought so, for this eminence was one of their favorite resorts.

Students of Indian lore say that this tribe had a number of strongholds to the south of Columbia, along the Susquehanna. Perhaps the best known of these was opposite Washington Borough, in York County. It is of interest to remember that the dispute between the heirs of William Penn and Lord Baltimore as to the boundary line between their provinces was caused by uncertainty as to which of several Susquehannock forts was meant when Penn agreed with Baltimore that one of these should mark the dividing line.

Other relics of the Indians are plentiful along these shores. Between Columbia and the mouth of the Conestoga are two great rocks whose flat surfaces are covered with picture writing. Just below the mouth of the Conestoga are Big Indian Rock and Little Indian Rock, both of great size, also used by the red men for their picture records.

The Conestoga Creek is another haunt of the Indian. The Conestoga trail led from Philadelphia through Gap to a point three miles above the creek. Some distance from the river was the site of Penn's Conestoga village, in the midst of a reservation set aside by him for his friends, the first owners of the country. For a time he dreamed of building at the mouth of the Conestoga a city which should rival Philadelphia, but he was compelled to be content with erecting the Indian village. To this settlement a road was begun in 1683, and completed in 1734. This followed, in a general way, the present line of the Lancaster road to Octoraro Creek. Near Christiana it turned south, finally reaching Wright's Ferry after passing through Conestoga and Blue Rock.

Conestoga was destroyed in 1763, when the Paxton Boys, in their search for Indians charged with murdering settlers, went there in force and killed most of the inhabitants.

Blue Rock, above the mouth of the Conestoga, once promised to become a town of importance. In 1788 John Penn wished to buy two hundred acres which commanded the distant banks of the Susquehanna, and several islands. These lands he thought might be "collected into one great prospect." But John Penn failed in his plans, as had William Penn before him.

Conestoga Creek and Lancaster County must be given a large place in the story of the development of water transportation. It was on this stream that William Henry, a native of the county, in 1763, made trial of his ingenious steamboat. His contrivance had paddle wheels of good design, but the engine was too heavy, and the boat sank. John Fitch, who for a season made a success of his steamer on the Delaware from Philadelphia to Burlington, once stopped to see Henry when on the road to Kentucky. The Philadelphia inventor, who was already making his own experiments, was deeply interested in Henry's drawings and patterns. Five months before the death of the Lancaster County originator, Fitch made a successful trial of his first boat on the Schuylkill, near the High (Market) Street bridge. The boat performed well, but most observers seemed doubtful of the practicability of the contrivance. J. P. Brissot de Warville in 1788 reflected public opinion when he said:

"I doubt not, physically speaking, the machine may produce part of the effects which are expected from it; for, notwithstanding the assurances of the undertakers, it must require many men to manage it, and much expense in repairing the damage occasioned by the volume and multiplicity of its parts."

Robert Fulton, too, was a Lancaster County man. He was born in the southeastern part of the county, but spent a portion of his youth in Lancaster, where he showed more interest in art than in mechanics. When he built his first steamboat he turned to the Hudson for its testing because the Susquehanna, by whose waters he had wandered many times, was too shallow, as were the waters of the creeks near his home.

In 1909, when New York was observing the centennial of the trial trip of the *Clermont*, a pilgrimage was made from Lancaster to Fulton's birthplace near Little Britain, on the Conowingo. A memorial tablet was dedicated there that day, and Lloyd Mifflin's tribute was read:

"A child of Lancaster, upon the land,
Here was he born, by Conowingo's shade;
Along these banks our youthful Fulton strayed,
Dreaming of Art. Then Science touched his hand,
Leading him onward, when, beneath her wand,
Wonders appeared that now shall never fade:
He triumphed o'er the Winds, and swiftly made
The giant, Steam, subservient to command."

It is remarkable that, of the "first" steamboats navigated in American waters before 1807, six of the trials took place in Pennsylvania streams.

The first iron steamboat ever constructed was launched on the Susquehanna opposite Marietta, in 1825. This was also the first steamer on this river. Phineas Jordan was the builder. The vessel, the *Codorus*, was sixty feet long, had a nine-foot beam, and was three feet high. Its weight, complete, was six tons, of which 1400 pounds were sheet iron, while the engines and boilers weighed two tons. The empty vessel drew five inches of water, and every ton of load caused it to sink an inch deeper.

The *Codorus*, named for the creek on which it was built, was brought overland to Marietta, where it arrived in a pouring rain. Yet the enthusiastic citizens were on hand in such numbers that they were able to draw it with a rope from the west side of the bridge to the upper end of Main Street in Marietta.

The speed of the marvel was supposed to be five miles an hour, but when it made three miles upstream, against the wind, in thirty-three minutes, this was thought to be a great performance. At this speed the river was navigated as far up as Owego and Binghamton. Yet the financial returns were so small that in 1827, when the vessel was rusting in the dock at York Haven, on account of insufficient water for the five-inch draft, an indignant stockholder wrote to ask what was the purpose of investing such a large sum as "between two and three thousand dollars," only to have an idle iron steamer. Probably he had some slight return on his investment when, in 1827, the *Codorus* was sold to a junk dealer for $600.

The time required for a trip down the Susquehanna from Columbia will be well spent, notwithstanding the fact that William Cullen Bryant permitted the statement to be made in "Picturesque America": "All the Susquehanna scenery is not beautiful. The ending is dull and prosaic; the long stretch south of Columbia . . . presents nothing worthy of commemoration by the pencil or comment by the pen." The author quoted this opinion to a conductor on the passenger train that runs every morning along the river bank, from Columbia to Perryville, Maryland. "Wait and see for yourself," he said. "I have been making this run twice a day, seven days a week, for ten years, and I can't see the river often enough. Just the other day I found something I had never noted before."

The trip is a long succession of surprises. The scenery is so varied that there is no excuse for weariness, all the way from Columbia to Peach Bottom. Bayard Taylor, who lived but forty miles from this section of the stream, declared that it went ahead of anything the Rhine could offer.

At Safe Harbor, where the Conestoga makes its entry through a wooded gap, the traveler is apt to rise to his feet in admiration, and when he comes to the mouth of the Pequea he does not know how to express himself. Here Tucquan Lake, as the backwater from the dam of the Pennsylvania Power Company, farther down, is called, covers the rocks and fills the channel from the rocky wall on the one side to the abrupt green slope on the other. Below the dam the rugged rocks and the wooded islands that bar the passage of the water trickling down look like a bit from the wilds of Canada.

Pequea Creek is another of the historic streams of Lancaster County. Far back in the glen through which it approaches the Susquehanna muskets were made for Washington's army. And seventy years earlier the valley was the scene of great activity, when 10,000 acres were bought by the Swiss Mennonites and the French Huguenots. Strasburg was the center of the colony. The Indians who lived at Conestoga said they would protect the settlers, who were known as the Palatines, and they kept their promise. Pequea Creek was named from the Piqua clan or totem of the Shawnee Indians. They had many Piqua towns. The name Piqua, in Ohio, is the survival from one of these.

York County shares with Lancaster the distinction of having on its border the delightful Susquehanna. The western banks are, as a rule, more rugged than the eastern, and seem more like a barrier to the rich country behind them. At Wrightsville, however, where the Lincoln Highway crosses the river, the shore is more hospitable, affording a pleasant portal to the comparatively easy grades of the road to York which the patriots followed in the darkest days of the Revolution.

Congress had no hesitation in going to York in 1777, since the loyalty of the citizens had been amply proved. The town furnished the first organized company for Washington's army and these first recruits were followed by many more. On July 7, 1776, the pastor of the Moravian church wrote:

"Yorktown seems quite deserted on account of the departure for the army of all men under fifty years of age. Our young men had to leave for Jersey."

At the time of the coming of Congress, in September, 1777, there were nominally about eighteen hundred people in York. The patriots met in the court house in Center Square, whose bell had pealed out the news that the Declaration of Independence had been signed. This bell is now in the cupola of St. John's Episcopal church, though the old court house disappeared in 1841.

There was not much to cheer the members of Congress who gathered daily from the shady streets into the assembly hall. The least of their troubles was that the eight dollars per day allowed them was paid in Continental currency, then worth but thirty cents on the dollar. Of the gloom that shadowed everything John Adams wrote, in October:

"The prospect is chilling on every side, gloomy, dark, melancholy, and dispiriting. When and where will light come for us? If Philadelphia is lost, is the cause of independence lost? . . . No, the cause is not lost. . . . We have as good a cause as ever was fought for."

One day during that same October Samuel Adams roused his associates by a ringing message:

"If we as delegates in Congress give up in despair, and grow desperate, public confidence will be destroyed and American liberty will be no more. . . . Though fortune has been unpropitious, our conditions are not desperate; our burdens, though grievous, can still be borne; our losses, though great, can still be retrieved. . . . We shall not be abandoned by the Powers above so long as we act worthy of aid and protection."

From the hall where these words were spoken went out, a few days later, the first Thanksgiving proclamation. Here the Articles of Confederation were ratified, and here was received the cheering news of Burgoyne's defeat and the later word from Franklin of the signing of the treaty with France. It was Saturday afternoon when the message from Franklin reached town, by way of Wright's Ferry. Congress had adjourned until Monday, but the members were called together by the joyous sound of the bell in the court house.

There was great enthusiasm when the news was announced throughout the town, but enthusiasm was still greater when, on June 20, 1778, it was shouted along the streets that Philadelphia had been evacuated, and that the way was open for the return of Congress to the historic meeting place on Chestnut street.

ALONG THE LINCOLN HIGHWAY

A tablet in Center Square records the fact that Congress met in York during the days when so much history was made. The traveler who reads the brief statements is interested to recall that the three habitations of Congress in Pennsylvania during the days of the Revolution were all on the line of the Lincoln Highway.

Like Lancaster, York was a receptive candidate for the permanent location of the capital. A committee was appointed to make a survey of a district ten miles square, of which the court house was to be the center. But, though York's claims were considered, a location on the Susquehanna seemed preferable to those who favored fixing the capital in Pennsylvania.

When hope of becoming permanent hosts to the nation was gone, the people of York turned with ardor to service for the country in other ways. The town prospered, and in its prosperity others shared. There were many instances of industrial activity that made distinct contribution to the country. For instance, Phineas Jordan, already mentioned as the builder of the *Codorus*, in 1831 constructed the first coal-burning locomotive. The Baltimore and Ohio Railway directors were in difficulty for lack of such an engine, and an offer was made of a prize for the best machine. Of the three engines built in response to the plea, Mr. Jordan's "York" was approved by the judges. To it the prize of $4000 was awarded because it burned coal, consumed its own smoke, could draw fifteen tons at a speed of fifteen miles an hour, did not weigh more than three and a half tons, and in pressure of steam did not exceed one hundred pounds to the square inch.

In 1832 the first steel springs used in America were

placed on the locomotive by Mr. Jordan. It was then in better shape than ever for the hard service expected of it. For many years this pioneer engine was kept on the road. It is now prized as a memorial of the early days of railroading.

From York to the western line of the county the road passes through country sometimes rolling, again quite rugged. The southwestward course is determined by the ridge that borders the valley of the Conewago, and a good opportunity to turn westward is not presented until after the head of the creek is reached.

Near the line of York County is Hanover, a town which was in Revolutionary days a worthy neighbor of York. More than two years before the adoption of the Declaration of Independence, on June 4, 1774, citizens of the town, in public meeting, resolved that, "in the event of Great Britain attempting to force unjust laws upon us by the strength of arms, our cause we leave to Heaven and our rifles."

When Adams County was separated from York County, the name of John Adams, who was President at the time, was given to it. The appropriateness of the choice became evident when, at Gettysburg, the Army of the North proved its loyalty to the country in a manner that would have delighted the heart of the Revolutionary patriot.

The twenty-five square miles of the battlefield, amid the picturesque hills and valleys south of Gettysburg, with its great National Cemetery which Lincoln dedicated in November, 1863, and its hundreds of memorials of the struggle that raged for three days in and about the Devil's Den, Round Top, Benner's Hill, Seminary Ridge, the Wheat Field, the Peach Orchard, and Cemetery Hill, make one of the nation's most

A PENNSYLVANIA SUGAR MAPLE TREE
Photo by State Department of Forestry

VIEW FROM LITTLE ROUND TOP, GETTYSBURG BATTLEFIELD
Warren Statue on Rock
Photo from Philadelphia & Reading Railroad

LOOKING UP SUSQUEHANNA RIVER TOWARD PENNSYLVANIA, FROM BALTIMORE & OHIO RAILROAD BRIDGE.
PERRYVILLE, MARYLAND
Photo by United States Geological Survey

sacred places, for this is "the final resting-place for those who here gave their lives that that nation might live." Every American should stand here at least once, that he may put in action the words of him who helped to make the field a shrine:

"It is rather for us to be here dedicated to the great task remaining before us, that from these honored dead we, take increased devotion to that cause for which they gave the last full measure of devotion; that we here highly resolve that these dead shall not have died in vain; that the nation, under God, shall have a new birth of freedom, and that government of the people, by the people, and for the people shall not perish from the earth."

"The Manor of Mask" was the name at first given to the Gettysburg country when those who settled there received their warrant from the Penns. One of these early settlers bought a farm of four hundred acres not far from the place where John Gettys later laid out his town, paying for the tract a pair of shoes. In 1843 it was a matter of wonder that the land was then worth all of twenty dollars per acre.

The ride from Gettysburg to Chambersburg will not easily be forgotten. The successive ridges rise higher and higher until the summit of South Mountain is reached, at an altitude of 1334 feet. This mountain barrier was a wonderful protection to the early settlers of Adams County during the French and Indian War of 1755 to 1758, when the savages swept into the valley of the Cumberland.

There were times, however, when the Indians managed to pass this barrier. In 1758 nineteen Delawares made their way across to the home of Richard Bard, where they took Bard, his wife, other members of his family, and a number of neighbors. The captives were hurried over South Mountain and then, approximately, over the route of the Lincoln Highway to Fort Pitt. Mr. Bard escaped and survived a nine days' journey back to Bedford County, his only food during the period of his flight being "a few birds and four snakes." Later he found Mrs. Bard at Shamokin (Sunbury) on the Susquehanna.

When the Indians led their captives over the mountains they must have passed near Caledonia, which is just over the line in Franklin County. Here is now a state park, but early in the nineteenth century the place was known as the haunt of Thaddeus Stevens, who had an iron furnace near. The office building in which he spent many years is still standing, while the old trolley station is the remnant of the blacksmith shop of the furnace.

Eight miles south of Caledonia is the spot where Captain Cook, one of John Brown's raiding party at Harper's Ferry, was captured. A marker by the road points out the spot.

Mont Alto, the town nearest the marker, is named from Mont Alto Park, which is said to be one of the most beautiful natural parks in Pennsylvania. It covers ground that once was very wild and almost impenetrable.

East of the highway, at Mont Alto, is the so-called "Valley of a Thousand Springs," where Antietam Creek, made famous during the Civil War, has its source.

At Mont Alto is also the South Mountain sanitarium for consumptives, operated by the state, as well as the School of Forestry from which the State Department of Forestry has sent out scores of trained men to assist in protecting the forests of Pennsylvania and increasing the forest acreage of the commonwealth. The South

Mountain State Forest reaches north as far as Caledonia, and those who use the Lincoln Highway have an opportunity to study the methods found successful in the nurseries from which seedlings are sent out to those who will help to plant forests.

Once Pennsylvania was practically covered with a dense forest growth; but, by wasteful lumbering operations and by fires which have been the result of carelessness, most of this valuable heritage has been lost. As a result climate has changed, streams have disappeared, floods have been caused, and the water supply of cities and towns has been threatened.

It is not many years since the people began to realize the seriousness of the situation created by their prodigal treatment of the priceless forests. From 1886 to 1897 a few far-seeing men worked through the Pennsylvania Foresty Association for the creation of a State Forestry Department. The first real sign of progress was the establishment in 1897 of the State Forestry Reservation Commission. Under its guidance the state began to buy back the lands from which lumber had been removed, though often it was necessary to pay a higher price than was received before the timber was cut. Two years later the first forest range was defined, and since that time progress has been rapid. The twenty thousand acres of forest land owned in 1899 became about half a million acres in 1903, while to-day the holdings are more than a million acres. The goal the Department of Forestry has set for itself is at least five million acres, though even this goal may be advanced in order to take in all the land in the state that is not suited to the growth of anything but trees.

There are now large reservations in every one of the old lumbering counties, as well as in other mountain counties and in Pike and Wayne counties. Millions of trees are growing under the care of scores of foresters, who are supervised by the State Forester; fires are prevented and subdued, and the water supplies of many cities are preserved from contamination. During one recent year 10,000,000 seedling trees were grown in the department's nurseries, 6,000,000 of these being used in the state forests, while 2,350,000 were distributed to private individuals, volunteers in the work of forest development, many of whom could read with understanding the lines of Joyce Kilmer:

> "I think that I shall never see
> A poem lovely as a tree;
>
> "A tree whose hungry mouth is prest
> Against the earth's sweet flowing breast;
>
> "A tree that looks at God all day
> And lifts her leafy arms to pray;
>
> "A tree that may in summer wear
> A nest of robins in her hair;
>
> "Upon whose bosom snow has lain;
> Who intimately lives with rain.
>
> "Poems are made by fools like me,
> But only God can make a tree."

The Department of Forestry looks forward to the day when every resident of the State of Pennsylvania will say, with Don C. Seitz's countryman in "Farm Voices":

> "Hardest thing in life for me
> To go out cuttin' timber;
> Allus hate to touch a tree,
> If we do need lumber.

"Want to leave them stand an' grow
  Tall an' green an' grand,
Like great giants in a row
  Guardin' of the land.

"While they spread their coolin' shade,
  Whisperin' to each other,
Shadowin' the forest glade,
  Brother nudgin' brother.

"Seem to hear the hemlock sigh
  An' the birches shiver
When they see the axemen nigh;
  Know the aspens quiver!"

The early settlers in Franklin County, like all pioneers, would have laughed at the idea of conserving forests. To them a tree was an enemy to be conquered. And they found plenty of trees along the valleys of the Conodoguinet and Conococheague creeks and in Path Valley, as the fertile ground between the latter creek and the Tuscarora Mountain is named. The Path Valley settlers were among the earliest arrivals in the county, and long before Chambersburg amounted to anything the "Conocojig settlement," as it was called, from Conococheague Creek, was a thriving though scattered community.

Perhaps the most interesting point in Path Valley is a mile from the village of Concord, where the borders of Franklin, Huntingdon, and Juniata counties touch. The corner of Perry County is also so near that one can readily see over the border.

Four miles from Concord are the headwaters of Tuscarora Creek. The stream, after passing through the Narrows, a wild gorge in the Tuscarora Mountain, flows through the length of Juniata County until it reaches the Juniata. Those who follow the stream along its entire course will see a section of unusual attractiveness, even for Pennsylvania.

For a long time roads were scarce in this mountain section. The first public road over the Kittatinny Mountains from Path Valley into Perry County was not built until 1820, though Concord dates from 1797. Lower down in the Path Valley settlers were found as early as 1746. They had a precarious foothold for some years, because of the enmity of the Indians, but by 1750 these same Indians were beginning to appreciate the blessings brought to them by the white men. In 1750 they asked for the improvement of the road through Path Valley, that traders might come in more freely. Unfortunately the traders did not bring over the road goods that pleased the Indians, so in 1750 a chief said, at a conference in Carlisle: "Your traders now bring scarcely anything but rum and flour . . . The rum ruins us. We beg you would prevent its coming in such quantities by regulating the traders."

A road much used in the later days of the Path Valley settlement passed from Baltimore, through Chambersburg, to Upper Strasburg and on by way of the valley of the Juniata to Fort Pitt. This was the shortest route to the Ohio River, and was chosen by thousands of drivers of pack horses. From this road can be seen the abrupt termination of one of the ridges of the Kittatinny Mountains, in a peak that is visible for many miles. From its summit a wide prospect is provided of the beautiful Cumberland Valley. At the foot of the peak—called Clark's Knob, for James Clark, the first settler, who made his home at Clark's Fancy, the present site of Upper Strasburg—is Clark's

Gap; through this the road finds its way into Huntingdon County.

When Francis Bailey, the English traveler, visited Chambersburg in 1796, the road to Pittsburgh most in favor was not that through Strasburg, but that over the Tuscarora Mountains to McConnellsburg and Bedford, the route of the Lincoln Highway. His astonishment at the traffic he told in his book of travels:

"I have seen ten and twenty waggons at a time on the way to Pittsburgh and other points of the Ohio, from there to descend that river to Kentucky. The waggons are loaded with the clothes and necessaries of a number of poor emigrants, who follow on foot with their wives and families . . . In this manner they will travel and take up their abode in the woods on the side of the road, like the gipsies in our country, taking their provisions with them, which they dress on the road's side."

In the building of the road which these emigrants traversed, Colonel Benjamin Chambers, founder of Chambersburg, gave much assistance to General Forbes, providing needed material and labor. Such leadership was expected of him by the people to whom he had been protector as well as friend. After Braddock's defeat, for instance, he built a stone house, roofed with lead, surrounded by water from Falling Spring as well as by a stockade. It is said that this stronghold was frequently attacked by Indians, but that no harm ever came to those who sought shelter within its walls.

By frequent conflicts with the Indians these hardy residents in Benjamin Chambers' town learned the value of security and freedom to such purpose that, when the Revolution made test of them, they stood in the forefront of the patriots who could be counted on to the last drop of blood. The community had no patience with a slacker. Once it was recorded in the

SEEING PENNSYLVANIA

minutes of the Falling Spring Presbyterian church that charges were presented against a man who was "strongly suspected of not being sincere in his profession of attachment to the cause of the Revolution."

The situation of the town near the Mason and Dixon Line, and on the direct road from Hagerstown to Harrisburg, made it second only to Gettysburg among the towns of Pennsylvania for its part in the Civil War. In the summer of 1859 John Brown, who called himself John Smith, and claimed to be a prospector for minerals in the mountains of Maryland and Virginia, appeared on the streets. Mysterious boxes (or boxes that might have been mysterious if they had not been thought to contain innocent supplies for the prospector) came to the town addressed "Smith and Son." These were called for by wagoners and were hauled away into the mountains, and down to a farm which John Brown had rented near Harper's Ferry. There they were opened, and the rifles, pistols, and ammunition in them were carefully stored for use when the raid on the arsenal should be made.

It has been claimed that the sufferings of Chambersburg at the hands of the army of the South during the Civil War were due to the town's failure to apprehend the unwise enthusiast and so prevent the raid.

On October 10, 1862, General J. E. B. Stuart with two thousand men reached town, the objective being the destruction of the military stores not long before taken from General Longstreet. Among other booty seized by the invaders were 1200 horses. Again, on June 15, 1863, a force of 1500 men plundered the town and remained for three days, then went on to Mercersburg, from there crossing Cove Mountain to McConnellsburg.

Less than a week later came the vanguard of Lee's army. For six days and five nights after their arrival, according to one who lived in the town at the time, "the legions of the South kept pouring through the main street—70,000 or 80,000 men."

General Lee, who came on the fourth day, was uncertain whether to go toward Harrisburg or toward Gettysburg. The roads forked at the Diamond; there he hesitated a long time before turning toward Gettysburg.

The last invasion was on July 30, 1864, when a call was made for a contribution of $500,000 in greenbacks or $100,000 in gold. Unless the sum was found within half an hour the town would be burned, the citizens were told. They refused to meet the demand, and fire was set to the homes. More than three million dollars' worth of property was destroyed.

Those days of destruction are only a memory. The city, which dominates the beautiful valley, is more than ever the pride of the residents of the county, who go there to do their marketing from Furnace Hollow and from Mercersburg, from Antietam Creek and from the "Conocojig."

It is remarkable that in the fourteen miles from Chambersburg to the banks of the Conococheague at Fort Loudon the net ascent is but fourteen feet. However, this must not be taken as an indication that the road is level, or that the scenery is lacking in charm. The view of hill and valley, so satisfying as Chambersburg is left behind, becomes more and more fascinating; all the way to Fort Loudon the prospect of distant heights and ridges, in which there seem to be no break, is compelling and restful.

On the highway, a mile east of Fort Loudon village,

a marker calls attention to the Fort Loudon monument, located not far away, on the site of the old fortress. This fortress, built in 1756 for the protection of the settlers against the Indians, was one in the long series of forts which stretched along the mountain barrier toward the Delaware River at Stroudsburg. General Forbes made use of it as he gathered troops and supplies for his expedition of 1758 against Fort Du Quesne.

Tourists will find difficulty in passing by this historic locality without lingering for a season of exploration. To the north the Conococheague and the Conodoguinet give mute invitation; Richmond Furnace, one of the best known of the haunts of the iron workers of early days, is but one of many points of interest that lie in that direction. The prospect from the top of Old Beaver Ore Washer, near the furnace, is up the valley to the point where a spur of the mountain divides Amberson's Valley from Path Valley. Back of the old furnace is another beautiful valley called Allen's Valley. Through this runs Aughwick Creek, long a favorite fishing place for trout and pickerel. Cowan's Gap, an opening from the valley to the western country, was visited by engineers in 1860, with a view to the building of a southern railroad through it which should shorten the distance to Pittsburgh. Farther north, near the Conococheague, another eminence, Jordan Knob, rises high enough to give a view of the whole country south toward the Maryland line.

That these valleys were familiar to the Indians is evident from the names of the two creeks that dominate the valleys: "Conococheague," with whose spelling the pioneer had as much difficulty as with the pronunciation, meant, "It is indeed a long way." "Conodoguinet" was still more expressive; its meaning is said to be, "It is a long way with bends." The course of the stream surely bears out the name. Along its banks the Indians went when they were traveling from the Susquehanna to the Allegheny by the Kittanning Path. In 1808 the legislature declared the stream a public course for floats and boats.

Farther south on the Conococheague is Mercersburg, where James Black settled in 1730. Among other early settlers was the Mercer family. General Hugh Mercer was perhaps the most famous of the family. For a time he was in charge of the fort at Shippensburg, to the north of Chambersburg, and later was engaged with Washington in important movements in the Revolution, whose climax was the battle of Princeton. With this battle his name will ever be connected because of his death on the field.

Black, the pioneer, must have had an eye for the picturesque. The site he selected for his home has mountains to the north and to the west, distant from two to five miles. And all this beauty he bought for a gun and a string of beads!

Among those whom the town attracted—though in their case, perhaps, for reasons of utility rather than beauty—were the parents of James Buchanan, who moved here in 1796, five years after the future President was born in a bit of Cove Gap, known as Stony Batter. A memorial in the form of a pyramid, built on the site of his birthplace, is not far from Foltz, on the highway from Mercersburg to McConnellsburg.

It is interesting to note that Buchanan, the only President from Pennsylvania, who was born in Franklin County, received his education in the adjoining county, Cumberland, and studied law at Lancaster, whose people sent him to the legislature and later—

acting with the voters of York and Dauphin counties—to Congress. It was in Lancaster County, too, that he spent his last years. His home, Wheatland, bought in 1848, is one of the show places of Lancaster.

Mercersburg claims distinction as the birthplace of Elizabeth Irwin, the mother of Benjamin Harrison, as well as of Jane Irwin, her older sister, who married William Henry Harrison, Jr., and was mistress of the White House during the presidency of her father-in-law in 1841. Their father, Archibald Irwin, was pastor of the Presbyterian church in Mercersburg when the Buchanans were members there. Three representatives, therefore, of this small community, spent terms in the White House.

When James Buchanan was born there was no road from Mercersburg to Stony Batter, though there was a favorite Indian trail. This trail was used by the pack horses long before the wagon road was built. The later turnpike, after following the Indian trail for a distance, turns to the left at Stony Batter, and for a space climbs the mountain by a series of easy grades, always keeping close to the old trail. Long before reaching the summit, however, it returns to the historic path.

The route followed by the Lincoln Highway from Fort Loudon to the westward is a few miles north of the historic Indian trail and its successors, the packhorse path and the roadway. For five miles it rises rapidly from six hundred feet to twenty-one hundred feet. The glory of the prospect to the rear increases as the height is reached, yet the traveler is hardly prepared for the vision that greets him from Tuscarora Summit, the Cumberland Valley on one side, and on the other the Cove Valley with McConnellsburg the chief jewel in a valley of green. It is a delight to stand on the height on a clear day, when fleecy clouds are passing before the sun. The waving of the distant grain and the alternations of light and shade, caused by the clouds reflected on the ridge, make a restful picture to be recalled in many later hours of weariness.

Thaddeus Mason Harris, one of the pioneers who passed this way, said that here on the summit "the view was still more diversified and magnificent, crowded with mountain upon mountain in every direction; between and beyond which were seen the blue tops of others more distant, mellowed down to the forest shade, till all was lost in unison with the clouds."

In 1794 Dr. Thomas Cooper said:

"It is impossible to pass this part of the journey without being struck with the perpetual succession of beautiful and romantic situations, numerous and diversified beyond what any part of England can supply within my recollection."

During the same year an officer who was on his way to help in quelling the Whiskey Insurrection stood on Tuscarora Summit where he saw "a prospect unexpectedly grand. To the north, south, and west appeared a little world of mountains, arranged in all the majesty of nature and destitute of a single sign of art or cultivation."

Robert Carleton, bound for the wilds of Indiana, also paused here to give expression to his wonder and delight. "Few are unmoved by the view from that top; as for myself, I was ravished," he wrote in his journal. "Was I not on the dividing ridge between two worlds—the worn and faded East, the new and magic West?"

The traveler who stands where the pioneers looked

down on what is now Fulton County saw a territory that was notable for its difficulty of access, even in that day when difficulties were commonplaces. The difficulty has not been entirely obviated in this day of easy transportation, for Fulton County is the only county in Pennsylvania without a railroad. "We thought we would soon be rid of that distinction," the keeper of a refreshment stand on Tuscarora Summit said to the author; "but many of those who were promoting the road that was coming here from the east have been accused of misappropriation of funds."

When this county was organized in 1850 the residents asked that the name Liberty be given to them. But the passage of the bill depended on a senator who would not agree to vote for it unless he was allowed to call the county Fulton. The county seat was fixed at McConnellsburg. Seated in the Great Cove Valley, it has the Tuscarora Mountains on the east and Ray's Hill on the west, with the Big and Little Scrub Ridge between. These mountains did not protect it from invasion from the South during the Civil War. On June 20, 1863, Confederate cavalry took possession of the town, and on a day in 1864, three thousand troops passed along the main street.

From the Great Cove Valley—which, for fertility and beauty, Thomas Bailey in 1796 compared to Kentucky—the highway leads on, across intervening ridges, to Ray's Hill, the western boundary of Fulton County. This hill, together with Sideling Hill farther east, furnished one of the dreaded passages for the pioneer. "We had been given a fearful description of it," Johan Schoepf wrote in 1788. Fifteen years after he owned that this assurance, spoken before the journey, "probably made it the more endurable." George Henry

ALONG THE RAYSTOWN JUNIATA, NEAR EVERETT
Photo by Lloyd M. Smith

MONUMENT ON THE SITE OF THE BIRTHPLACE OF PRESIDENT JAMES
BUCHANAN, FULTON COUNTY
Photo by Lloyd M. Smith

WEBSTER MILLS BRIDGE, FULTON COUNTY
Photo by State Highway Department

Loskiel, pilgrim from Reading, wrote of his experience on this ridge:

"A wilderness of rocks is here,
Both high and rugged, dark and drear,
Wherever we our eyes may rest,
By nothing but gray rocks they're met.

"'Tis Sideling Mountain; but the name
Of Mount Patience fits the same;
For, haste the traveler as he may,
The summit still seems far away.

"The prospect from the summit here
Was beautiful, immense and clear;
A pity, though, it makes us feel,
America's unfinished still."

The highway records of the state show that in 1787 an order was issued concerning the section of the road of which the rhymester wrote so disrespectfully. This directed that it "be cleared and made good and sufficient, to be twelve feet wide on the side of the hills among the rocks, and not less than twenty feet wide on the other ground, and room to be made for not less than three wagons to draw opposite one side of the narrow places at a convenient distance for others to pass by, and the water to run next to the hill side."

Thus the designers of this Pennsylvania state road set a good precedent for their successors of to-day, the State Highway Commission, which has done so much to make the Lincoln Highway within the state a road so easy that it is difficult to appreciate the trials of the pioneers on these same mountains.

From this slope down into Bedford County there is a panorama of striking beauty toward Everett and Bedford. In the distance ridge rises on ridge, like a series of steps. In the foreground lies the Raystown Juniata, a stream whose poetic beauty cannot be fittingly described. Rufus Putnam, as he drank in the scene when on his way to Ohio in 1794, could only call this comprehensive view the most picturesque his eyes had beheld, while Francis Bailey in 1796 spoke of it as "one of the most enchanting and romantic scenes" of which he knew. Then, more particularly, he described what is certainly one of the choicest vistas of a marvelous state. "The hill terminates at the river, and the road down to it is a narrow winding path, apparently clipt out of the mountain." The defile was gloomy, but soon light broke on him, "and the first thing that presented itself was the Juniata River, flowing gently between two very steep hills, covered with trees to the very top."

The crossing of the Juniata (Raystown Crossing) is made by a covered bridge of unusual interior construction; half way across it widens, and the single passage is divided by a partition.

This is a region where it is wise to linger. Every turn in the road affords glimpses that have charms of their own, ever changing. This road, as Francis Bailey said, is "carried along the side of a tremendously high hill which seemed to threaten us with instant death if our horses should make a false step."

Four miles from the Juniata crossing, along a nicely level road, elevated about one thousand feet, is Everett, where the Juniata takes advantage of a passage through Warrior's Gap. Once the town was called Bloody Run, because Indians there killed a party of traders whose traffic they wished to prevent.

Of Everett's many famous visitors Christopher Gist was not the least. In November, 1750, he reached

Warrior's Gap, passed eastward over the old Indian path on the site of the present highway, then on to Shannopin Town (Pittsburgh), his mission being to "search out and discover" lands for the Ohio Company.

The first attempt to make a road through the fertile lands and rugged mountains of Bedford County was in May, 1755, when the province of Pennsylvania sent a party of three hundred men to clear the trail from Fort Loudon to Braddock's road at Turkey Foot, in Fayette County. James Smith, the eighteen-year-old brother of one of the commission in charge of the road cutters, has left a record of an interesting incident of the heroic attempt:

"We went on with the road, without interruption, until near the Allegheny Mountains; when I was sent back, in order to hurry up our provision wagons that were on the way after us. I proceeded down the road as far as the Crossings of Juniata, when, finding the wagons were coming on as fast as possible, I returned up the road again toward the Allegheny Mountains."

About four miles above Bedford, he was captured by three Indians and was carried by them to Fort Du Quesne. Two years passed before he regained his liberty.

Colonel Bouquet and General Forbes were later identified with the opening of the road. At first it was known as the "Raystown road" (Raystown was the old name of Bedford) but later it was called the Forbes road. The name is preserved in Forbes Street, the Pittsburgh end of the route.

Later the Glade road, from a point east of Bedford to Somerset, Connellsville, Uniontown, and Brownsville, shared the popularity of the Forbes route. In 1820 the Somerset *Whig* advertised:

SEEING PENNSYLVANIA

"Glade Road Turnpike. Cheap and pleasant Travelling. Waggoners, travellers and the Publick in general, are now informed that the two mountains, the Allegheny and Laurel Hill, are now Completely turnpiked, and ... the road is so well improved that it can be travelled with more ease both to the horse and to the rider than any other road across the mountains."

Partly because of its situation just east of the junction of the Glade road and the Forbes road, Bedford was the chief stopping place for packers and travelers between Fort Pitt and Chambersburg. Sometimes there were as many as a thousand pack horses in the town. One man might have in his charge one hundred of the animals. Each pack train had three guards who went all the way to Fort Ligonier.

Bedford has a most advantageous situation. The hills almost entirely surround it. The Juniata winds through the valley as if it had ample leisure for the trip. To the north, beyond the ridge, Morrison's Cove, eight miles wide, extends into Blair and Center counties. To the south are the famous Bedford Springs, on the side of Evitt's Mountain, near Dunning's Creek, where hill and dale, rocky ridge and tree-covered slope combine to make a perfect picture.

The country to the south will repay examination across the line to Cumberland, Maryland, either by the road or by the railroad. One of the landmarks on the way is Buffalo Mills, not far from Bedford Springs, where, it is said, the last buffalo in the county was killed. To the north of Bedford, also, either the road or the railroad should be taken through a country too seldom seen by the tourist. There is a choice of routes—along George's Run and through Morrison's Cove by Pine Ridge and Dunning's Mountain to Hollidaysburg and Altoona; or by the valley of the Raystown Juniata, where the Huntingdon and Broad Top Railroad shows the way to mountain marvels. Of the many heights to be seen from these choice roads, Blue Knob is most notable, for this is 3136 feet high, the greatest elevation in Pennsylvania.

From Bedford the highway leads across a ridge into the Quaker Valley, 1210 feet high, in which Schellsburg has its seat. Just beyond is Chestnut Ridge. Here, on the summit, one of the early travelers, the record of whose experiences is interesting reading to-day, was overtaken by the night. "The road was narrow and bounded by frightful precipices," he declared. "If I attempted to advance, a sudden and rapid death was unavoidable; or if I remained where I was wolves, panthers, and tiger cats were at hand to devour me. I chose the latter risk as having less of fatal certainty in it."

A clearing on the mountain road has been made that the eye may take in Grand View. Here, from a point 2350 feet high, there is an inspiring panorama of cultivated fields and forests for twenty-five miles; the best view east of the Rocky Mountains, it has been called, not without reason. This point, from which seven Pennsylvania counties are to be seen, is called David Lewis's Outlook. David Lewis was a gentleman outlaw who frequently came to this point to descry ill-fated travelers as they come straight toward the gold-hungry highwayman.

Just before the Somerset County line is reached, after Grand View is passed, a succession of ridges clear to the Maryland line and beyond is in sight. Then comes the rapid ascent to the summit of the Allegheny Mountains, 2850 feet high. This ascent is gradual. At one point the road runs straight ahead, up hill and down,

SEEING PENNSYLVANIA

like a drive in a park; this section is known as the Seven Mile Straightaway.

Stoyestown's steep main street, which is the route of the highway, is a vantage point for an impressive outlook over a valley where cultivated farms take full advantage of the fertile lands. These well tilled farms are to be seen on both sides of the road on the top of the mountain near Stoyestown. At this point the Glade road, where it passes through Somerset, is but five miles distant. The county-seat town was an important point on the road which, on account of its surface of soft earth, was chosen by many drovers for the passage of cattle and hogs from the Ohio Valley to Baltimore and Philadelphia. Sometimes as many as four or five thousand hogs were seen on the road in a single drove.

Somerset may well be called a highland county. Even the valleys are high. The road from Stoyestown to Jennerstown is comparatively level for five miles, though the elevation is more than eighteen hundred feet. Soon, however, it climbs rapidly nearly nine hundred feet to the summit of Laurel Ridge, the last great summit on the route.

A few miles below the point at which the highway crosses Laurel Ridge is Laurel Summit station, on the railroad from Ligonier to Somerset. This is in the heart of the Westmoreland-Somerset forest reserve, where, in 1909, the State Forestry Department acquired 8500 acres, largely of cut-over, burned land. Laurel Summit station is near the head-waters of Linn Creek. The stream, in its course to Loyalhanna Creek, cuts a deep gorge where the lover of the unusual in highland scenery can have his fill of delight.

From Somerset County the highway passes into Westmoreland County, "the garden of western Pennsylvania," known once for the salt wells along the Conemaugh, later for its coal mining and gas wells. The first of the gas wells was driven in 1875. The flow was tremendous, but for five years no capitalist could be found who was willing to invest the necessary $200,000 for pipes to lead the flow to the mills.

Not far from the base of Chestnut Ridge, Ligonier has its most pleasant setting in the valley of the Loyalhanna. Here was Fort Ligonier, an important link in the chain of defensive works erected in the days when French and Indians were allied against the Pennsylvania pioneers. A tablet in the city square tells the story of the first English fort west of the Allegheny Mountains, built near the square in 1758:

"Here General Forbes, with the aid of Colonels George Washington, Henry Bouquet, and John Armstrong, assembled an army of 7850 men, constructed the Forbes road, compelled the evacuation of the fort, Nov. 25, 1758, thereby overthrowing French and establishing English supremacy in this region.

"Here Colonel Bouquet reorganized the expedition for the relief of Fort Pitt, and, while on the march, at a point 27 miles west of this, fought the battle of Bushy Run, August 5 and 6, 1763, defeating the Indian chief Guyasutha, in one of the best contested actions ever fought between whites and Indians."

Ligonier is noted as the residence, after the close of his military career, of General Arthur St. Clair. He lived a mile and a half north of town, where a tablet tells the passerby the main events of his life. Here he became a bankrupt, his difficulties having come as a result of his purchasing supplies, from his own pocket, for the blockhouses of Westmoreland County at the outbreak of the Revolution. Later he advanced some of the money Washington needed to carry on his work, though part of the sum so advanced was later returned to him. Again, in 1791, finding the amount furnished by Congress insufficient for the expense of his campaign against the Indians, he guaranteed the payment of many bills himself. When judgment was given against him for the debt so contracted (some ten thousand dollars) his failure followed. His home was taken from him, and he became dependent on a pension from the state, and on another from the United States. His last days were spent in the home of his son on Chestnut Ridge, not far from the highway. There he made his living by caring for travelers in his log cabin. He was buried at Greensburg.

The Loyalhanna opens the way for the passage of the highway from Ligonier to Greensburg and Pittsburgh, by a gap through Chestnut Ridge, called "The Narrows."

The Loyalhanna is not the only notable stream of Westmoreland County. On the western border is the Youghiogheny, and its chief tributary in the county is Jacobs Creek. This creek has a place in the history of the regions bordering on the highway because on its banks was built the first furnace west of the Alleghenies, and because over it was constructed, in 1801, the first chain suspension bridge in the United States, at a cost of $600.

The broken country about Ligonier, so quietly beautiful at every turn, is typical of Westmoreland County. The section of the county covered by the highway contains some of its most pleasing vistas of fertile farm lands, protecting hills and secluded valleys.

Not far from the western border of the county, but over the line in Allegheny County, is Turtle Creek, the scene of Braddock's disastrous defeat at the hands of

BUTTERMILK FALLS, LIGONIER
Photo by W. T. Brown

SUSPENSION BRIDGE ON FOUR MILE RUN, NEAR LIGONIER
Photo by W. T. Brown

OHIO, ALLEGHENY AND MONONGAHELA RIVERS, PITTSBURGH, FROM SOUTH SIDE
Photo by John C. Bragdon

ALONG THE LINCOLN HIGHWAY

the French and Indians, in 1755. Francis Parkman says that the events of that day were fraught with momentous consequences for America, for there the colonists discovered that they were not inferior to the British soldier. Besides, that day also made known to them their future leader, George Washington.

The region known as Braddock's Field would have had a place in the history of western Pennsylvania, even if the Indians had not come upon Braddock here, most unexpectedly stealing down from a ravine similar to hundreds of others which are a delightful feature of Allegheny County scenery. For here, in 1742, when the Delawares and their queen, Allequippa, held this region, John Frazier, the first settler west of the Alleghenies, built his cabin. This stood on the site of the great Edgar Thomson steel works.

On March 4, 1791, a deed was signed by the governor of Pennsylvania, giving title to three hundred and twenty-eight acres of a "certain tract called Braddock's Field." The price was less than half a dollar an acre. The state reserved "the fifth part of all gold and silver ore!"

The next appearance of the field in history was in 1794, when some eight thousand farmers and distillers who opposed the whiskey tax gathered here to resist the forces of Washington. Fortunately there was no conflict; they dispersed without resistance, and the Whiskey Rebellion was at an end.

Washington's first important visit to the site of Pittsburgh was made two years before his fortunate escape on Braddock's Field, where he had four bullets through his coat while two horses were shot under him, though he escaped unhurt. Then he was acting for the Ohio Company. After viewing the site at the junction of the Allegheny and Monongahela he wrote that he thought the ground extremely well suited for a fort and for a city. His judgment was later approved by the French.

Fortunately the French did not long possess the strategic site. On November 25, 1758, General John Forbes took Fort Du Quesne, and the name Pittsburgh was later given to the first permanent white settlement at the forks of the Ohio. This was "the end of the death struggle between France and England for the valley of the Ohio."

Very soon far-seeing visitors declared their belief that Pittsburgh would become a great center of population and industry, and as the years passed there was even greater assurance that this county of steep hills and great ravines, of fertile uplands and navigable rivers would have a place of distinction in the country's history.

In 1836 the man who wrote under the *nom de plume* Peregrine Prolix said, "Pittsburgh is destined to be the center of an immense commerce, both in its own products and those of distant countries." In 1841 the editor of the Wheeling *Times*, after a visit to Pittsburgh, called it "the great manufacturing city of the West," and told of climbing to the hills and looking down on a sea of smoke which "lay like the clouds upon Chimborazo. No breath of air moved the surface; but a sound rose from the depths like the roar of Niagara's water or the warring of the spirits in the cavern of storms." Finally he said that, "as a citizen of the West," he was proud of Pittsburgh.

The Wheeling visitor knew where to go for his view of the city. The hills, especially those on the South Side, have some wonderful points of vantage from which the panorama of rivers and heights and bustling city can be seen. A European artist who spent a season in Pittsburgh in 1854 chose Coal Hill, opposite the Monongahela House, for his view. When he came down he spoke of the likeness of the scene to that from the hill of Pera, opposite Constantinople. "The distances are on a smaller scale." he wrote, "but the heights are not dissimilar." He said he never saw two scenes more alike. To him the Bosphorus was represented by the Ohio, the Propontus or Sea of Marmora by the Allegheny, and the canal by the Monongahela. Allegheny City represents Scutari, and there is a bridge crossing the canal at about the same distance from the point as that over the Monongahela. Old Fort Du Quesne stood at the point just as the Seraglio stands in Constantinople. "The time will come," he added, "when the rich colors of sunset, caused by the smoky atmosphere (and they are of wonderful beauty), will be as famous and as much sought for as a sight of the Golden Horn."

Not only the hills, but some of the high buildings and the tower of the court house, invite the visitor to take a view of the industrial city where, in a recent year, before the war, were fifteen of the fifty Pennsylvania industrial establishments employing over one thousand men each; and these fifteen made use of more than seventy-two thousand of the one hundred and thirty-five thousand assembled in such establishments throughout the state. Pittsburgh has a right to its smoke; it is the city's badge of honor.

But the smoke does not keep the tourist from appreciation of the city's claim to beauty of landscape. Walk along her boulevards, study her river banks, go through Schenley Park, visit the East End, penetrate the recesses of the ravine through which the Baltimore and Ohio Railroad passes to the valley of the Monongahela from the tunnel under the park, take one of the South Side inclines, and watch the city as it falls away from underneath, stand on the point bridge and look up and down and all around, cross to Allegheny and persuade that section of the old city to give up its secrets; then say if Pittsburgh is not worthy of a place near the end of this great Pennsylvania section of the Lincoln Highway, as Philadelphia is worthy of the place at its beginning!

ROUTE II
BY THE NATIONAL ROAD TO WHEELING AND PITTSBURGH
ABOUT 480 MILES

"SO you are from Philadelphia?"

The greeting was made to a traveler by an old man who was shaking his head sadly as he thought of the past.

"No, Philadelphia will never be the same," he continued dolefully. "Once, when on the roads there was one long, long train of Conestogas carrying freight that brought prosperity to the city, it was in a fair way to become great. But the railroads came, and they took off the wagons. When the wagoners lost their jobs, the country was forsaken, and the city began to go down. These modern improvements, as they call them, have a lot to answer for!"

The seventy-five years since the ancient made his moan for the departed past have seen the recovery of the roads as well as the prosperity of both city and countryside. The products of farm and factory have grown so rapidly that railroads can no longer take care of them adequately, and the highways have again been called into service. Instead of the picturesque Conestoga wagon—with its curved bottom that prevented freight from slipping out of place on mountain roads, its bright blue paint, and its four to eight horses—the great automobile truck, well able to move several tons on the heaviest grade, appears in convoys of ten, twenty, thirty, or more, just as did its lordly forerunner. Once more the drivers camp by the way, or gather in the roadside taverns, which are still to be found, though most of these have disappeared, and their picturesqueness is a memory.

One of the routes most favored by the motor-conestoga of to-day is the old National Road which leads from Wheeling to Baltimore, for nearly one hundred miles within Pennsylvania and over one hundred more so close to the southern boundary that it is really a Pennsylvania road as far as surroundings are concerned. Even this stretch would have been in the state but for the result of the boundary dispute between Pennsylvania and Maryland. William Penn claimed the thirty-ninth degree as his southern boundary, but in 1750 the present boundary was agreed to. Thus the state is narrower by three-fourths of a degree than Penn's interpretation of the charter of 1681 indicated.

Not only is the National Road from Hagerstown to the point where it crosses the state line in Somerset County a Pennsylvania road by contiguity, but it has had so much to do with the development of western Pennsylvania and it is such a favorite with the motorists of the state in their journeys to the West that readers of this volume will be asked to follow the author along its inviting grades and over its staunch stone bridges.

The approach of the road may be made by the King's Highway from Philadelphia to Chester and on to Gap by a circuitous route, then to Lancaster, Harrisburg, Carlisle, and Chambersburg to Hagerstown.

The journey to Chester is through one of the state's most historic regions. Along this road Washington passed repeatedly when going from Mount Vernon to Philadelphia and New York. This way also went the patriot army when it sought Lord Howe, who had landed

IN THE HEART OF PHILADELPHIA, FROM RITTENHOUSE SQUARE
Photo by Bell & Fischer

SYCAMORE MILLS, NEAR MEDIA
Photo by J. E. Green

ON RIDLEY CREEK AT IRVING'S MILLS, CHESTER
Photo by J. E. Green

ROAD TO WHEELING AND PITTSBURGH

at Head of Elk. In November, 1777, Cornwallis led his men by this road to Chester, and from there crossed the Delaware in order to reach Red Bank.

Cornwallis's progress was not undisputed. His troops were fired on when they were passing along what is now Woodland Avenue, Philadelphia, by a picket who took refuge in Blue Bell Tavern. This old building still stands sentinel over the road at Seventy-second street. At that time the two-story section of the present deserted tavern stood alone, having been erected in 1766. The enlargement dates from 1801.

The first part of the road is too far from the Delaware to enable the traveler to see the great Hog Island shipbuilding plant without a detour. But this historic island should be seen. During the Revolution it was used for military purposes of a very humble nature, but during the European War it was the scene of unexpected activity. On September 22, 1917, workmen began to transform the eight hundred and forty-six acres of marshland into a gigantic ship works. A force frequently as large as fifteen thousand men worked throughout the winter to prepare the ground for the great burden it was to carry. Often steam was used to break the frozen soil. Within nine months there were on the site fifty shipways, and the first 7500-ton vessel had been launched. Back of the yard a little city had been built, with two hundred and fifty buildings, which included everything required by an up-to-date municipality. Thirty thousand men and women were employed, and the pay roll was more than one million dollars weekly.

Below Hog Island is Tinicum Island, the scene of the first settlement of Europeans in Pennsylvania. The Swedish governor, Printz, had his park here. A part of

SEEING PENNSYLVANIA

his orchard became an aviation field during the war. Joran Kyn occupied a tract of land, granted to him by the Crown, whose bounds were the Delaware, Ridley Creek, and Chester Creek.

The entire Chester area, from Eddystone to Marcus Hook, has become one of the most intensively industrial sections of its size in the world. There are two shipbuilding plants, in addition to that farther north at Hog Island, as well as steel mills, munition works and locomotive works.

The river widens toward Chester; there it is 6600 feet to the New Jersey shore, and it is a delight to survey the broad sweep of the tide-influenced stream. Chester, once called Upland, is the oldest town in Pennsylvania. In 1668 it was the chief village of Sweden's settlements on the Delaware. It might have been chosen by Penn as the site for his new city, if he had not been uncertain as to his southern boundary. The town has had a checkered history. First it lost its importance as county seat of Chester County when what is now West Chester grasped the honor. Then it enjoyed another period of county-seat life, for Delaware County was organized almost at once by a state legislature that received with great complaisance the appeal of the old town by the river. The day came when Media, five miles distant, deprived Chester of its second county-seat honors. There were those who said the town was doomed. Events proved them wrong; for factories came, and Chester grew rapidly from its seven hundred people to many thousand. The growth is now more rapid than ever, for it is becoming one of the great manufacturing centers of the state.

The final removal of the county seat has brought to the people of Chester another benefit—the necessity of making trips with more or less frequency along the beautiful route through valley and over hill to Media. The charm of this trip to the town where Benjamin West was born gives such a good impression of inland scenery that an extension of the journey to West Chester is an easy matter. This will be, approximately, over the same route as was taken in the days when Chester's citizens, indignant at the efforts to take away her precious county seat, sent an armed party to tear down the temporary jail and court house constructed at West Chester.

From West Chester it will be difficult to resist the temptation to save a few miles by going directly over to the Lancaster pike. But this neighborhood should not be left until a bit more of the country to the southeast is seen. Let Marshallton be the first stop, for near the town, at Northbrook, Humphrey Marshall was born in 1722. A tablet on a rock by the roadside, some distance from the birthplace, calls attention to the place where the author of the first American botanical treatise began his life. Another tablet marks his home at Marshallton, where he toiled to such purpose that he was able to call attention to the astonishingly varied flora of Chester County; this territory, but one-sixtieth of Pennsylvania, has within its borders more than fourteen hundred specimens of flowering plants, while the entire state has only about twenty-two hundred.

About his home he lovingly tended a garden and an arboretum that were the admiration even of those who knew best the garden of Marshall's cousin, John Bartram, in Kingsessing. The latter, though in a sadly neglected state, is a landmark to the left of the King's Highway, not far from the Blue Bell Tavern in Philadelphia, on the banks of the Schuylkill.

Marshall's book, "Arbustum Americanum," was translated into a number of the languages of continental Europe, where the genius of the author was lauded by many savants.

The name of the "gardener of Marshallton" should be remembered by every lover of trees, for he was really the first Pennsylvanian to advocate the very work that the State Department of Forestry is now doing so efficiently. In the preface of his book he made statements that must have had an odd sound to the residents of a state that was so well covered with primeval forests. Looking into the future he saw his beloved state "scored by the hand of man and swept nearly clear of the giant trees of the forest," and he expressed the hope that, "if one wishes to cultivate timber for economical purposes," he would turn to the pages of the "Arbustum" and "be informed about our valuable forest trees."

Thus he was more than a century ahead of his time. But the day came when his vision of desolation became actual, and the cultivation of trees was pushed with might.

A short distance from Marshall's home, where there may still be seen a few remnants of the trees of his planting, the road crosses the sinuous Brandywine, one of whose admirers, Bayard Taylor, has written of it:

"And once thy peaceful tide
Was filled with life-blood from bold hearts and brave;
And heroes on thy verdant margin died,
　　The land they loved, to save.

"These vales, so calm and still,
Once saw the foeman's charge,—the bayonet's gleam;
And heard the thunders roll from hill to hill,
　　From morn till sunset's beam.

"Yet in thy glorious beauty, now,
Unchanged thou art as when War's clarion peal
Rang o'er thy waves, and on yon green hill's brow
    Glittered the serried steel.

"And still thy name shall be
A watchword for the brave of Freedom's chime,
And every patriot's heart will turn to thee,
    As in the olden time."

Some distance down the stream lies the field of Brandywine, where Washington made such spirited resistance to the British forces, and where Lafayette was wounded. The chief points of the historic field are plainly marked.

When crossing the Brandywine one must also cross that remarkable bit of railroad construction, the Wilmington and Northern—a system which follows the western Brandywine for more than fifty miles. W. W. MacElree, the Boswell of the Brandywine, has said of this road:

"In the main it consists of a collection of curves: curves of low degree and high degree, harmonious and irregular, sinister and dextral, curves with functions, and curves without function, curves that find their expression in algebraic symbols, and curves which transcend the powers of mathematics to express them—all are here in profusion: parabolic forms for geometers and diabolic forms for passengers. Travelers taking the road for the first time have been heard to say there are no two consecutive points lying in the same direction from Wilmington to Reading. It is not unusual to find a passenger train occupying three of these curves, while a freight train often lengthens itself out over four or five. It is asserted that a great many of these were introduced for the purpose of enabling its passengers to see both sides of the road at the same time, but I have heard it maintained that the comfort of the passengers was not considered at all, the aim of the engineers being rather to demonstrate that in railroad construction a straight line is unnecessary and useless."

One thing is certain, however. A ride over the line furnishes a trip whose unusual features will be recalled with appreciation and delight, for it passes through the heart of one of the finest agricultural regions in the state, where Nature vies with herself to make the quiet beauty of one mile exceeded only by that of the next mile.

Southwest from the railroad of curves and the river of romance is the town where Bayard Taylor built his mansion Cedarcroft. Here he spent some of the pleasantest years of his life. There is little opportunity to wonder why he chose this spot after seeing the property, still the pride of the town.

Once, when the wife of the poet-novelist journeyed to Cedarcroft, she wrote lines that are among the best available descriptions of Chester County scenery:

"The countryside through which our primitive road led us after we had left the Delaware was so lovely, so idyllic, that I forgot how bad it was underfoot. We skirted hills and valleys, tilled land and green woods in changeful succession; hedged fields with here and there a single wide-branched tree casting its broad shadow, and meadows, through which a brook fringed with willows meandered along, where fine herds of cattle were grazing or resting in the lush herbage. Anon we passed gentle slopes overgrown with bowers of foliage, of maple, sycamore, walnut, chestnut, locust, and sassafras. Tangled thickets intwined with grapevines climbing to the treetop, and in dark hollows an exquisite wilderness of flowers and ferns ran riot. Nestled among sheltering clumps of trees the farmhouses lay scattered here and there, surrounded by orchards and barns which were often larger and more pretentious than the modest dwellings."

And the writer was fresh from the charms of Europe!

Some twenty miles after leaving Kennett Square on the road to Gap, one more of the delightful streams of Chester County is reached—the Octoraro. This section of the creek has long been a center of the fox-hunting sport. The hunters from the Rose Tree Hunt of Media have often ridden to Pine Hill, an eminence near Octoraro, a town to the left of the road—by the way, one of the oldest post offices in the country. An enthusiastic fox hunter who knows Pine Hill well once broke into rhyme as he thought of the sport:

"And surely never yet was heard,
From tongue of man, or throat of bird,
From reed or tuba, or string or key,
From all the craft of minstrelsy,
More stirring, joy-inspiring sounds
Than one such orchestra of hounds
Pours o'er the listening land,
As if the muses' sylvan powers
Went choiring through the matin hours
At Dian's fond command."

Christiana, the last town before the Lancaster road is reached at Gap, is noted for something more serious than fox-hunting. A monument at the corner of the Pennsylvania railroad subway hints at the story of Edward Gorusch, Castner Hanway, and others who followed their lead. The time was 1851; the place was the humble house of an ex-slave, who was sheltering four fugitive slaves. When the marshal came he defied them. "There will be no slaves taken back from here while I am alive," were his words. One Marylander was killed in the melée that followed.

The case became famous, not only in this country, but in Europe as well, for it was the first instance of open resistance to the authority of government in the anti-slavery agitation.

Thirty-eight of those who resisted the officers were put on trial for treason, but all were eventually released. While some of them were in Moyamensing prison, Philadelphia, awaiting trial, John G. Whittier wrote his "Lines" to them:

> "God's ways seem dark, but soon or late
> They touch the shining hills of day.
> The evil cannot brook delay,
> The good can well afford to wait.
>   Give ermined knaves their hour of crime;
> Ye have the future grand and great,
>   The safe appeal of truth to time."

A number of other Chester County towns were prominent in the great movement of aiding escaping slaves from the South to Canada. Kennett Square and West Chester as well as Christiana sheltered and passed on many of the refugees. Lancaster, too, was a point of importance on the remarkable and mysterious "underground railroad."

There is characteristic Lancaster County landscape all the way from Gap to Elizabethtown, a town noted in the early days of the New Orleans trade for its boat-building activities, and later for the building of canal boats. Conewago Creek, which forms the northern boundary of Lancaster County, has supplied both power and access to the Susquehanna for these and other purposes.

The approach to the Conewago is impressive. The road descends one hundred and twenty-five feet to the water, and again ascends after crossing the creek. The valley between the hills that define the fertile valley is four miles wide.

STONE BRIDGE CROSSING THE COCALICO, NEAR EPHRATA
Built in 1800
Photo from Philadelphia & Reading Railroad

ALONG SWATARA CREEK
Photo by J. Horace McFarland Company

ROAD TO WHEELING AND PITTSBURGH

Near Middletown—so named because of its situation half way between Lancaster and Carlisle—the Susquehanna is first seen from this road. This, the oldest town in Dauphin County, has been prominent in the development of Pennsylvania because of its unique situation. During the Revolution a commissary boat was located here; supplies were sent by it to Wilkes-Barre for the use of General Sullivan's expedition against the Six Nations. There was also a lead refinery, used under direction of Congress for the preparation of ammunition for Washington. Later the Union canal, the first in the United States, was built down the Swatara, to connect with the Pennsylvania canal up the Susquehanna.

If plans made by George Washington had been carried out Middletown would have been the hub of Pennsylvania, at least so long as canals remained the chief means of freight transportation. In 1784, after an exhaustive investigation, he recommended to Governor Harris of Virginia a system of canals and river transportation of which Middletown was to be the center. The routes he outlined as desirable were:

1. Up the Swatara to Philadelphia, by way of the Quitapahilla and the Schuylkill canal to Philadelphia. The distance would have been 140 miles.

2. Middletown to Havre de Grace; 54 miles.

3. To Pittsburgh, along the Juniata, and other streams; 285 miles.

4. By way of Susquehanna, Sinnemahoning, and Allegheny, to Presque Isle (Erie); 420 miles.

5. An alternative route to Presque Isle by the Allegheny; 421 miles.

6. By North Branch of Susquehanna, the Tioga, and other streams to Lake Ontario; 382 miles.

7. To Otsego Lake; 359 miles.

At that time Robert Fulton shared with Washington enthusiasm for canal building. Many times the two exchanged ideas on the subject, and in 1796 Fulton sent to Washington a copy of his "Treatise on the Improvement of Canal Navigation." On the title page he wrote:

"I beg leave to present you with this publication: Which I hope will be honoured with your Perusal at a Leisure hour; the object of Which is to Exhibit the Certain Mode of Giving Agriculture to every acre of the immense Continent of America; By means of a creative System of Canals."

The measure of Fulton's startling program is revealed by the final chapter in the volume, written on blank pages, for Washington's eye only. In this he proposed to make the horse path of the leading canals sufficiently wide for a road for horsemen. In their passage the canals "would water the cities and towns, clens them of Filth and Sprinkle them in seasons of derth." Every farmer would be able to irrigate his land, and to have a private water wheel for the production of power to thresh, cut straw, break and clean flax, grind apples, mash turnips, wash, churn. In conclusion Fulton said:

"Thus we See the Infinite Advantage to be derived from a Judicious use of the Streams which nature has lifted to our Mountains, Streams by which the demand for horses May be much diminished, and America Rendered Like one Continual Garden of Which every Acre would Maintain its Main Stream which would produce Abundance and every one of them having the Necessaries and Conveniences of Life Within their easy Reach would be Left to their discretion to Use them like Rational Beings."

Little was destined to come of this wonderful vision

of Lancaster County's child, who, eleven years later, was to put on the Hudson a vessel that would show railroad builders the way to relegate canals to the background. But much of Washington's more practical program was realized, as a study of the relief map of the state in this volume will show.

Canal and river, railway and highway are side by side all the way from Middletown to Harrisburg. This bit of country has lost none of its attractions since 1788, when John Penn wrote of it:

"From the vast forest and the expansive bed of the river, navigable to its source for craft carrying two tons burden, the ideas of grandeur and immensity rush forcibly upon the mind, mixed with the desert wildness of an uninhabited scene."

But the wildness of the country was not to be to him an argument against this region, any more than it was to William Penn nearly a century earlier. Soon after Penn landed in Pennsylvania, he showed his desire to secure the title to the Susquehanna country. In 1696 he succeeded in making a lease for one thousand years from Thomas Dongan, once governor of New York, the price being £100 and annual rent of a "pepper corn," if demanded. Later, absolute title was given by Dongan. The Delawares, who claimed an interest in the lands, transferred their title in 1736, yet it was 1784 before all dispute to the ownership of the territory west of the Susquehanna was finally ended.

Penn asked £5000 of John Harris, the first settler on the present site of Harrisburg, for all the land from the river to Silver Spring, and across the Cumberland Valley from mountain to mountain, but the bargain was concluded for £3000.

John Harris was a trader, and the attraction for him

was the Indian village on the river. His son, John Harris, who laid out the town in 1784, lived the quiet life of a ferryman; the famous "Harris Ferry," which was mentioned as a candidate for the national capital, having been founded in 1753. The town became the county seat in 1785, and it was made the capital of the state in 1812, after a contest in which it won over Northumberland and Reading by a single vote.

John Harris may have been a trader, but money was not his idol. He was a thoroughgoing patriot. Although he was at first opposed to the passage of the Declaration of Independence, he and Mrs. Harris later lent the colony £3000 for the expenses of the war, making known the fact that they were ready to give the sum outright, if need be.

Visitors to Harrisburg are tempted to agree with Mrs. Annie Royall, who, in 1828, called the site of this city one of the most charming spots on the globe. She echoed the sentiments of Thomas Ashe, the traveler of 1806, who declared that "the breadth and beauty of the river, the height and grandeur of its banks, the variety of scenery, the verdure of the forests, the murmur of the water, and the melody of the birds, all combined to fill my mind with vast and elevated thoughts."

A walk along the river front, where there is a drive of which any city in the world might be proud, is a pleasure that should be long drawn out. Features in the prospect are the gracefully curving banks, the silvery sheet of water (a mile wide), the green islands, the tree-clad slope beyond, and the bridges, chief among them being that at Market street, a successor of the old wooden "camel-back" structure, begun in 1813. At the portal of this bridge stand two of the columns rescued from the fire that destroyed the old capitol in 1896.

ROAD TO WHEELING AND PITTSBURGH

Next comes the natural park site of twelve acres, not far from the center of the city. From this the vista of river and mountain is a joy that is ever new.

Then climb to the dome of the capitol. Look out on the broad Kittatinny Valley, in which the city is situated by the river bank. See the Susquehanna sweeping to the northward, and on to the southeast. Follow the mountains that encircle the city, now close at hand, now farther away. Look off to the gap through which the river breaks a way through the Blue Mountains. Let the eye rest on the small islands that dot the river, and the larger Duncan's Island, where David Brainerd visited the Indians. Look across to the Cumberland Valley, between the Conodoguinet and Yellow Breeches Creek. Yes, look, and look again, and say if it is not good to be alive in a world of which, when God had made it, he said that all was very good.

Beauty is not left behind when the river is crossed and the road is taken down the Cumberland Valley toward Carlisle. On the right, just at hand, are the graceful curves of the Conodoguinet. Farther to the right is the seemingly endless ridge of the Blue Mountains. To the left are fertile farms. Everything, everywhere, gives emphatic testimony to the wisdom of the pioneers who braved the perils of the frontiers, to make their home in this favored valley.

Along this road—the "great road" of the middle eighteenth century, which was made a turnpike in 1813—George Washington traveled in 1794, when he went to the West to put down the Whiskey Rebellion. And in 1863 an invading force from the South marched down the road toward Harrisburg, to Camp Hill, within sight of the city.

Carlisle, too, had its experience during the same

June week. Confederate cavalry entered the town and remained for three days. On July 1 the town was shelled, and when it refused to surrender the shelling was renewed, and much damage was done by fire. But the troops retired without taking possession.

Revolutionary history also was made here. Three of the signers of the Declaration made their homes in Carlisle—George Ross, James Wilson, and Thomas Smith. Bullets and cannon were manufactured for the army, and officers were trained in a building long used as the Indian school, and—during the Great War—as a reconstruction hospital for invalid soldiers. This institution, located just at the edge of town, on the highway to Harrisburg, looks out on the ever glorious Blue Mountains.

After the Revolution the town once again knew the tread of soldiers, for thirteen thousand men were quartered here in 1794, while Washington was making preparation to march against the misguided men who inspired the Whiskey Rebellion.

But long before the days when Washington visited Carlisle armed men were a familiar sight. The early stockade, where twelve men made their headquarters, was succeeded by Fort Louthier in 1753; in this fifty men were on duty. That was the year of the treaty of friendship with the Ohio Indians, whose representatives came to the fort to meet the three commissioners of the colony, of whom Benjamin Franklin was one.

In 1764 Carlisle was the scene of one of the most affecting incidents of early Indian warfare. During that year the Indians sent here many captives, some of whom had been held for years. That these might be returned to their homes Colonel Bouquet sent word about the countryside that parents who had lost children in Indian raids should appear to identify them. Among those who applied was an eager old woman who told a moving tale of a daughter whom the Indians had kept from her for many years. In vain she looked at all the released captives; in none of them could she recognize the features of her lost daughter. In her sorrow she told Colonel Bouquet that when her daughter was small she had been accustomed to sing to her a song that became a favorite with the child.

"Suppose you sing it now!" the colonel suggested. With eager but faltering voice she did sing:

"Alone, yet not alone, am I,
   Though in the solitude so drear;
I find my Saviour always nigh,
   He comes my dreary hours to cheer."

At the first note one of the unclaimed women started. An instant later she was on her feet. And before the last note was sung she rushed to the singer and cast herself into the arms that had been empty so long—the arms of her mother. The song learned in childhood had bridged the gap of years.

Carlisle has other reminders of the heroic days of old than such incidents as that cited above. All about the town are places famous for their connection with the events of those days, as well as remarkable for the beauty that has survived and will survive. On the north is Wagner's Gap in the Blue Mountains, and on the northeast Sterrett's Gap provides a ready-made outlet for a roadway; while Carlisle Springs is within four miles of the city in the same direction. Southeast, on Yellow Breeches Creek, is Boiling Springs, whose bubbling water fascinated the Indians as it attracted the first settlers. On the banks of the Conodoguinet, not far away, is a remarkable limestone cave where generations of boys have explored, imagining marvelous adventures.

From Newville a road leads eight miles north through Doubling Gap, which was used for the passage of an Indian trail, long before the coming of the white men. The gap is on the upper border of the interesting hairpin loop in the northern boundary of Cumberland County, made necessary by the unusual configuration of the mountain range at this point.

Doubling Gap was one of the favorite haunts of David Lewis, the gentleman outlaw who roamed the country from Somerset to Carlisle in his search for victims—victims whom he would rob but would not kill; he drew the line at bloodshed because of his uncomfortable memories of the story of Cain and Abel, once read in his hearing when he was a lad. He has been compared to Sir Walter Scott's "Rob Roy," for he stole from the rich to give to the poor. For years efforts to catch him were in vain, because he could retire at will into some mountain fastness where no one was able to discover him. Yet the day of his capture came. The cave he used to seek above Doubling Gap when he was in his glory in 1815 has been filled up, and David Lewis, the outlaw, is a memory still used by unwise people to terrify the children.

This Rob Roy of Cumberland County must often have haunted the old Three Mountain Road. This led from Shippensburg—except York, the oldest town in Pennsylvania west of the Susquehanna—to Fort Littleton in Fulton County. Eventually the pioneer road was extended to Pittsburgh, where it entered the city on the site of Penn avenue, leading to the foot of the hill where the Pennsylvania Railroad station now stands.

ROAD TO WHEELING AND PITTSBURGH

Not far from Shippensburg, in the midst of a landscape whose charms must always be a subject of delighted comment, was the home of Alexander Thomson, a Scotchman. In 1771 he bought a farm on Conococheague Creek, where Scotland village now looks out on the valley. An English traveler who once visited him described his log cabin as a house "built of square blocks of wood, worked or indented in one another." Then he quoted from a letter written by the proprietor to a friend near his old home. This letter is evidence that the pioneers were not so occupied by the stern realities of daily life that they were unable to appreciate those common blessings money cannot buy:

"While I and my son are clearing ground, and go for a while to walk or rest ourselves in the forest among the tall oaks on a summer day, the sight of the heavens and the smell of the air give me pleasure which I cannot tell you how great it is. When I sit down to rest, the breezes of the southwest wind, and the whispering noise it makes in the top of the trees, together with the fine smell of the plants and flowers, please us so exceedingly that we are almost enchanted, and unwilling to part with such a pleasure."

Two pioneers of a different sort located in 1843 near Greencastle, some miles south of Chambersburg, attracted there by just such a scene of delight as that about Scotland. These men proved to be missionaries of the church of Latter Day Saints, and it was their purpose to lay the foundation of a colony of Mormons. A farm was bought on the banks of a tributary of the Conococheague, and two hundred settlers followed. A city and a temple were planned for the future, but for the time being a barn served as temple. A paper was even published at Greencastle. But financial difficulties overtook the missionaries. They could not live on the beautiful scenery within the shadow of the Cove Mountains. When the mortgage on the farm was foreclosed they gathered up their possessions and stole away to the West.

Originally Greencastle was called Conococheague Settlement. At the demand of the settlers who wished to market their produce in Baltimore, a road was laid out over the site of what became Waynesboro, through Nicolas's Gap in South Mountain, and on toward the East.

Waynesboro, was named for "Mad Anthony" Wayne, under whom a son of the founder, John Wallace, served during the Revolution. The citizens of the town always have been proud of its location, and for this they can readily be excused. Surely they have a right to be proud of the unique composite of glen and ravine, of forested heights and sloping valley, of the winding Antietam Creek and the haughty mountain above them from whose height they secure the most satisfying vision of their great possessions.

In the list of things that invite the Waynesboroites to spend much time out of doors are the limestone caverns all about the town. The largest of these is on the Maryland line, a little more than a mile southeast. A subterranean stream adds mystery to the cavern. Then there is Nicolas's Gap, long the haunt of outlaws, where even to-day the Pennsylvania State Police need to keep their eyes open. Through the gap passes Mason and Dixon's line. This way led many of the Indian trails, and here scouting parties innumerable had their rendezvous. The engineers of the Western Maryland were glad to choose this pass for the construction of the line through a difficult country, and the Tapeworm Railroad "wriggled hitherward," in the expressive phrase of a local historian.

SUSQUEHANNA RIVER AT HARRISBURG
Photo by State Department of Forestry

A PEEP INTO THE VALLEY, CUMBERLAND COUNTY
Photo by State Department of Forestry

THE ONLY STONE TOLLHOUSE ON THE NATIONAL HIGHWAY
STILL STANDING IN PENNSYLVANIA, AT ADDISON
Photo by State Highway Department

OLD VIADUCT ACROSS TOMS CREEK ON TAPEWORM RAILROAD
Photo by State Department of Forestry

ROAD TO WHEELING AND PITTSBURGH

The Tapeworm Railroad (properly the Gettysburg Railroad) was Thaddeus Stevens's pet project. By it he hoped to connect with the Baltimore and Ohio Railroad, and market the product of his iron furnace, farther north. He was a member of the state legislature, and he found it an easy matter to induce his fellow legislators to make appropriations for the road; at last, however, when nearly a million dollars had been swallowed up by the line, appropriations ceased. So Waynesboro was without a railroad until 1878, the year of the completion of the Mont Alto Railroad from Scotland.

The situation of Waynesboro on the border made the town an easy mark for invaders from the South. Before the battle of Gettysburg, troops were in the town, and the people were compelled to furnish supplies to them. After the battle the retreating men were engaged near Waynesboro by the Army of the Potomac.

The point where the road to Hagerstown crosses the Mason and Dixon line is about half way between Greencastle and the junction with the National Road. This historic line is marked by pillars. The original stones, brought by the surveyors from England, were a foot square, four feet and a half high, and weighed five hundred pounds. It is not strange that many of these stones were removed from their places during the long years between the first survey and the resurvey by Maryland and Delaware in 1900 and 1901. These recent surveyors searched for the missing stones and found many of them. "One was found as a door step; another was in a bake oven; two were in a foundation for a church." Whenever it was possible, the old stones were returned to their former location.

Hagerstown is the first town on the National Road so

justly famous in the early development of the Ohio Valley country. Although the section from Hagerstown to Cumberland, like that from Hagerstown to Baltimore, was not constructed by the United States, as was the section from Cumberland to Wheeling, and the later section to Indianapolis, the entire route became known as the National Road because the roads from Baltimore already constructed were joined to and made a part of the work of the government engineers.

The National Road, or the Cumberland Road, as it was often named, has been called "the longest straight road ever built in the world," since for seven hundred miles it "marks the course of the Star of Empire in the advance from the East to the West."

Almost at once after leaving Hagerstown the reason becomes apparent for urging that, so far as scenery to the north is concerned, the next sixty miles of this turnpike be considered a Pennsylvania road. To the right the eye has many a glimpse into the state to the north; sometimes these glimpses become vistas of astounding extent and charm. As an instance, there is, from a hilltop five miles from Hagerstown, opportunity for such an alluring study of the windings of the Conococheague (which flows the length of Franklin, the county of sparkling streams and cooling springs), that there is apt to be born a longing for the time when its course can be followed through all its windings. And why not? Think of a week's tramp from this point or, better, from the Potomac to a place near the source of the Conococheague; then a cross-country, around-the-mountain ramble to the headwaters of Sherman's Creek; then along this stream the length of Perry County, to the Susquehanna, not far from the mouth of the Juniata!

But now the National Road is calling—on from the hill overlooking the creek of many windings to Fairview Mountain and through the gap between the barrier and Boyd Mountain. From here, where the road ascends to a height of about one thousand feet, the way is through the mountains for sixty miles or more.

Gradually the traveler approaches closer to the state line. Tonoloway Ridge is followed by Sideling Hill, perhaps the most dreaded of the ridges crossed by the emigrants who ventured this way before good roads were built. To-day one does not need to dread Sideling Hill, though the grades are steep—in a mile and a half the ascent is seven hundred and sixty feet. But the steeper the grade the more comprehensive and varied the view is apt to be.

Sideling Hill Creek is crossed by one of the monumental stone bridges that are so characteristic of this road, most of them bridges that date from the year when Henry Clay, then at the height of his fame, stood by the project for the National Road against all opponents. The story is told of one of these old bridges that it resisted the fearful pressure of an immense steel truss, torn from its fastenings by a flood, until the steel was twisted into such a shape that the waters could force it through the arches.

After crossing Polish Mountain the road descends to Flintstone, an ancient village in Warrior's Gap. Near by the Indians picked their way through the mountains into Pennsylvania, which is here but little more than a mile distant. At Cumberland, twelve miles farther on, the state line is five miles away.

The contracts for the ten miles of road leading out of Cumberland were signed in 1811. The town was left behind by a route over Wills Mountain that corresponded almost exactly to the track taken by Braddock in 1753; but more than twenty years later it was relocated through the Narrows, the passage at grade, along Wills Creek, through the mountain. This is a gorge that will stand out in the memory of those who have the privilege of passing through it—as will many other features of the next few miles, particularly St. John's Rock on Big Savage Mountain. This is a point of vantage for a view of mountain scenery that is not excelled along the route, unless one goes to Dans Rock, on the top of Dans Mountain, seven miles southeast of Frostburg, from which large parts of Pennsylvania, as well as of Maryland and West Virginia, can be seen. Robert Bruce, in his book, "The National Road," calls this "one of the finest views in the Appalachians." Unfortunately, as there is not yet a good road to the eminence, those who are able to enjoy the panorama spread out on a clear day are comparatively few.

Little Savage Mountain comes next. This is crossed at a height almost as great as the loftiest point on the Lincoln Highway, many miles to the north. Following the mountain comes a remarkable bit of road-building, "the long stretch," as the traveler of early days called it. For two miles and a half there is not the slightest deviation from a straight line.

Near the beginning of "the long stretch," Fishing Run is crossed, a creek worth noting because this is the first stream which the changing watershed turns northward toward the Monongahela. Waters crossed hitherto have turned toward the Atlantic. Then near the end of the stretch is Two Mile Run, not far from the spot where Braddock's Road crossed the route taken by the National Road. The hollow through whose center the creek flowed was dreaded by the pioneer wagoner,

ROAD TO WHEELING AND PITTSBURGH

by reason of the dense pine forests, since cut away, which made the glen so dark that it was called "the shades of death."

Castleman River is crossed by a fine stone arch bridge. This was Little Crossings of Braddock's day. When the unfortunate general passed the stream, the country was a famous hunting ground, where bear and elk and deer were numerous. On November 8, 1751, Christopher Gist, who was making a journey to the Monongahela for the Ohio Company, wrote that he "killed several Deer, and Bears, and one large Elk."

A tablet set in a rock on the right hand side of the road, just after it passes into Somerset County, Pennsylvania, calls attention to the fact that this way went Washington and Braddock.

It was in 1754 that Washington made the adventurous passage of which Sparks says:

"So many obstacles intervened that progress was slow. Trees were to be felled, bridges made, marshes filled up, and rocks removed. In the midst of these difficulties the provisions failed—the commissioners having neglected to fulfill their engagements—and there was great distress for lack of bread. At the Youghiogheny, where they were detained in constructing a bridge, Colonel Washington was told by the traders and Indians, that, except at one place, a passage might be had by water down that river. To ascertain this point—extremely advantageous if true—he embarked in a canoe, with five men, on a tour of discovery, leaving the army under the command of a subordinate officer. His hopes were disappointed. After navigating the river in his canoe more than thirty miles, encountering rocks and shoals, he passed between two mountains, and came to a fall that arrested his course. He returned, and the project of a conveyance by water was given up."

The start for this vain canoe journey was at Confluence, not far from Addison, a little town some distance beyond the state line, made noteworthy for the traveler by the curious stone toll house by the roadside, one of three toll houses still standing on the road in Pennsylvania.

The crossing of the Youghiogheny at Somerfield has always been known as Big Crossings. It will be remembered that Castleman River, which enters the Youghiogheny not far north of Somerfield, was left behind at Little Crossings. By road it is not much more than twenty miles between the crossings, but by water the distance is more than twice as great.

Perhaps it will not be thought strange that there was much uncertainty about spelling such a difficult name as Youghiogheny. Christopher Gist called it Yaughaughanny, while Youghhannie, Yok-yo-gane, Yaw-yaw-gany, Yoh-w-gain, and Yox-i-geny are other forms.

On the far side of the substantial bridge at Big Crossings—one of whose walls carries a tablet calling attention to Colonel Washington's passage of the stream a short distance beyond—the road passes into Fayette County.

A succession of grades all the way from Somerfield to Farmington give vantage points for repeated studies of the rugged but fertile lands of southern Fayette.

West of Farmington, between the fifty-second and fifty-third milestones, are the fields of rolling green where Washington fought his first battle and made "his first and only surrender." This site he called the Great Meadows, and the fort which he built to oppose the advancing French he called Fort Necessity. A tablet on the site of the fort records the fact. Washington had four hundred men; nine hundred French regulars,

ROAD TO WHEELING AND PITTSBURGH

together with their Indian allies, opposed him. Yet he managed to hold out for nine hours against this superior force.

Thirteen years after the surrender Washington became owner of three hundred acres including the site of Fort Necessity, paying for the tract less than one hundred dollars. He was still in possession of the land when he died. In his will he spoke of the tract as being worth six dollars per acre. Then he described it:

"This land is valuable on account of its local situation. It affords an exceeding good stand on Braddock's Road, from Fort Cumberland to Pittsburg; and besides a fertile soil, possesses a large quantity of natural meadow, fit for the scythe. It is distinguished by the appellation of the Great Meadows, where the first action with the French in 1754 was fought."

Less than a year after Washington's defeat at Fort Necessity, General Braddock passed the site of the fort, on his way to Fort Du Quesne, where he was sure he would have a glorious victory. But a few days later, fatally wounded, he was carried by some of his men back to the Great Meadows. When he died his body was buried in the middle of the road and the wagons of the expedition were driven over the grave, lest the Indians should discover and desecrate it. Washington himself conducted the services of burial. In 1804 the body was taken up and reinterred a few rods away, near Braddock's Run, between the fifty-fourth and fifty-fifth milestones, only about a mile from Fort Necessity.

In 1871, when the grave was marked only by an old stump, a Pittsburgh nurseryman who visited the spot decided to mark it by trees appropriately chosen. Because it was an English general who died fighting against the French intruder on American soil, he chose, first, two English elms, two English larches, and two Norway spruces. All these were imported from England. Then came a weeping willow from the tomb of the first Napoleon at St. Helena, and a selection of American shrubbery. The trees, planted in a square about the grave, grew splendidly. Until a few years ago, surrounded by a board fence, they were a landmark. But in 1913 twenty-three acres, including the grave, were bought by the General Braddock Memorial Park Association, and a monument was erected on the site. The association was made up in great part of people from Uniontown and Fayette County. To-day the lines of Stephen Tilden are more true to fact than when they were written:

> "Beneath this stone brave Braddock lies,
> Who always hated cowardice,
> But fell a savage sacrifice,
>   Amidst his Indian foes.
> I charge you, heroes of the ground,
> To guard the dark pavilion round,
> And keep off all obtruding sound,
>   And cherish his repose."

In this vicinity stood one of the most famous and most prosperous taverns of the staging days. It is recorded that in a single year the profits were $4000, and that on one morning seventy-two passengers took breakfast there. In the days when this inn was in its glory the turnpike "looked like the leading avenue of a great city rather than a road through rural districts." One man in 1848 counted one hundred and thirty-three six-horse teams passing along the road in one day, and took no notice of many more teams of one, two, three, and four horses. It looked "as if the whole earth was on the road—wagons, stages, horses, cattle, hogs, sheep, and turkeys without number."

One Fayette County wagoner said that on a night when he stopped at a mountain inn there were thirty six-horse teams in the wagon yard, one hundred Kentucky mules in an adjacent lot, one thousand hogs in other enclosures, and as many fat cattle for Illinois in adjoining fields.

Those were the days when the driver of the stage coach acted like a monarch. A traveler of 1848, in his history of the road, told of one coachman who, in passing an orchard, halted in spite of the protests of his passengers, climbed a "snake" fence, and proceeded to fill his pockets with apples. The impatient passengers called to him, but he paid no attention. So a man on the driver's seat urged the horses on. The driver pursued in vain: "The road was now on the side of Chestnut Ridge (six miles from Uniontown), and the descent was rapid. In a few minutes, when turning a curve, the coach swayed over, and fell down a precipice ten feet, almost perpendicular, rolling twenty feet further, till brought up by the trunk of a locust tree." There was half a day's delay. That night, when the stage reached its stopping place, beyond Uniontown, many of the passengers had black eyes and bandaged heads.

One more tale of the road—a tale of the days before the way was made easy for stage drivers and wagoners to be monarchs. Near the summit of Laurel Hill (Chestnut Ridge) John Slack had a tavern. When he learned that a new road was proposed, he was loud in his opposition. But in spite of his protestations the improvement was made. Later, when he was asked the reason for his opposition, he said:

"Wagons coming up Laurel Hill would stick in the mud a mile or so below my house, when the drivers would unhitch, leave the wagon in the mud, and bring their teams to me and stay with me all night. In the morning they would return to their stranded wagons, dig and haul them out, and get back to my house and stay with me another night. Thus, counting the wagons going east and west, I got four nights' bills from the same set of wagons. Now the wagons whip by without stopping."

But just as there were those who opposed the construction of the turnpike because they thought the improvement would be an injury to them, so there were those who fought the railroads, and for the same reason. When the railroads began to take away the traffic from the road the wagoners had a song whose chorus was:

"Now all ye jolly wagoners,
   who have got good wives,
Go home to your farms, and there
   spend your lives;
When your corn is all cribbed,
   and your small grain is good,
You'll have nothing to do but
   curse the railroad."

There came a day, however, when the wagoners were called back from their farms for a brief renewal of their reign on the turnpike. Word was passed that there was a break in the Pennsylvania Canal, and that the whole system, including the Portage Railroad, was paralyzed. For a time all western freight had to go over the National Road in wagons. The news was brought to the scattered farms by the drivers of the stage coaches, and within a few days the road had resumed its old-time activity.

After many years of comparative quiet the National

THE GREAT MEADOWS, WITH FORT NECESSITY OUTLINED IN CENTER
Photo by James Hadden

WASHINGTON'S MILL, OWNED BY WASHINGTON AT THE TIME OF HIS DEATH.
BUILT 1776
Still standing, twelve miles north of Uniontown
Photo supplied by Dr. F. C. Robinson

TURKEY'S NEST BRIDGE, FAYETTE COUNTY
Photo supplied by Robert Bruce

IN WASHINGTON COUNTY
Photo by State Highway Department

ROAD TO WHEELING AND PITTSBURGH

Road is alive once again. Automobiles are so many that old roads have been opened and new hotels have been built. The most magnificent of them is the Summit Hotel, on the crest of Laurel Ridge. From this favored resort there is a glorious view of the Monongahela Valley. The pleasure afforded by the survey of the countryside may be prolonged with profit by a short side trip from the hotel to Washington Springs, a mile distant, and Jumonville, two miles farther on. Here Washington, a little before his disappointing defeat at Great Meadows, gained a slight success. Learning of the presence of a party of French under the leadership of Jumonville, he went with a few of his men to Washington Springs, where he found a company of friendly Indians. Their counsel led him to seek Jumonville and attack him. The French leader was killed, as were several of his followers; the rest were captured.

Now comes a bit of the road where the automobile is a hindrance rather than a help. To enjoy to the fullest extent the vistas that follow one after the other in startling variety, one should not ride down the three-mile slope to the foot of the ridge; he should walk, and he should take from one to two hours to accomplish the descent—twelve hundred feet within three miles. Near the end of the grade is a bridge of unusual design, out of all proportion to the size of the stream crossed. This is the Turkey's Nest bridge, built in 1818, on a curve, with stone walls, massive but graceful. The trees on either hand, growing from the banks of the little stream, make the spot look like the work of a master of parkway construction and landscape gardening.

If the National Road had been constructed as it was first planned, the traveler would have missed the satisfaction of seeing the country toward the Monongahela

SEEING PENNSYLVANIA

from Summit; he would have missed Turkey's Nest, and he would have missed Uniontown. Originally the route was to have been more direct toward Wheeling, but when Pennsylvania gave permission for the construction of a part of the turnpike within her borders, the stipulation was made that the route should be changed, if possible, so as to include Uniontown and Washington.

To have missed Uniontown would have been a calamity, for it proved to be one of the chief points on the road, by reason both of interest and business. The tourists of to-day marvel at the city in its setting of green amid the hills; many of them know beforehand that Uniontown is an important center, but few are prepared to see one of the most pleasing cities in the state. The taste of the citizens is apparent on the streets, in the residences, in the business buildings.

Times have changed since 1784, when General Ephraim Douglass wrote from here to General James Irvine at Pittsburgh. He said of the settlement, then seventeen years old:

"This Uniontown is the most obscure spot on the face of the globe. I have been here seven or eight weeks without an opportunity of writing to the land of the living; and, though considerably south of you, so cold that a person not knowing the latitude would conclude we were placed near one of the Poles . . . The town and its appurtenances consist of . . . a court-house and school-house in one, a mill, and consequently a miller, four taverns, three smith shops, five retail shops, two Tanyards, one sadler's shop, two hatters' shops, one mason, one cake woman, two widows and some maids. To which may be added a distillery.

"I can say little of the country in general, but that it is very poor in everything but the soil, which is excellent, and that part contiguous to the town is really

ROAD TO WHEELING AND PITTSBURGH

beautiful, being level and prettily situate, accommodated with good water and excellent meadow ground."

But better days came. The settlers had freedom to develop the country and to care for their homes. The road was built, and with it arrived tens of thousands of brave men and women who did not falter at the prospect of going to the West, where they, too, would have some of the very problems that conspired to make life so difficult for Fayette County folks in the days before the road went through.

The number of emigrants and other travelers became so great at one time that a resident of Uniontown wrote, "Scarcely an hour of the day passes when a stage coach may not be seen passing through the town."

Stage coaches meant taverns, and Uniontown had a number of famous hostelries. There were also stage yards, where horses were changed and coach supplies were kept. In connection with one of these stage yards a story is told of Dr. John F. Braddee, a famous criminal whose case demanded the attention of the United States courts for some time.

The doctor's medicine was in demand. Patients, it is said, came hundreds of miles to see him. At the trial it was stated that fifty horses had been seen around his office at one time.

Yet the fees that came from his patients did not satisfy him. He wanted easier money. And he proceeded to get it. The sight of the mail bags carelessly thrown at the feet of the drivers of the coaches stirred his cupidity, and he laid his plans to get hold of some of them.

First he bought the property next to Stockton's stage yard. This was a place much frequented, for at the time (1840) there were usually thirty coaches a day in either direction. Then he scraped acquaintance with one of the caretakers of the teams during their moments of pause in the town. When the time was ripe he proposed to the man to let him get hold of the mail bags, promising him an equal share in the profits. The proposition was accepted; the two men agreed to work together.

Various methods were used. Sometimes the driver would leave behind, at the inn where he changed horses, one of the bags which he had reason to believe was the most valuable in his care. Again, the doctor would send a message after the driver. The man would bring back to him a bag which the driver conveniently dropped.

The scheme might have been worked indefinitely, but the doctor failed to keep his word as to the division of profits. Detectives who were on the track of the culprit managed to secure possession of one of the two men who knew the doctor's secret. The trial was fiercely contested, but the criminal was convicted and sentenced to prison for ten years.

From Uniontown to Brownsville there are a number of the dignified old stone taverns, some of which may have been, without the knowledge of the proprietors, scenes of the doctor's nefarious operations. Perhaps the most noted of these relics is the Searight House, six miles from Uniontown, at a crossroads, and on the north side of the pike. It is now the home of a great-grandson of the original proprietor, who was for a long time a commissioner charged with the upkeep of a section of the road. Another member of the family was Thomas B. Searight, the author of "The Old Pike," the most exhaustive of the books on the route. The body of Mr. Searight, who asked to be buried near the road in which he took so much delight, was placed in Oak Grove Cemetery, a short distance west of Uniontown, the grave being within sight of those who pass by.

There is a combination of the old and the new at Brier Hill, Peter Colley's tavern, built in 1796, and the modern town, built up by the coke industry. The coke furnace here is one of the most important in the region.

The short space from Brier Hill to Brownsville provides a succession of satisfying views, the last of them the best of all—from Sandy Hollow over to the Monongahela River. The rapid descent (three hundred feet within two miles) increases road difficulties, but it adds decidedly to the pleasure of the trip.

The last stop leads into the heart of Brownsville, one of the earliest settlements in western Pennsylvania. In pioneer days it was called Redstone Old Fort; and thus it was named on the tract laid out by Nemacolin from Winchester, Virginia, to the Ohio in 1749. Five years later Washington came this way. From here some of the troops of George Rogers Clark embarked for the Falls of the Ohio, where that far-seeing man had planned his expedition against the strongholds of the British in Indiana and Illinois. From here General Rufus Putnam and his heroes, many of them survivors of the Revolutionary War, took boat, bound for the Ohio country and the founding of Marietta. Uncounted thousands of other emigrants preceded and followed him, Redstone Old Fort being the lure that beckoned them across the seemingly endless mountains with the promise that here, on the bosom of the Monongahela, would begin the last and easiest stage of the journey.

Naturally boat-building early became a prominent industry here. The first flat-boat to descend the Ohio was constructed at Redstone Old Fort, while the first steamer on the Monongahela, the *Enterprise*, was launched here. This boat was also the first steamer to go from Pittsburgh to New Orleans and to return up the Mississippi.

Redstone Old Fort was an old Indian fortification, no one knows how old, said to have stood on the left of the turn made by the pike as it seeks a parallel route with the river through the business section of Brownsville. In 1758, after the capture of Fort Du Quesne, a fort was built on this site, and this too was called Redstone Old Fort. Later the town that sprang up about the fort was called Brownsville, after the founder.

In 1860 there was talk of reviving the historic and appropriate name of pioneer days. Bancroft, the historian, and many others who learned of the proposal, were delighted. Evidently, however, the preference of those most concerned was not consulted, for when the legislature acted favorably on the suggested change, there was such a united protest from the citizens of the town that "Brownsville" was restored to the atlas.

Of the town's many distinctions not the least is that here the Whiskey Rebellion was born, and here it received its death-blow from the thoughtful citizens and others who came here at their invitation. July 27, 1791, was the date of meeting when the organized trouble began. At that time an indignant company talked over their grievances. Why should they pay the new tax of fourpence per gallon on whiskey they distilled? They could not use all the corn they raised, and there was no market for the remainder. They could not send it to the East as corn, but they could send it as whiskey; for, while a horse could carry but four bushels of corn over the mountains, he could carry twenty-four bushels in distilled form. Then was not the tax an invasion of personal liberty?

These were the arguments presented that day, when it was decided to hold a larger meeting at Pittsburgh, on September 7. At the latter meeting so much resentment was stirred up that various sorts of disorder took place, including the capture of a revenue collector, who was not released until his hair had been cut and he had been tarred and feathered.

For three years the trouble continued. At length, in 1794, a committeee of sixty men met at Redstone Old Fort and decided to recommend submission to law. So, when Washington's army of fifteen thousand men approached, there was nothing for them to do but to return to the East.

While the fort which gave the name to the old settlement has disappeared, there is another relic that bids fair to last yet many years—the iron bridge over Dunlap's Creek only a few rods before it enters the Monongahela. This, the first cast-iron bridge built west of the Allegheny Mountains, has an interesting history. A local historian says:

"It is tradition that Henry Clay, on one of his journeys, overturned in the bed of the stream, and that he gathered himself up with the remark that Clay and mud should not be mixed in that place again. The rest of the story is that soon after his return to Washington there came, unsolicited, the order for the iron span, carrying the road high above the stream."

Until 1910 there was a second historic bridge at Brownsville, a covered structure, built in 1833, though not by the Government—the one exception to the rule that all bridges on the National Road were government bridges. This carried the turnpike across the Monongahela to West Brownville, the birthplace of James G. Blaine. In 1914 it was replaced by the present steel bridge.

From the new bridge or from the heights above the town the Monongahela presents a spirited scene, especially during seasons of high water, when the coal tows pass this way on the journey to Pittsburgh, the first stage in the longer voyage to Cincinnati, Louisville, and New Orleans. Locks and dams at frequent intervals facilitate the transport of the bituminous coal from the Uniontown field and from West Virginia mines.

At West Brownsville the turnpike climbs the ridge that borders the river, and follows it for some distance. The prospect up stream to the bend, and beyond to the hills on the horizon, is not the least of the glories of Brownsville.

It is difficult to speak in any detail of the country from here to Washington. All the way the road leads along the ridges and into and out of the valleys. Fields and forest combine to make a series of landscapes that keep the traveler in an expectant attitude; he knows there must be something still better beyond, yet he wonders how there could be anything better.

The man responsible for naming Scenery Hill—it is possible to see thirty miles to Laurel Ridge if the day be clear—showed his appreciation of the glory around him, and the officials who chose the site for the triangulation station of the United States Geological Survey had an eye to beauty as well as to utility. Here the elevation is 1467 feet—the highest point between the Monongahela and the Ohio.

Praise must be given also to the man who chose the site of Washington—Little Washington, as the town is affectionately called in western Pennsylvania.

The distant view of this old college town claims the attention just after Laboratory is passed, and the eye cannot well leave it until the rapidly descending grade leads one into the heart of the classic streets, within two squares of Washington and Jefferson College, part of whose campus was once owned by George Washington.

Of those days an early writer says:

"No daily stage rattled along at the rate of ten miles an hour, no commodious Conestoga wagon, even, creaked along the road with its three tons of goods—no steamboats came up from New Orleans in two or three weeks' passage."

During this period salt was the most precious commodity, and it had to be brought from a long distance. Every family collected what could be obtained throughout the year:

"In the fall, after seeding time, each family formed an association with some of its neighbors, for starting the little caravan. A master-driver was selected from among them. The horses were fitted out with pack-saddles. The bags provided for the conveyance of the salt were filled with feed for the horses. On the journey part of the feed was left at convenient places on the way down, to supply the return of the caravan . . . Each horse carried two bushels of alum salt, weighing eighty-four pounds the bushel. The common price of a bushel, at an early period, was a cow and a calf. Until weights were introduced, the salt was measured into the half-bushel by hand, as lightly as possible. No one was permitted to walk heavily over the floor while the operation was being performed."

The Washington County pioneers for whom it was necessary to get produce to market in such primitive fashion found trying conditions still more difficult because of the uncertainly as to whether Pennsylvania or Virginia had jurisdiction over them. There were a number of reasons for Virginia's claim to a part of the territory which is now included within the bounds of Pennsylvania. One of these grew out of the mistake made when the southern boundary of the northern colony was fixed by means of the "Circle Line" which is the northern boundary of Delaware. According to the grant, this southern boundary was to begin where the circle drawn within a radius of twelve miles from New Castle should intersect the parallel marking forty degrees of north latitude. The two do not intersect, however. So there were misunderstandings with Maryland as well as with Virginia.

For some time before 1775 Virginia had been attempting to govern the territory claimed in Pennsylvania. Western Pennsylvania had long been looked on as a part of Augusta County, but in 1775 the district of West Augusta was spoken of, and this was divided into the counties of Ohio, Monongalia, and Yohogania. These counties included what are now Greene, Washington Fayette, Beaver, Allegheny, and Westmoreland counties.

For some time the courts of West Augusta exercised authority over the territory, and the records show some curious things. For instance, there is the order "that the Sheriff Imploy a Workman to build a Ducking Stool at the Confluence of the Ohio with the Monongahela."

At the call of Governor Patrick Henry of Virginia a council was held at Catfish Camp, the present site of Washington, to see what could be done by the residents of the district for defense against the Indians. But when matters were talked over it was decided that neither Virginia nor Pennsylvania could be looked to for protection. Accordingly a petition was sent to Congress requesting the organization of "the Province and Government of Westsylvania," which should be the fourteenth province of the Confederation. Within its bounds should be a country about two hundred and forty miles long and seventy or eighty miles broad, from the mouth of the Scioto to the summit of the Allegheny Mountains, "fertile and healthy even beyond a Credibility."

The reasons for the request were appended to the petition. There could be neither security nor comfort "whilst annexed to or dependent on any Province whose seat of Government is . . . four or five hundred miles distant and separated by a vast, extensive and almost impassable Tract of Mountains, by Nature itself formed and pointed out between this County and those below it."

Congress took no action, probably for two reasons: Its attention was taken by the problems of the Revolution. Then nothing could be done until the Atlantic Colonies should cede to Congress their claims to western territory. This was not done until 1784.

In the meantime the Virginia Assembly had made to Pennsylvania a proposition to compromise her claims to territory claimed by that colony, so as to include only the present Green, Fayette, and Washington counties, the latter in part.

The matter was finally left, in 1779, to arbitration, when many propositions and counter-propositions were made. Pennsylvania offered to accept a large portion of West Virginia, south of Green and Fayette counties. Virginia proposed to concede part of the territory to the south, on condition that Pennsylvania would accept as western boundary a line exactly parallel with the windings of the Delaware, at every point five degrees from the corresponding point on the right bank of that river.

At length the present western and southwestern boundary was arranged, the famous Panhandle of West Virginia being provided for.

Although Pennsylvania promptly ratified the agreement, Virginia delayed, in the meantime trying to dispose of certain lands on the Monongahela. For a time there was fear of violence. At length Congress interfered, and the vexed question was settled.

George Washington was one of the landowners whose claim to western Pennsylvania lands was derived from Virginia. In 1774 he secured 2813 acres in Cecil and Mount Pleasant townships, north of Washington, on Miller's Run, a branch of Chartiers Creek—or, as Washington called it, "Shurtees Creek." On the land a number of settlers squatted. Washington's business representative tried to bring them to terms, and when he failed he advised that his employer visit the men in person. The visit was accordingly made in 1784. To those who had made homes on the land he offered to sell this for twenty-five shillings per acre, or to lease the property to them for 999 years. They said they would stand suit before they would pay so much. Suit was therefore entered and judgment was given for Washington. Later the entire tract was sold for $12,000.

When problems of government and land had been settled satisfactorily, the people of Washington County were ready to make internal improvements. A number of roads were built, but the talk of the National Road made them hungry for more. In 1808 it was learned that, while the route as far as Brownsville had been decided on, it was not yet settled what should be the course from there to the Ohio River. Washington's determination to secure the pike was finally successful, though for a while it looked as if a route several miles south of the town would be chosen.

There is one curious connection between Washington and the turnpike that is not widely known. The drivers of the Conestoga wagons liked to smoke, and they wanted a cheap smoke. A cigar manufacturer of Washington made an effort to supply the demand by rolling a long cigar which he could sell four for a cent. The new cigars became so popular with the men on the road that they were given the name Conestogas. That word was as long as the cigars, and it was soon shortened to "stogies," or "tobies."

Through many years drivers of Conestogas filled their pockets with this special brand of long cigars and enjoyed them thoroughly on the rolling uplands that are so characteristic of the pike from Washington westward. The oil derricks are a modern growth; of the houses, many have changed, but the country is the same.

So is the old S-bridge which leads across Buffalo Creek, six miles from Washington. It would be interesting to know the origin of the name as applied to this stream; perhaps it was given in days when the coming of the buffalo to drink in its waters was not a mere memory.

Claysville, a town named for Henry Clay, and West Alexander are the last towns of importance in Pennsylvania. West Alexander is on a high hill overlooking a bit of the Panhandle of West Virginia. On the main street of the old town where beautiful views of the surrounding country are to be had for the gazing, is a tavern whose proprietor proudly shows the room in which the Marquis de Lafayette slept in 1825. The town was thirty years old when the French friend of America passed over the road—time enough to have given to it such suggestive nicknames as The Three Ridges, Hard Scrabble, Gretna Green, and Saints' Rest.

No traveler can be content to go as far as West Alexander without going on to Wheeling. The distance is but twelve miles, but in this short space the pike affords one of its greatest treats—a ride through the narrow valley of Middle Wheeling Creek, where pike and trolley, creek and railroad dispute the passage at almost every one of the numerous turns. There are steep green slopes—first on one side, then on the other, then on both sides at once. There are chasms and gorges, and tributary runs which after a rain of only an hour or two may become raging torrents. There are bridges of a sort to make the modern stonemason look in wonder. There is—just before Middle Wheeling Creek enters Big Wheeling Creek at Elm Grove—the monument to Henry Clay on the lawn of the old Shepherd house where Clay and Webster, Andrew Jackson and James K. Polk, William Henry Harrison and General Houston were welcome guests.

From Elm Grove to Wheeling is but six miles. From this metropolis of West Virginia the route chosen leads south, then west to Waynesburg, the county seat of Greene County. Soon after turning eastward Big Wheeling Creek is encountered. All the way to Waynesburg the country is not unlike that which the National Road traverses in Washington County—pleasing uplands and fertile valleys, rugged slopes and tree-clad summits.

Waynesburg is most attractively located on Ten

WATERFALL ON RAVINE TRIBUTARY TO MEIGS CREEK, WASHINGTON COUNTY
Photo by State Highway Department

OVER THE GREENE COUNTY HILLS
Photo by State Highway Department

ROAD TO WHEELING AND PITTSBURGH

Mile Creek, whose valley is one of the notable scenic features of the county. Along this stream Indians prowled in the days when men and women who settled here took their lives in their hands.

The town was named for General Anthony Wayne, an honor it shares with Waynesboro in Franklin County. Both towns chose the name Waynesburg, and in the contest between them for the retention of the name the Greene County town was successful.

At one time it was thought the National Road would pass through Waynesburg. Though the route as finally fixed was to the north, Waynesburg was not deprived of a large amount of highway traffic. Through the town passed a road that was chosen by many drovers, in preference to the stone-surfaced pike, for driving herds of cattle toward the eastern markets.

From Waynesburg north to Washington are two roads either of which leads through a region so alluring that one ought to take them both. At any rate he should walk leisurely along the mile that connects them at Waynesburg; from the ridge on which this road is located there is a panorama of farm and forest of such an impressive nature that one old man who enjoyed the walk just once, and that more than sixty years ago, has never forgotten what he saw.

For a few years it looked very much as if Waynesburg's only outlets to the outside world would continue to be the turnpikes. Once the Baltimore and Ohio Railway talked of building through Waynesburg, using the country to the west by the valley of Wheeling Creek. Opposition developed, however, from farmers and others who feared that the coming of the railroad might mean the loss of revenue secured from those whose flocks and herds used the highways.

Yet the day came when another road was proposed—to Washington, twenty miles distant in a direct line. The easiest possible course would have been by the Chartiers Valley, but this route was opposed by the farmers who lived there. The railroad, therefore, found a wonderful route over the hills. This has been described humorously by a local historian, who told of a journey from Washington southward:

"In passing over the road into Greene County for the first time, there is a constant cloud of uncertainty hovering over one. For a while he seems to be leaving Washington behind him, and he feels sure that in the scheduled time he will arrive in Waynesburg. But he has not gone many miles before the sun, which was full in his face at starting out, is now at his back, and he is haunted with the suspicion that he has taken the wrong train, and is on his way to Pittsburg. But while he casts an admiring glance at the landscape, changing at every instant, and presenting an endless variety of hill and valley and winding stream, he suddenly finds himself turned quite round, and he is making direct for Ohio, and begins to fear that he is on his way to the far West. But that solicitude has scarcely had time to get a lodgment before the train, by a miraculous transformation, is turned completely about, and is rushing on directly for the Delaware Water Gap. In his perplexity he is just upon the point of calling the conductor and inquiring where he is really going to, when the train pulls around, and seems to be making in the direction of his destination. . . . But all at once it starts off on a cruise, and when it has made the complete circle . . . Waynesburg breaks on the view. The road is indeed a marvel.

> 'It wriggles in and it wriggles out,
> And leaves the matter still in doubt,
> Whether the man that made its track
> Was going out or coming back.''

ROAD TO WHEELING AND PITTSBURGH

This was in 1874, when the road was first built. It has been much straightened, but still it is a remarkably picturesque line.

From Washington there is a road up the Chartiers Valley whose course is through the rolling lands to Canonsburg, the site of the first academy west of the Allegheny Mountains. A short distance northwest of the village are the lands so long owned by George Washington.

The approach to Pittsburgh through the industrial section of southern Allegheny County is different from that afforded by any other road. The city itself is hidden until the last ridge is crossed. Then, from the height, there bursts on the vision that unrivaled panorama

> "Where the Monongahela's meet
> The Alleghany's waters fleet,
> And there the two th' Ohio make."

ROUTE III

FROM PHILADELPHIA TO PITTSBURGH
BY WAY OF READING, HARRISBURG AND THE WILLIAM PENN HIGHWAY
ABOUT 370 MILES

In a curious old book called "Historic Tales of Olden Times Concerning the Early Settlement and Progress of Philadelphia and Pennsylvania," published in 1832, wonder is expressed at the marvelous progress in methods of transportation to and from Philadelphia. The author says that his mother had often told him how, in days before the Revolution, the mail was brought to Penn's City by a postboy who rode on horseback. "A small affair then," is the comment; "now it requires a four-horse stage."

In 1855 a reader of this volume penciled in the margin "And now!!!" Whereupon another reader, in 1872, wrote in his turn, "And now again!!!"

Between the two scribblers who were so prodigal of their exclamation points came another who spoke of the tremendous strides made in the satisfaction of demands for increased transportation facilities. One day in 1861 a venturesome traveler took what he called "the lightning line" from Philadelphia to Pittsburgh, making his start from the awesome depot at Eleventh and Market streets. But he was wordier than the man of 1855 who made such demands on the stock of what, in the printing office, are called "astonishers." For he said:

"Then comes the tap of the bell—a rush of negro porters—a shout by the conductor, and the long line of mules apply themselves to their task, and, with a jerk

IN JENKINTOWN
Photo from Philadelphia & Reading Railroad

ON THE PERKIOMEN AT COLLEGEVILLE
Photo from Philadelphia & Reading Railroad

upon their iron chain, start the car on its journey of three hundred and fifty-four miles to Pittsburg. Rather slow work, this mule locomotion, but allowable, as it only has to be borne during ten minutes, required to haul the train to the outer depot in West Philadelphia . . . As you rattle along at a dog trot, view the car in which you are ensconced, note the solidity and strength of its construction, and think of the care which was exercised to prepare the vehicle destined to carry thousands of miles in the course of the year."

At last the great West Philadelphia depot was reached which "cost a power of money, and will last forever."

Just so to-day it is a common thing to boast that the transportation equipment in which we take so much pride must be the last word in progress. And it *is* the last word—as surely as the postboy of 1776, the four-horse stage of 1832, the mule-power tramway of 1861, and the curious locomotive of 1872 were last words!

What changes have taken place in the ways of the people since the never-changing hills that command the Schuylkill first looked down on the pioneers who ventured into the interior toward Norristown and Reading! What stories the valley could tell of the years before the making of straw printing paper at Manayunk began the pollution of the crystal stream that led the shad to desert it; of the time when the green slopes of Laurel Hill were innocent of monumental stones; of the turning, at Norristown, of the first spade of earth for what it was hoped would prove the first public canal in the United States; of the heroic shivering during long winter months of Washington and his men on the beautiful hills and in the alluring glens of Valley Forge; of the hunting and trapping of Audubon along the winding Perkiomen; of the peaceful life of Muhlenberg at Trappe, where he trained a son who was to become one of the picturesque leaders of the Revolution; of the coming of John Potts to build his iron works at what is now Pottstown; of the sorrow of the Indians as they looked at the inroads of the settlers on the inviting lands along the broad reaches of the shining river or back among the hills from which such breath-taking visions of the valley may be secured.

The charms of the Schuylkill Valley many times lured William Penn, as well as later scions of the Proprietor's family, from their seat at Philadelphia. Once William Penn lost his way among the hills overlooking the river, but he did not lose appreciation of their peculiar appeal. Many years later Thomas Penn followed the river up from Philadelphia, and called the region from Norristown to Reading "a very pleasant country." "The character of it is the beautiful," he added, "a little heightened in some places by the sublime. It is, indeed, perfect, especially as you approach the Schuylkill about Pottsgrove [Pottstown]. . . . The river adds to the beautiful disposition of the ground and to the picturesque form of the horizon." Later, in viewing the high hills toward Reading, he said that they made him think of "Pelion upon Ossa."

Just as enthusiastic were the words of that later nature-lover, Bayard Taylor, who repeatedly made his way along the stream which the Indians called "Man-ai-unk." He had viewed the most notable places in Europe, but when he came to Reading, he said of the scene spread out before him:

"Never had I seen or imagined anything so beautiful. The stately old town lay below, stretched at full length on an inclined plane, rising from the Schuylkill to the base of the mountain; the river, winding in abrupt curves, disclosed itself here and there through the landscape; hills of superb undulation rose and fell, in inter-locking lines, through the middle distance. . . . It was not ignorant admiration on my part, for one familiar with the grandest aspects of Nature must still confess that few towns on this side of the Atlantic are so nobly environed."

When Thomas and Richard Penn encouraged the building of a town where ridges of the Blue Mountains cross the Schuylkill they decided to hold to their title to the ground. They knew that its productiveness, coupled with the beauty of the surroundings, would attract settlers. They were right. The town which began in 1748 with one house had one hundred and thirty dwellings in 1751, and it continued to grow rapidly. Those who stand on Mount Penn, on whose slopes part of the city lies, and look away to the valley far below, will not find it difficult to understand the reason. On one side are the Irish Hills, then appears South Mountain, and finally, to the northeast and west, are the straggling Blue Mountains. Shut in by these encircling mountains is the delightful Tulpehocken Valley, stretching away toward Harrisburg. The meandering river makes its way from the north, while the Tulpehocken's course from the west is marked by the banks of vivid green and bordering trees whose branches bend protectingly over the stream, as well as over the old Union Canal. This artificial waterway united with the Schuylkill Canal, which followed its companion stream from Port Carbon to Philadelphia, as well as with the natural waterways of Berks County, to provide abundant transportation facilities and water power for the region.

Power was needed, too, for the industries that early found congenial homes in this favored section. The chief of these industries was long the preparation and fashioning of iron. In early days there were as many as sixteen furnaces clinging to the various streams. In a number of these were made during the Revolution many of the cannon whose excellence led the British captain to ask a soldier:

"Where do you get your big guns?"

"We make them," was the reply.

"Where do you get your patterns?" was the next question.

"From Burgoyne at Saratoga!" the undaunted prisoner responded.

Even in the bustling surroundings of Reading there are so many quiet nooks that it is easy to picture the easy-going days when both canals were crowded by the slow-moving coal boats and passenger packets, and when on the roads stage coaches and postboys bade less lordly traffic keep out of the way. The weekly two-horse coach of 1789 required two days for the trip to Philadelphia.

Gradually the demand for increased speed became greater, until, in 1842, the valley was invaded by its first railroad, whose opening as far as Pottsville was celebrated by 2150 persons, who loaded themselves into 75 passenger cars, drawn by a single engine. The size of the cars may be judged from the fact that in a train following were 52 burden cars, which carried all of 180 tons of coal. For a long time after that day passengers realized that they were only an incident on the road; the distance between the tracks was too small to permit the running of regular passenger cars. When, at length, it became necessary to make provision for the passengers who demanded transportation through the beautiful valley, a car of wonderful proportions was devised. On one side of the aisle were seats for two passengers, while on the other side but one traveler could be accommodated in each seat. Not until 1862 were the tracks separated enough for cars of ordinary construction.

A passenger car is a good place from which to see the famous Tulpehocken Valley—that is, if a better vehicle cannot be found. One needs to be in the open, with the privilege of looking to right, to left, ahead, behind, and above if he expects such a richly endowed region as this to yield its secrets. The sweep across to the encircling mountains is too broad to be limited by the frame of a car window, and the valley is crossed too soon if the space is covered by the steady progress of an express train. In the garden of Berks County time is a necessity to one who would make the most of his opportunity of looking so that the picture will remain with him during days of toil when he is far from the valley's restful surroundings.

Ten miles of green glory—glory of fertile field, of stately forest, of tree-clad hills near at hand and other hills receding into the dim distance! Then the eye rests on the buildings of the famous hospital at South Mountain where the state cares for hundreds of those who are called incurably insane. The location of the hospital has been admirably chosen, for, if anything could restore these people, surely such scenery as this in which they live should do the work. From every building, from all corners of the great farm, they drink in the beauty that gives calm and poise, quiet and repose. The managers of the hospital have taken the best means to make the surroundings effective; they provide regular work for all, and so they have been able to put to a real test the idea that a home like this should be made self-supporting. In their efforts they have been so successful that visitors from abroad have more than once found their way to this retired valley that they might learn the reason for the success of the South Mountain Hospital. When word of the results obtained here were carried across the water, the London *Lancet* wrote, "The example of Wernersville might with advantage be followed in a systematic way by institutions in Great Britain."

Eyes that have long been lifted to the encircling hills are soon attracted to a roadside tablet erected to Conrad Weiser, Indian interpreter, whose old home stands a few rods from the tablet, back among the trees.

When Conrad Weiser first saw the valley it was still in the hands of the Indian owners. In 1723 a party led by his father, John Weiser, floated down the Susquehanna, then ascended the Swatara from Middletown. Their cattle they drove overland. Six years later Conrad made his home half a mile east of Womelsdorf. He had been there but two years when Shikellimy asked him to go to Philadelphia as interpreter. This was the first of many similar missions, for he gained and retained the confidence of both Indians and white men to such an extent that he soon became the accepted mediator between the races.

The house by the Tulpehocken roadside gave evidence to the fact that the honesty and faithfulness of its owner did not make him popular with all about him. His capable services, as justice of the peace, angered some fellows of the baser sort. One night some of them approached the house, barred the windows and guarded the doors, then set a fire against the front entrance. A child, startled awake, gave the alarm, and the family managed to escape through a window that had not been barred as well as was thought.

VALLEY CREEK, NEAR VALLEY FORGE
Photo by Miss L. A. Sampson

ON THE ROAD TO VALLEY FORGE
Photo by Miss L. A. Sampson

THE GOLF CLUB AT WERNERSVILLE
Photo by J. Horace McFarland Company

OLD CORNWALL FURNACE
Photo from Philadelphia & Reading Railroad

Treatment of this nature was an exception. In the province Weiser was so much appreciated that once, when he presented a bill for £36 18s 3d, for personal service, this was passed without question, and the sum of thirty pounds in addition was voted to him. The Indians, too—who called him Tarachawagon—honored him; they dreaded the day when he would be taken from them. "When he goes the long road," they said, "it will be time enough to look out for another. While he is here there is no room to complain."

Whenever Tarachawagon had opportunity he liked to tramp over the corner of what is now Lebanon County, south of his home, to the gap in South Mountain. This way led the trail of his friends, the Indians, from their village of Shamokin (Sunbury) to the Penn treaty ground on the Delaware. From the summit on the left of the gap, Eagle's Peak, there may be secured a fine view of the valley to the north. This is certainly one of the finest views in the state. On March 22, 1755, Henry Melchior Muhlenberg climbed to this point of vantage. Later he spoke of the "splendid panorama for a distance of thirty miles . . . limited to the west and southwest by the Blue Mountain chain."

Not far from the gap is the town that boasts of having had the first water works in the United States. Since 1753 Schaefferstown has secured its water supply from a spring on the top of Tower Hill. This is one of the heights in the neighborhood which afford prospects that cannot be forgotten. From Cemetery Hill there is spread out a typical agricultural view—probably just such a view as Emerson had in mind when he wrote of a charming landscape, "indubitably made up of some twenty or thirty farms. Miller owns this field, Locke that, and Manning the woodland beyond. But none of them owns the landscape . . . This is the best part of these men's farms, yet to this their land deeds give them no title." It will add to the enjoyment of a trip through this country if preparation is made by reading Emerson's essay, "Nature."

Not far away are the famous Elizabeth furnaces, where guns and ammunition were made during the Revolution; while further to the west are the great Cornwall ore banks. These have been called the great metallic curiosity of the state. But they are more than a curiosity; they contain the most extensive deposits of iron ore east of the Mississippi and south of the Great Lakes. They are located on knobs of South Mountain, Grassy Hill, Middle Hill, and Big Hill. Here, too, guns and ammunition were made for Washington's army.

Cornwall Furnace dates from 1742, and Colebrook Furnace, six miles to the southwest, was opened in 1781. Their location has been celebrated in the lines:

"Colebrook Furnace in Cornwall stands,
Crouched at the foot of the iron lands."

On a spur of South Mountain is Mt. Gretna, the beautiful resort of the Pennsylvania National Guard, whose commanding situation and pleasing surroundings have made it famous.

It is a temptation to go on over the line into Lancaster County, and visit Manheim and Lititz and Ephrata, towns that glory in the stories of sturdy pioneers and strange sects, then on to the valley of the Conestoga. But the call is heard to go back to the direct road to Harrisburg, at Lebanon, where old houses compete with the surrounding mountains for the attention of the traveler. The mountains are apt to win, especially if it is possible to go north far enough to see the gap of

PHILADELPHIA TO PITTSBURGH

the Swatara, another of the landmarks of the Indian path to Shamokin. One of the attractions of this region for the red man was the beautiful cascade, a few miles north of the gap. Still farther on there is a ridge from which it is possible to look southwest to the Susquehanna Gap near Harrisburg, as well as north to Swatara Gap. These gaps are proportioned in size to the streams that pass through them, but both compel attention without regard to their size. The commanding height from which they are visible was resorted to by the Indians when they wished to display their signal fires to their tribesmen and their allies in time of danger. Another height favored by the Indians was Bunker Hill, near the Swatara, some seven miles from Lebanon.

The road to Harrisburg crosses the Swatara at Hershey, the model milk chocolate town, where, through the efforts of the company, the banks of the stream have been beautified, schools have been improved in a marked manner, and many farms have been bought that the milk supply for the families of the factory workers might be made pure.

Not long after the Swatara has been left behind the ever glorious Susquehanna greets the eye. This is the stream which Alexander Wilson apostrophized in 1804:

"Hail, charming river, pure transparent flood!
Unstained by noxious swamps or choking mud;
Thundering through broken rocks in whirling foam;
Or pleased o'er beach of glittering sand to roam;
Green be thy banks, sweet forest-wandering stream!
Still may thy waves with finny treasures teem;
The silvery shad and salmon crowd thy shores,
Thy tall woods echoing to the sounding oars;
On thy swol'n bosom floating piles appear,
Filled with the harvest of our rich frontier:

Thy pine-browed cliffs, thy deep romantic vales,
Where wolves now wander, and the panther wails,
Where, at long intervals, the hut forlorn
Peeps from the verdure of embowering corn,
In future time (nor distant far the day)
Shall glow with crowded towns and villas gay;
Unnumbered keels thy deepened course divide;
And airy arches pompously bestride;
The domes of Science and Religion rise,
And millions swarm where now a forest lies."

When John Harris came to the banks of the Susquehanna he too felt the prophetic impulse. "This spot of ground seems destined by Nature for the seat of a town," he wrote. So he laid the foundation of Harrisburg, attracted by the healthy, pleasant, high situation, "the easy connection by water with a great part of the country," and the situation "on the main road through the Continent."

There are few finer river prospects in the state than that gained from the great stone bridge at Rockville, five miles from Harrisburg, where the Pennsylvania Railroad crosses to the right bank. Both up and down stream the view is marvelous.

At this point the Blue Mountains, the first of the Alleghenies, are entered through the portal of Rockville Gap. And for nearly two hundred miles the traveler by this route will continue to pass through and over the mountains. All the way from Harrisburg to Blairsville there is—except when the summit is crossed—a continuous chain of gaps where watercourses seek a way through the mountains. Both railroad and turnpike follow closely the picturesque windings of the streams, first the Juniata, then the Little Juniata, then, after an interval of summit conquest, the Conemaugh.

Perhaps the Rockville Gap is not so impressive as

NEAR RUTHERFORD
Photo by J. Horace McFarland Company

ROCKVILLE BRIDGE OVER THE SUSQUEHANNA, NEAR HARRISBURG
Photo by J. Horace McFarland Company

THE RAVINE, COVE FORGE, NEAR THE MOUTH OF THE JUNIATA
Photo by J. Horace McFarland Company

other gaps which follow in rapid succession; the river is nearly a mile wide at this point. But the stream is much narrower at Dauphin, where is the gap through Second Mountain, and as a result the opening seems much more majestic. A few miles farther on, near Duncannon, is still another gap that can best be seen from a point below the town. A spur of the mountain here is called Profile Rock, because of its resemblance to a human face.

Beyond Duncannon the broad river makes room for fertile Duncan's Island, or "Juneata Island," as David Brainerd called it in 1745 when he visited the Indian village here. The devoted missionary agreed with later visitors as to the wondrous beauty of the surroundings, but he turned sadly away from the Indians because even his optimism was dismayed by the heathenish practices which seemed the more awful because of the favored locality they had chosen for a home.

Duncan Island marks the point where the Juniata mingles its mountain-tossed waters with those of the Susquehanna. From here the route is never far from the stream which inspired the song:

"Wild roved an Indian girl,
Bright Alfarata,
Where sweep the waters
Of the blue Juniata,
Swift as an antelope
Through the forest going,
Loose were her jetty locks
In wavy tresses flowing.

"Gay was the mountain song
Of bright Alfarata—
Where sweep the waters

Of the blue Juniata.
Strong and true my arrows are,
In my painted quiver—
Swift goes my light canoe,
A-down the rapid river."

The triangle between the rivers, the northeast portion of Perry County, is a region most surprisingly picturesque. From the railroad this triangle is seen from one side, while the turnpike traveler looks from the other side. Perhaps those who choose the highway have the better view, for they follow the Susquehanna as it breaks through the barriers of the Cove Mountain.

One of the most noteworthy of the covered bridges for which Pennsylvania is remarkable is just west of Duncannon, the Clark's Ferry bridge, which has eleven piers. From this bridge the eye leaps to what is perhaps the most pleasing of the many knobs along the bank; from one point of view this is almost a perfect pyramid. Like many more of the eminences above the river, this does not crowd closely upon the bank. A few miles farther on, however, at Millerstown, the last town in Perry County, the mountains press close on either bank, forming the Tuscarora Gap. Here there seems to be scarcely room for the railway, the river, and the canal.

In the days when the canal was in its glory there was a pool below Millerstown formed by a state dam in the river. On this pool boats passed "by means of an endless rope stretched across the river and passing round a large pulley on the canal side." When a signal was given, one of the pulleys was turned by water power; this put in motion the rope and the boat attached to the rope was moved in its turn. This was one of the interesting sights of travel by canal that led N. P. Willis to write, in 1840:

"Of all the modes of traveling in America, the least popular—and the most delightful, to our thinking—is traveling on the canal. The packet-boats are long drawing-rooms, where one dines, sleeps, reads, lolls, or looks out of the window; and, if in want of exercise, may at any time get a quick walk on the tow-path, and all this without perceptible motion, jar, or sound of steam . . . It is always a reasonable query to any, except a business traveller, whether the saving of time and fatigue in the wonderful improvements of locomotion is an equivalent for the loss of rough adventure and knowledge of the details of a country acquired by hardship and delay. Contrast the journey over a railroad at a pace of fifteen [!] miles in the hour, through the rough, the picturesque valley of the Susquehanna, with a journey over the same ground ninety years ago."

In 1836 a passenger who knew how to enjoy the leisurely canal boat told of his joy in seeing the country from the mouth of the Juniata to Lewistown:

"We had reached a most romantic region, having the Juniata and the ever-changing scenery of its bold and picturesque banks constantly in view; now swelling into gentle hills, partly in culture and partly in woods; now rising abruptly into mountains, whose primeval forests seemed untrod by man; now subsiding into little plains and valleys occupied by villages and towns."

But not all canal-boat travelers were ready to enjoy these privileges. One early author lamented:

"Great men of steam and iron, Thomson, Stockton, Stevens, what do we not owe you for lifting us out of the miseries of packet-boat travelling! What boots it, that the railroad car does seize upon its victims and carry them off? What boots it that the locomotive, bisecting the orchard, cutting up the garden, ruining the village-green, narrowly escaping the grave-yard, shrieks in sermon-time, startles the calves in the midst of Windham, crushes a 'good-bye' under its iron wheels, and puffs a sob into profound silence? People dream it thunders, when the train is coming; fancy the wind is rising, when the train is going; the clocks are all set, not by immemorial noon-marks, but by train, and everybody obeys the sign at the 'crossing,' and 'looks out for the cars' when the bell rings."

The road toward Pittsburgh, along which the Juniata canal once carried the tourist, next leads across one of the lozenge-shaped counties which at once attract the eye as one glances at the map of Pennsylvania. This peculiar shape is due to the configuration of the land; in each county there is a long valley, shut in by parallel ridges of mountains. The geologist says that originally these long valleys were much wider; after the Appalachian region of Pennsylvania was thrust up, it was subject to crushing and compression until "a tract of the earth's surface measuring originally one hundred and fifty-three miles from southeast to northwest" became but sixty-four miles wide. In one place ninety-five miles have been compressed into sixteen miles. Juniata County has been compressed in this way; the land is all there as in ages long gone, but much of it is in the shape of mountains instead of valley.

The length of Juniata County is about forty miles, but the average width is but nine miles. The Tuscarora and Shade mountains enclose the valley of Tuscarora Creek, whose lands are so fertile that an early historian, after telling of vain search for a fabled silver mine in the county, said, "The best mines to get opened in Juniata County are on those lands that yield twenty-eight or thirty bushels of wheat to the acre."

Bordering on these central mountain counties are

PHILADELPHIA TO PITTSBURGH

long mountain ridges in which there is hardly a break. Communication has always been along the central valleys, except where the Juniata has shown the way to the railroad to move in a circuitous course from east to west, between the broken mountains, many of whose tree-clad slopes are cared for by the Department of Forestry.

Interest attaches to the trip of Philip Fithian along the Tuscarora Valley in 1775. He spoke of it as "a most stony valley; two mountains on every side. The passage is so narrow that you may take a stone in your right hand and another in your left and throw each upon a mountain, and they are each so high that they obscure more than half of the horizon."

One day Fithian sat on the banks of the Juniata and wrote:

"Fair genius of the water, wilt not thou, in some future time, be a vast, pleasant, and very populous country? Are not many large towns to be raised on these shady banks? I seem to wish to be transferred forward only one century. Great God! America will surprise the world!"

Mifflintown is the delightfully situated county seat of Juniata County, though it is natural to think of it as a Mifflin County town. Once it was, but the division of the county carried it along to its new neighbor. From Mifflintown to Lewistown the Juniata breaks through a succession of mountains, some of them rugged and high. In Lewistown Narrows, once known as Long Narrows, Black Log Mountain and Shade Mountain rise to about one thousand feet above the river—"the brave little river," as Ex-Governor Brumbaugh once called it, because, "instead of winding its way toward the Susquehanna around the high mountains," it "breaks its way through thirteen separate mountain ranges between Huntingdon and Juniata Bridge."

Lewistown Narrows is a gorge four miles long. From here through the entire length of the country the river flows through a valley so fertile and so wonderfully beautiful that it has been compared to the Wyoming Valley. At the lower end of this valley the stream makes a sharp turn to the west and enters Huntingdon County through a gap whose attractions are known to comparatively few, because it is so far from the ordinary routes of travel. Just beyond the gap the winding Raystown Branch enters the parent stream from the south.

The windings of the river find fitting company in the strangely angular western boundary of Mifflin County. The zigzags are a reminder of the dispute among the early settlers. Huntingdon claimed the lower section of Mifflin County, but the claim was stoutly resisted, even to the arrest of the sheriff of Huntingdon County when he attempted to serve processes in the debated territory.

The first settlers came the length of the county, after crossing the mountains from the Conococheague Valley in Franklin County, and made their home on the present site of Lewistown, induced, no doubt, by the exceedingly attractive location on the ground that rises from the river toward the hills to the north. One who takes in the prospect of the valley from these hills cannot wonder at the choice of the pioneers.

Just above the settlement stood Fort Granville, where a garrison protected the settlement. A year after their arrival, during the harvest of 1756, the garrison was guarding the men in the grain fields, when the Indians approached the fort by means of the Juniata and a convenient ravine and succeeded in capturing it and,

THE ROAD TO MIFFLINTOWN
Photo by State Highway Department

ALONG THE JUNIATA
Photo by State Highway Department

JACK'S NARROWS, FROM MOUNT UNION BRIDGE
Photo by State Department of Forestry

JUNIATA RIVER, MIFFLIN COUNTY
Photo by State Department of Forestry

later, taking many prisoners. Twelve years passed before the treaty of Fort Stanwix made renewal of the settlement safe.

A few years after this new settlement at Lewistown, an English emigrant wrote home enthusiastically:

"This is the best part of the Country that I have Ever seen for industrious People of Every Trade . . . This is a fearful Country for wild Creatures, such as Dears, Bars, Wolves, and Panters, the Dears meet yoused for Beef or Venison, and Bears Meet good Bacon. Fishes in Great plenty. This is a fine Country for Roots and Vegetales. I shall send you a small account of them. Cow cumbers, Water Mellens, Squashes and Pompcans, with a variety of Beanes, such as ye have none in England, with others too tedis to Name. All rises from the Ground without much troble and come to Great perfection."

This settler might have written of another crop that grew plentifully in the streets of the Lewistown of his day—stumps. These were so plentiful that the recognized fine for drunkenness was the digging up of a stump. It is said that a ravine near the center of the town was filled with stumps pulled in this way.

Lewistown is surrounded by scenes of grandeur. Not content with the valley to the south and the Narrows to the east, the town has, several miles north, the rocky gorge of Jack's Creek. This leads to a valley girdled by hills. Still farther on are the Seven Mountains, with Milliken's High Top last of all. Kishacoquillas Valley stretches off to the west. To make the picture complete, there is Jack's Mountain to the southwest, followed by ridges that reach as far as the eye can see.

In the midst of these attractions is Reedsville, situated at the point where the William Penn Highway makes a sharp turn on itself, famous as the location of the spring which was one of Chief Logan's favorite resorts. Logan, who was named for James Logan of Philadelphia, was a son of Shikellimy, but not a friend of the whites like his brother, Captain Logan, though he boasted, "I appeal to any white man to say, if ever he entered Logan's cabin hungry, and he gave him not meat; if ever he came cold, and he clothed him not."

James Reed, the founder of Reedsville, once had a narrow escape from taking the life of this red man. He was at the spring, drinking, when he saw the reflection of an Indian in the water. Quickly he sprang for his rifle, but Logan made himself known in time.

North of Reedsville is the most famous of the many limestone caves in Mifflin County—Naginey Cave. This, as an enthusiast has said, ranks with the caverns of Virginia and the Wyandot Cave of Indiana, and surpasses others in Pennsylvania, except Penn's Cavern in Center County. It is said that Edgar Allan Poe once visited it and was delighted with the beauty of its interior. He also visited Winegartner's Cove, a sink in the hill back of the cave where ice has been known to remain throughout the summer.

Each mountain, valley, cove, and stream of all this highland territory has its story to tell of the Indians who roamed here in the days of long ago. Mount Union, for instance, is proud of the fact that Nit-a-nee the beautiful Indian girl, is said to have lived near the present site of that picturesque town on the banks of the Juniata. For her the Nittany Mountains and the Nittany Valley in Center County were named. To this country the people of her chieftain father were driven by Indians from the South, who succeeded in conquering the people of Nit-a-nee only after they had

PHILADELPHIA TO PITTSBURGH

made spirited and long-continued defence of the haunts in which they delighted.

Mount Union is notable because it is at the entrance to Jack's Narrows, the gap in the mountains of which the Juniata takes advantage for its passage through Jack's Mountain. Originally the name of this great gorge was Jack Armstrong's Narrows, so named for an early trader who was killed here by the Indians.

More fortunate were two later travelers, who came this way in 1754, Conrad Weiser and John Harris. They came from the South through a wild country. A pleasant day may be spent in following the trail, past Trough Spring, some twelve miles southeast of Mount Union, the majestic Shape Gap in the Shade Mountains, where a branch of Aughwick Creek steals through (in that day this was called "The Shades of Death)," the Black Log, near Orbisonia, the Three Springs, not far from the borough so named to-day, and Aughwick, on the present site of Shirleysburg. Ordinarily a list of names means little, but in this instance even the names give an invitation to take the prolonged ramble outlined through some of the most majestic regions of Huntingdon, a county that lies entirely within the mountains.

Four years after Harris and Weiser made their historic trip, Richard Bard and his wife came this way from their home in Adams County, but not willingly. They were captives in the hands of the Indians. After crossing the Tuscarora Mountains into Huntingdon County, Bard succeeded in escaping. On his return to civilization, in eighty-eight stanzas of awful construction he told the story of his enforced journey, his escape, and his reflections. This poem of pioneer days should be read as a whole. Here are a few samples:

SEEING PENNSYLVANIA

"On a woeful day the heathen came,
    And did us captive make:
And then the miseries commenced,
    Of which we did partake . . .

"At three roods distance from a run,
    Encamped the night are we:
But when for drink they do me send
    No more they see of me.

"Alas! for me to go 'tis hard,
    Since with them is my wife,
Yet 'tis the way that God ordained,
    For me to save my life.

"O'er hill that's high, and swamp that's deep
    I now alone must go:
Travelling oh, I suffer much,
    For bruise my feet I do.

"Amazingly my foot is swelled,
    With heat 'tis in a flame;
And though I'm in the desert land
    Can't walk, I am so very lame.

"But lest my foot I further hurt,
    My breeches tear I do,
And round my foot I do them tie
    That I along may go.

"The time since first I captive was,
    This is the fourteenth day;
Five with the Indians, and nine since
    From them I ran away.

"And now from bondage though I'm freed,
    Yet she that's my beloved,
Into the land that's far remote
    By Indians removed."

From such poetry—and such callousness—it is a relief to look again at the beauties of nature along the Juniata from Mount Union toward Mill Creek. The sharp bends here are explained by the sight of Sideling Hill and Terrace Mountain, for these compel the stream to turn south, and so add to the delights of the railway tourist and make the travelers by the turnpike who enter Mill Creek from the northeast wish to go down into Trough Creek Valley, south of the town. This valley, the boyhood home of Ex-Governor Brumbaugh, presents a wonderful assortment of varied attractions that make one wish that railroads and highways led to every corner of the region.

Fortunately there is a railway down the valley of the Raystown Branch, so that it is possible to follow the crooked course of this tributary of the Juniata as far as Breezewood on the Lincoln Highway. This ride over the celebrated Huntingdon and Broad Top Railway is the more inviting because of the possibility of returning, by way of Bedford and the railroad thence to Altoona, through a wild section of Bedford and Blair counties, whose grandeur makes us all the more ready for the quieter scenes spread out in the valley of the Frankstown Juniata, the branch of the mountain river that parallels the Raystown Juniata, at a distance of from seven to ten miles, across two ranges of mountains.

The start for the round trip through the valleys of the two branches is Huntingdon, the town named by its founder—Dr. William Smith, first provost of the University of Pennsylvania—for the Countess of Huntingdon. The Indian name for the place was the more picturesque Onojutta, or "Standing Stone." The "standing stone," an ancient memorial of the Indians, stood within the limits of the present beautiful city. It was originally fourteen feet high and six inches square, and was covered with hieroglyphics. The Indians removed it in 1754, but its memory persists, helped by a tablet erected on its site in 1896 and the representation of the monolith on the seal of the borough. The Juniata, too, helps to keep green the memory of the "standing stone," for Juniata is derived from the musical Onojutta. Huntingdon is located in this valley, and is surrounded by wooded slopes and fertile fields so attractive that it is difficult to decide which way to turn. To the southwest is Great Terrace, to the east and southwest the lordly range of Jack's Mountain. Other majestic mountain views are toward the gap of Mount Union and the Lion's Back.

There is a most attractive road from Huntingdon to the northeast that parallels the William Penn Highway from Reedsville, though with a ridge of high mountains between. This gives access to a region whose wild gorges, steep hillsides, and rocky wilderness combine to make what will prove a pleasing detour. Greenwood Furnace, one of the famous charcoal forges of other days, is found at the end of eighteen miles of the route. The site of the furnace is included in one of the great properties of the Pennsylvania Forest Reserve.

Fortunately it is possible to return from Greenwood Furnace by a route that joins the main highway some six miles beyond Huntingdon,—a route so abounding in pleasures for the eye that it is easy to forget the difficulties of a path that has not yet received the final touches given by the State Highway Department to so many of the state's roads.

In following the main highway from Huntingdon toward Hollidaysburg a scenic feature three or four miles on the way is the great Pulpit Rocks, forty or fifty feet high, on Warrior's Ridge; while a few miles farther on is Water Street, so named by the early settlers because the pioneer road led for some distance through a narrow defile, along the bed of the stream. This stream is probably Sinking Creek, which flows from Arch Spring, a few miles northwest of Water Street, but nearer Birmingham. Arch Spring—so called because it is in a large limestone arch, through which the water flows—is one of the favorite resorts in these mountains. After leaving the spring the stream runs along amidst the wildest scenery. It receives additions from smaller springs, when finally the whole volume of water disappears in a large cavern, and again enters the bowels of the earth. In the inside of this rocky cavern the stream continues from eighteen to twenty feet wide. The roof declines gradually, and a ledge of loose rugged rock keeps in tolerable order upon one side, affording means to scramble along. The opening continues for several hundred yards, when the cavern opens into a spacious room. At the bottom is a great vortex, into which the water is precipitated, and whirls around with amazing force. The stream is supposed to pass several miles under Brush and Cove mountains, and to reappear by two branches, which empty into the Frankstown Branch of the Juniata.

Those who have opportunity should take the road that leads northeast from Water Street, up Spruce Creek Valley, to Pennsylvania Furnace. Near by are "the Indian Steps," a series of stone steps over the Tussey Mountains, made famous by the titanic struggle of 1635, when the Susquehannocks and the Leni Lenapes fought for the possession of these mountains. In the battle—which Colonel Henry W. Shoemaker, a man who knows every mile of this mid-mountain territory, says was equal to any of the great conflicts of the Civil War, both in fierceness and in the number of men engaged—the Susquehannocks, under their chief Pipsisseway, were victorious, and the Lenni Lenapes sadly turned to the lands to the north.

From Water Street two routes are open to the west. One of them follows the Little Juniata, familiar to those who ride along its banks on trains of the Pennsylvania Railroad toward Tyrone, and then to Altoona, while the second keeps near the Frankstown Juniata all the way to Hollidaysburg, a town built on a spot where Adam Holliday, in 1768, said to his brother, William, "Whoever is alive a hundred years hence will find here a considerable town." It is a pity that the lower route to Hollidaysburg is not better known, for it leads through a brilliant succession of valleys and mountain gorges.

Those who used the old Pennsylvania canal enjoyed the beauty of the lower route, from Petersburg, as did the Indians who picked their way along the Frankstown trail, which gives its name to old Frankstown, near Hollidaysburg. There it succeeded the Indian village Assunepachla, a town that dates from 1750. Perhaps half way between Petersburg and Hollidaysburg is the Beaver Dam country, a wild region famous for its primeval forests. Not many miles from here, near Williamsburg, William Penn made one of his fortunate investments in real estate, the fertile Morrison's Cove Valley. For this he paid £400!

The section of canal that led along this route to Hollidaysburg was an important link in the combined route of the Pennsylvania Canal and the Portage Railroad from Philadelphia to Pittsburgh, the predecessor of the Pennsylvania Railroad. The complete route of this historic waterway-railroad was from Philadelphia

ARCH SPRING, NEAR BIRMINGHAM
Photo supplied by Dr. Alvin R. Grier, Birmingham School

OLD STONE ARCH, PLANE NUMBER TEN, PORTAGE RAILROAD, NEAR DUNCANSVILLE
Photo by Stouffer

STONE SLEEPERS, FOURTEEN MILE LEVEL, OLD PORTAGE RAILROAD, LOOKING TOWARD MINERAL POINT
Photo by Stouffer

AT SALTSBURG ON THE KISKIMINETAS
Photo supplied by Dr. A. W. Wilson, Kiskiminetas School

by rail to Columbia, by canal up the Susquehanna to the mouth of the Juniata, up the Juniata and the Little Juniata to Hollidaysburg, by the Portage Railroad to the Conemaugh, then down the Conemaugh, the Kiskiminetas, and the Allegheny, to Pittsburgh. This made a roundabout journey. But the trip, once taken, could not be forgotten.

Perhaps the best idea of traveling by the canals and the Portage Railroad was given by a traveler of 1836 who called himself Peregrine Prolix. First he described his accommodations:

"A canal packet boat . . . is nearly eighty feet long and eleven wide; and has a house built in it that extends to within six or seven feet of stem and stern. Thirty-six feet in length of said house are used as a cabin by day, and a dormitory by night; the forward twelve feet being nocturnally partitioned off by an opaque curtain, when there are more than four ladies on board, for their accommodation . . .

"This machine is dragged through the water at the rate of three miles and a half per hour by three horses, driven tandem by a dipod with a long whip, who rides the hindmost horse. The rope, which is about one hundred yards in length, is fastened to the side of the roof, at the distance of twenty feet from the bow, in such fashion that it can be loosed from the boat in a moment by touching a spring."

Prolix mourned that he missed the last eighteen of the twenty-eight miles of interesting scenery because of darkness. So he lamented that there was not, for the accommodation of those who wished to see Pennsylvania, "a line of canal packets traveling only by day, drawn by five horses at the rate of five miles per hour; starting at 5 a. m. and stopping at 7 p. m. at good hotels in pleasant places; furnishing breakfast and dinner on board. Such a line would draw such a concourse of pleasure-seekers as would soon fill the packets of the enterprising proprietors."

At length the packet reached Hollidaysburg. There, in a commodious basin, the eastern section of the Pennsylvania Canal terminated. In this basin "the goods destined for the West" were taken from the boats and placed "in Burthen Cars which are to carry them over the mountains, by means of the Allegheny Portage Railroad." This railroad led "by a gently rising grade, four miles from the foot of the mountain, whither the cars are drawn by horses."

Unfortunately this master of the art of racy description did not continue his journey to Pittsburgh by way of the Portage Railroad. A few weeks later, however, he crossed the mountains from Johnstown to Hollidaysburg by this route, and he left an account of the trip, which is good reading at this point, even if it was taken toward the east instead of toward the west.

The paragraph telling of the mountain experience was introduced by an execrable attempt at punning:

"We incline to be very plain in explaining the nature of these planes, and to prevent our readers from complaining of the little light we may shed on the subject when we shall be passing this miracle of art, we shall keep our eyes, ears, and mouth wide open."

The western end of the Portage Railroad was reached at Johnstown. A level of four miles led to the foot of the first plane. This was covered in horse-drawn cars, at a speed of six miles an hour. The ascent was one hundred and one feet. During the passage of the level there was much excitement:

"In six hours the cars and passengers were to be raised eleven hundred and twenty-two feet of perpendicular height, and to be lowered fourteen hundred feet

PHILADELPHIA TO PITTSBURGH

of perpendicular descent, by complicated, powerful and frangible machinery, and were to pass a mountain, to overcome which, with a similar weight, three years ago, would have required a space of three days. The idea of rising so rapidly in the world, particularly by steam or a rope, is very agitating to the simple minds of those who have always walked in humble paths."

At the foot of the first plane "the horses were unhitched and the cars were fastened to the rope, which passes up the middle of one track and down the middle of the other." After this the cars were drawn up sixteen hundred and eight feet, for a rise of one hundred and fifty feet, in four minutes, the motive power being a stationary steam engine.

Then came a journey by horse power "through a magnificent tunnel nine hundred feet long." Next "the train of cars were attached to a steam tug to pass a level of fourteen miles in length, with a rise of one hundred and ninety feet."

"The valley of the Little Conemaugh is passed on a viaduct of the most beautiful construction. It is of one arch, a perfect semicircle with a diameter of eighty feet, built of cut stone, and the entire height from the foundation is seventy-eight feet six inches."

An hour brought the passengers to the foot of the second plane, seventeen hundred and sixty feet long, with a rise of one hundred and thirty-two feet; then:

"The third level has a length of a mile and five-eighths, a rise of fourteen feet six inches, and is passed by means of horses. The third plane has a length of fourteen hundred and eighty feet, and a perpendicular height of one hundred and thirty. The fourth level is five miles long, rises nineteen feet and is passed by means of horses. The fourth plane has a length of two thousand one hundred and ninety-six feet, and a perpendicular height of one hundred and eighty-eight. The fifth level is three miles long, rises twenty-six feet, and is passed by means of horses. The fifth plane has a length of two thousand six hundred and twenty-nine feet, and a perpendicular height of two hundred and two, and brings you to the top of the mountain.

"Three short hours have brought you from the torrid plane, to a refreshing and invigorating climate. The ascending apprehension has left you, but it is succeeded by the fear of the steep descent . . . And as the car rolls along on this giddy height, the thought trembles in your mind, that it may slip over the head of the first descending plane, rush down the frightful steep, and be dashed to a thousand pieces . . . The descent on the eastern side of the mountain is much more fearful than is the ascent on the western, for the planes are much longer and steeper, of which you are made aware by the increased thickness of the rope; and you look down instead of up."

The last of the five levels which alternate with the descending planes was nearly four miles long. This led to the basin at Hollidaysburg. Along it the cars traveled by the force of gravity.

When the road of which Prolix wrote so enthusiastically was built a journalist of the day wrote:

"The design was originally entertained of connecting the main Pittsburgh route by continuing the canals with locks and dams as far as possible on both sides, and then to tunnel through the mountain summit, a distance of four miles! Fortunately, however, this extravagant idea was abandoned, and surveys for the railroad were commenced in 1828 . . . Sylvester Welch . . . has immortalized his name by a work equal in importance and grandeur to any in the world. He has raised a monument to the intelligence, enterprise and public spirit of Pennsylvania more honorable than the temples and pyramids of Egypt or the triumphal arches and columns of Rome.

PHILADELPHIA TO PITTSBURGH

"In October, 1834, the portage was actually the means of connecting the waters of eastern Pennsylvania with those of the Mississippi . . . Jesse Christian, from the Lackawanna, a tributary of the North Branch of the Susquehanna, loaded his boat, named *Hit or Miss*, with his wife, children, beds, and family accommodation, with pigeons, and other livestock, and started for Illinois."

He planned to sell his boat at Hollidaysburg, but enthusiasts persuaded him to take it over the mountain. A special railway car was prepared. The boat was placed in this, and was carried over the rugged Allegheny, without disturbing the family arrangements for cooking, sleeping, etc. They rested at night on the top of the mountain, and next day descended to the canal and proceeded by water to Pittsburgh and the Ohio.

The day came when the state decided that the planes must be abandoned. So, in 1855, there was completed a new Portage Road for canal boats, between Hollidaysburg and Johnstown. The old line had been sold to the Pennsylvania Railroad. For less than two years the new road was operated in competition with the private corporation; but it proved unprofitable, and was abandoned—to the sorrow of employees who were able to take many privileges in those free-and-easy days. A local historian tells of some of these:

"After dark the officials were not particular what their employees did with the engine, and frequently they would raise steam and set it off to attend a country frolic, and leave the locomotive standing on the main track, without guard or light, as no lamps or torches were provided for night work. On Sunday the engine would be taken out at the pleasure of the crew, who would go where they desired."

The inconvenience of such actions may be guessed from the fact that on parts of the route the new Portage Railroad used the same tracks as the Pennsylvania Railroad!

The Portage Railroad passed into history in 1857, but there are relics of its brilliant career. There are a number of towns along the route, once prosperous, now abandoned or moribund, though some of them have continued to prosper. Then in the Carnegie Museum at Pittsburgh there is a section of rail and stone blocks used on the line. But best of all are the remnants of the stanch bridges, the mark of the right of way, and the stone sleepers still to be seen by one who follows the old course from Hollidaysburg over the mountains.

To discover some of these relics, leave Hollidaysburg and walk a mile or more across the fields, past Duncansville. You will presently find your further progress barred by an extensive chain of high hills, rising almost to the dignity of mountains. Here on the hillside is plainly visible a long, smooth incline, climbing by an easy grade a distance of half a mile. This is plane number ten, the first eastern plane of the old Portage Road.

From Hollidaysburg to this plane the bed of the old road is still in view by the Newry branch of the Pennsylvania. It is a climb of half a mile to the top of plane number ten. Then comes a level space a mile long to the foot of plane number nine—a mile made memorable by the towering mountains on one side and the view of the valley spread out below. The pilgrimage should be continued up planes nine, eight, and seven. To the right will be seen Blair's Gap, while the old Pittsburgh turnpike is far below in the valley.

At the foot of plane number six the turnpike crosses

the old Portage route on a stone bridge. At the end of plane six is the summit, the highest ground in Cambria County. Summit village is a little farther on, on the level stretch between planes five and six

The new Portage Railroad did not climb so far as this, but turned aside at plane number eight, and crossed the mountain by a tunnel at Gallitzin. The Pennsylvania Railroad also reaches Gallitzin, but by the easier grade of which the Horseshoe Curve is an important link. The original Portage road, however, pointed the way for its present-day successor to cross the valley at Kittanning Point; here there was one of the great engineering triumphs of the road, a semicircular track of eighty feet span, which cost $54,562—a large sum for those days.

The eyes of the average traveler who rides around the Horseshoe Curve are turned downward so that he fails to grasp the rather intricate engineering problem solved when this bit of the road was built. An official publication of the Pennsylvania Railroad describes this:

"The valley the road has followed for six miles here separates into two chasms, neither of which can be made available for further progress. Another opening into the giant barriers must be gained, and engineering science proved equal to the task of reaching it. By a grand horse-shoe shaped curve, the sides of which are parallel with each other, the road crosses both ravines on a higher embankment, cuts away the point of the mountain dividing, sweeps around the stupendous eastern wall, and leads away to a more tractable pass."

The great Kittanning Indian trail crosses the mountain by this gorge, using the northeast gap. The southwest gap was called Burgoon Gap; through it led a variation of the Kittanning trail.

SEEING PENNSYLVANIA

Think of it! Within a short distance of each other are five great routes of travel—the trail of the Indian, the old Pittsburgh pike, the old Portage road, the new Portage road, and the Pennsylvania Railroad.

As the train emerges from the tunnel at the summit of the Allegheny mountains the brakeman shouts "Gallitzin." Some of the passengers who have passed that way before give no heed; others look eagerly from the windows and wonder at the strange name of the station. It was evidently named for some man. But who was he? Indian? Explorer? Soldier?

Gallitzin was neither Indian nor soldier. He was something of an explorer, but only as his duties led him into the mountain fastnesses of an unknown section of the country. He was a humble missionary, whose life in the Pennsylvania wilderness was a marvel of self-sacrificing endurance. Yet his name is all but forgotten, and the few stories of his life which have been written are difficult of access. When they are asked for at the library, the inquirer is usually informed that they are out of print.

This Pennsylvania missionary of more than a century ago was born a prince. His father, the head of a rich and noble Russian house, once ambassador to France and to Holland, owned landed estates, near Warsaw, which were larger than the state of Pennsylvania. His mother was the daughter of one of the field marshals of Frederick the Great.

The father was an infidel, while the mother, during the earlier years of her life was "scarcely better," as one writer says. The training of the young prince can be imagined. However, in 1787, when he was seventeen, "he accidentally picked up in a bookstore a copy of the Bible, which he purchased, and great was his satisfaction in the secret perusal of a volume so rich and wonderful." The reading led to his conversion.

When twenty-two years old he was preparing to go to Vienna, where he was to put on the uniform of a colonel in the Austrian army. This was to be the first stage in a splendid military career which his father had mapped out for him. But political considerations made it impossible for him to go as planned. So it was thought best to devote the next few years to foreign travel, without which no gentleman's son was considered educated. He was, therefore, sent to America. The voyage was made in the company of a young minister, whose example and consecration fired the zeal of the young prince. He determined to turn his back on the world and its allurements.

The first step in his new life was to seek admission to a theological seminary at Baltimore. After his ordination, in 1795, he was sent as a traveling missionary to Conewago, Pennsylvania, and to "different towns and stations in Maryland, Virginia, and Pennsylvania." In 1799, determining to centralize his work, he chose a location on the western slope of the mountains, where he built a log church. From the home field he made hundreds of journeys to minister to scattered settlers, when "the bare floor was frequently his bed, the saddle his pillow, and the coarsest fare his food."

At Loretto, several miles from Gallitzin, he determined to found a colony. He planned to purchase lands at his own expense, sell them in small farm lots at a nominal price, or give them away. "He erected gristmills, sawmills, and other facilities for subsistence, in a region whose settlers had been wont to travel thirty or forty miles to grind their breadstuffs and procure the necessaries of life." Thus he became responsible for a large sum of money.

The devoted missionary was in the midst of his work when his father died, and he was summoned to return to Russia and claim the estates. He would have been glad to do this, but no one could be secured to take his place, even temporarily, and he felt that he could not leave alone the colonists whom he had invited into the wilderness. Accordingly "he wrote to his mother that whatever he might gain by the voyage from a temporal point of view could not, in his estimation, be compared with the loss of a single soul, that might be occasioned by his absence." He therefore asked that agents be appointed to look after his interests, and secure any portion of the estate they could.

The courts, however, declared that the absence of the prince in America, and his religious faith, disqualified him for inheritance, and the estate was given to his sister. The sister promised to make the matter right by a will in his favor. At her death, some years later, a fraudulent document was substituted, and he was given nothing. Although his case could easily have been won, he refused to make a contest, saying, "an investigation must injure some one, and he could endure wrong and hardship, but would inflict none."

Depending upon the sale of goods left him by his mother, he continued his work, spending about one hundred and fifty thousand dollars, all for the benefit of others:

"No portion of this was spent for his own pleasure or comfort, as his personal habits were peculiarly plain and simple. His food generally consisted of coarse bread and garden vegetables, his clothing was of the plainest and simplest homespun, and his house was a rude log cabin, whose door was always hospitably open to the poor and the stranger. To complete his self-abnegation, he dropped the noble name of Gallitzin, and passed among his people as plain Mr. Smith, a name assumed as a safe disguise to shield him from the inquiries which even in that remote corner of the earth pursued the princely missionary."

The dishonesty of relatives at home kept from him some funds on which he had counted, and he became financially embarrassed. A friend of his boyhood—at this time the king of Holland—learned of his need and sent him a considerable gift, insisting on its acceptance. The Russian minister at Washington sent him five thousand dollars. With such assistance, and by strict self-denial, he was able to keep his head above water.

But nobles and kings were not the only men who helped him. It is related that "when the laborers on the Pennsylvania canal, then building, learned that his house was to be sold by the sheriff, they raised the money and paid the debt."

In 1837, when a friend urged him to return to Europe and make another fight for his patrimony, he answered, "Being in my sixty-seventh year, burdened moreover with the remnant of my debts, I had better spend my few remaining years, if any, in trying to pay off that balance, and in preparing for a longer journey." He died three years later, after forty-five years of self-sacrificing toil for his fellow-men.

Prince Gallitzin knew how to choose a good town site. When he wanted to start a colony he turned his steps to the neighborhood of the only gap in the mountain range between what is now Altoona and the Maryland line, by which a railroad could cross the divide—except for the notch made by the Castleman River, used by the

Baltimore and Ohio Railroad in its progress from Cumberland to Pittsburgh.

Not far away from Gallitzin, and four miles from Ebensburg, is a ridge from which a close observer may note the water on one side that flows into tributaries of the Susquehanna, and so into the Atlantic, while on the other side he can see water that is bound for the Gulf of Mexico by way of the Ohio River.

Wales as well as Russia had a part in the settlement of Cambria County. In fact, the name of the county tells of the Welsh settlements; it was so named for the mountain region of Wales, of which the new country was a constant reminder. Ebensburg, too, was named by Welsh settlers, who delighted in the commanding view of the country round about afforded from the site of the town, at the top of one of the ridges of the Alleghenies, and only seven miles from the summit. The elevation here is about two thousand feet, and the descent to the surrounding valleys is often abrupt. At almost every turn the highway—this leads through Ebensburg instead of following the valley of the Conemaugh from Gallitzin to Johnstown, as does the railroad—gives glimpses that are sufficient explanation of the fondness of the Welsh settlers for this highland section.

Within three miles of Ebensburg there is a village that is another reminder of the Welsh of early days. Beulah Road is all that is left to tell of the town of Beulah, laid out in 1796 by Rev. Morgan John Rhys, on land purchased from Benjamin Rush of Philadelphia. The plan was quite ambitious; the right-angled streets were copied after Philadelphia. This was to become a great city in the land of Jordan. It did prosper for a time. At length there were sixty log houses on the site, as well as a school, a church, and a library of six hundred volumes. But when Cambria County was formed Ebensburg became the county seat, and Beulah lost its population. By 1808 all had left. Ebensburg grew slowly until the completion of the Portage Railroad, when it became a popular summer resort.

Though the sightly old Welsh town continues to prosper, the Portage Railroad has been all but forgotten for three quarters of a century. Yet there are, on the western side of the mountain, as well as on the eastern side, reminders of the day when the railroad was in its glory—as, for instance, the old tunnel at the head of plane one, near Johnstown (said to have been the first tunnel through a hill for railroad use on the continent) and the remnants of the wall protecting the railroad on the south side of the Conemaugh.

It is claimed by some that all ocean steamers which depend on bulkheads for safety in time of collision owe a debt to the Portage Railway. At first the goods brought to either end of the railway by the canal had to be transshipped for the mountain passage. Captain John Dougherty of Hollidaysburg studied long the problem of ways and means of saving the time and expense of the double transfer of shipments. As an experiment he devised the three-section canal boat. When the basin at the beginning of the mountain section was reached, the boat could be divided into sections. Then, loaded with goods, the sections could be transported to the beginning of the next section of canal. In 1834 he sold his patent, but in 1842 he surprised the purchaser by offering for use on the canal a four-section boat. This improvement was quite successful, and the idea was later incorporated in the great steamships.

The water for the Pennsylvania canal was supplied, in

dry seasons, by the South Fork dam, begun in 1835. Twice this dam gave way—once, in 1862, when the water was so low that little damage was done in the valley, the second time in 1889. Then it had been swollen by heavy rains, and without warning it sent the impounded water from its five-hundred-acre lake upon the doomed thousands who could not escape to the hills in season.

At Johnstown there was a large basin in the center of the town, formed by damming the Conemaugh. In this the boats waited their turn to pass on over the mountain. There were frequently scores of boats, and the surrounding warehouses and boatyards were kept busy. One of the conveniences arranged here was an apparatus for landing and hauling up the section boats, that they might cross the mountain on trucks.

Before the days of the canal-boat railway Johnstown was a vital point between the east and the west. Arks and flatboats were here prepared for transfer to the Juniata and its waters, or were received after the journey across the mountains. This was done by means of the Kittanning trail, then by the Frankstown road, then by a turnpike, and finally by the railroad.

The Conemaugh is not much of a stream till it comes to Johnstown, the steel city. There it becomes broader and deeper, as if realizing the importance that was given to it in the past, that will perhaps belong to it at some time in the future. The town was originally named for the stream on whose banks it stands. But it is not fair to Stony Creek to speak of the larger stream as if it were the only channel there. The name Stony Creek was given to the smaller stream because it was filled with great rocks. In and near the town many of these were removed. Those who would see what the creek looked like two generations ago should go fifteen miles north and see the large rocks still to be found there.

From Johnstown the Conemaugh flows northeast through a number of gorges and gaps to Blairsville. The one hundred and ninety miles of mountain scenery are soon to end, and in this twenty-four-mile section the river makes the most of its opportunities. Canyons, ridges, and valleys succeed one another with bewildering rapidity. Four miles from Johnstown is Sang Hollow, through Laurel Hill. Fifteen miles farther on is Packsaddle Narrows, through Chestnut Ridge. Through these magnificent regions the railroad descends rapidly, though not so rapidly as did the canal. Between Johnstown and Blairsville the old canal descended two hundred and twenty-three feet by means of thirty-five locks, five dams, and three aqueducts.

One of the remarkable caves of the state is in the limestone rock on the side of Chestnut Ridge, about five miles south of the Packsaddle, near Hillside station. Great Bear Cave has a number of passages which lead over deep chasms where running water is heard far below, to vast chambers in the heart of the mountain. But the best part of the visit to the cave comes when one steps from the darkness within to the light of the mountain side, and looks with dazzled eyes out over the Conemaugh as it winds through the valley to the north and east.

The Conemaugh Valley becomes much more sedate after Blairsville is left behind. It continues along the southern boundary of Indiana County, joins the Loyalhanna that comes in from Latrobe and so forms the beautiful Kiskiminetas—a stream which was an important link in the system of water transportation between the western terminus of the Portage Railway and the Allegheny River.

In the days of the construction of the canal, Blairsville was a town of importance. In fact, it was almost a boom town during the early thirties, though after the completion of the waterway Johnstown became a much more important center, because it was the terminus of its western section.

One of Blairsville's most exciting days was in 1834. The Blairsville *Record* of June 11, 1834, tells the story:

"Last week a steam canal boat [the *Adelina*] came up from Pittsburgh and went on to Johnstown. She returned on Sunday morning with a load of more than forty thousand pounds of blooms, passing the place handsomely at the rate of rather more than three miles an hour."

Before the period when iron blooms were made in the Conemaugh Valley, salt was a product of importance. In 1813, when salt was high, many wells were sunk along the river in a most laborious manner. A common stone chisel attached to poles was used to cut a channel from two to three inches in diameter, and 300 to 600 feet deep. As the work was done by hand, the chisel being struck smartly for each slight gain in depth, progress was slow. Sometimes a year or even more was required to drill a single well. Fresh water was excluded by means of a tube, and salt water was drawn from within the tube by pumps, operated either by horse power or by steam. The salt water was boiled and left standing until the salt crystallized. Thirty gallons were evaporated to make a single bushel of salt. Yet one well could produce from fifteen to twenty barrels a day. The price, however, was frequently but one dollar per barrel.

PHILADELPHIA TO PITTSBURGH

Not many miles from Blairsville the William Penn Highway joins the Lincoln Highway, and follows the same route into the metropolis of the Allegheny Valley, whose surroundings are as attractive to-day as they were in 1806 when Thomas Ashe said, "Perhaps no inland town in the United States, or perhaps in the world, can boast of a position superior to this, both as to the beauty, and also the many advantages with which it is attended."

ROUTE IV

THROUGH THE PENNSYLVANIA HIGHLANDS

FROM HARRISBURG TO OLEAN AND ELMIRA, NEW YORK, AND BACK TO HARRISBURG, BY WAY OF WILKES-BARRE

ABOUT 530 MILES

IT is far from a misfortune to be asked to go a second time over the thirty miles of road from Harrisburg north to Liverpool, where the William Penn Highway turns to the west and the Northumberland Road leads northeast. For those miles are along the queenly Susquehanna through scenes that would satisfy the desires of any seeker after the picturesque in landscape.

The highway is constructed in many places on the bed of the old canal that followed the course of the river. This fact can be appreciated best from the railway, to the east of the road. The substantial masonry that supported the canal has been built higher, so that the surface is on a solid foundation. Farther on, the canal route can be traced by the stone aqueducts by which it crossed little streams, and the tall trees growing from the abandoned bed.

Only a few miles from Harrisburg is the gap at Dauphin, where the river turns to the south after making its graceful curve to the east. A few miles farther up stream, to the north of the Juniata covered bridge, a lingering backward look discloses a marvelous composition that defies description. It is a view that should be seen from both sides of the river. At this point the highway crosses to the west side, but if a journey can be made up the east side as well the traveler will be well repaid for the extra effort. Fortunate are those who are able to stand at one end of the rear coach of the train to Northumberland, on the journey northward. They can turn the eye at will down the stream, or across the broad surface to the villages and fields on the west, or inland. Some of the most striking vistas of the journey will be the reward of the gaze inland, for from the east flow one after another a series of creeks whose ravines, valleys, and gorges surprise by their variety and beauty. Stony Creek, Clark's Creek, and Powell's Creek are succeeded by the Wiconisco, along whose banks the railway to the famous Lykens Valley coal region—one of the earliest roads in the state—picks its way. Then comes the Mahantango, with its corresponding stream, the West Mahantango, across the river.

A magazine writer of seventy years ago was thinking primarily of this section of the Susquehanna when he spoke of it as "the Alpha and the Omega of Nature's gifts to the state—the first and noblest in beauty as it is in extent and position." Then his thoughts turned to the stream in its entirety:

"From its rippling mountain springs to its vast and swelling *débouche*, every step of the noble river is amidst the picturesque, whether flowing in broad and placid expanse through the great sunlit valleys, or gliding in ghostly shade at the base of lofty hills, or wildly disputing its way with obstructing rock and precipice."

William Cullen Bryant's enthusiasm led him to statements even more emphatic. He says that the tourist who has been enraptured by the Susquehanna would be loath to exchange its mountain scenery "for mountains that invade the skies, and whose sullen peaks are covered with a snow mantle fringed with glittering glaciers."

To appreciate the truth of Bryant's words one needs only to take a good look at the gap below Millersburg, the town at the mouth of the Wiconisco, which might well belong in a section of country much more rugged. The gap can be seen to better advantage by a backward look from Liverpool, a pleasing town on the west bank.

Across the river from Millersburg, and on the line of the highway, is Buffalo township—a reminder that this valley was once a part of the range of vast herds of buffalo. W. T. Hornaday says that the animals used to roam from Harrisburg to Sunbury and on up the West Branch of the Susquehanna. It is probable that as late as 1773 there were twelve thousand bison in the herds that came to this part of the country. Union County, a few miles farther north, has named three of its nine townships for the awkward looking animals, while a fourth is named for the deer that once frequented the valley. This county has also Buffalo Cross Roads, Buffalo Gap, and Buffalo Path Run. Along the latter, according to Henry W. Shoemaker, the path taken by the buffalo is still plainly marked, although none of the animals have tramped over it for more than a century.

The country between Buffalo township in Perry County and the three Buffalo townships in Union County, and westward in north Snyder and south Union Counties, will ever be memorable in the minds of sportsmen because here was the scene of the last stand of Pennsylvania's dwindling herd of bison. December, 1799, was the time of the disaster.

Nearly four hundred animals, unable to escape because of settlements on all sides, had remained hidden in the fastnesses of the mountains to the west of Snyder and Union counties. The severe winter of the closing year of the eighteenth century made them desperate; and, in search of food, they braved the dangers of the valley of Middle Creek, whose winding stream entering into the Susquehanna may be observed by the wayfarer as he comes to Selinsgrove, a few miles below Sunbury. Soon they scented the barnyard haystack of a settler, broke through the stump fence, and in a few moments were devouring the hay, after trampling the cattle and sheep in the enclosure.

The owner of the hay, assisted by a neighbor, managed to kill four of the beasts. The shots and the barking of the dogs drove them farther down the valley to the cabin of the neighbor who had helped the owner of the stack. This cabin stood near Troxelville, in the northwest part of Snyder County. There the wounded leader of the herd broke down the door and took refuge in the cabin. Of course the herd followed until no more could enter; thus they were jammed in the cabin "as tightly as wooden animals in a toy Noah's ark." Neighbors were summoned, the cabin was torn down, the buffalo were released, and the dead bodies of the wife and children of the owner of the cabin were found.

The residents of the valley at once decided to avenge the victims by exterminating the herd. Fifty men were brought together by messengers who went out, one toward the headwaters of Middle Creek, the other toward the Susquehanna. In the meantime the bison had fled to the mountains. At the end of two days the hunters found them, buried to their necks in snow that had fallen since the tragedy at the settler's cabin. The spot was near Weikert, in the "Sink," in the southwest corner of Union County, the "tight end" of Buffalo Valley. Handicapped by cold and hunger, as well as by the snow, the buffalo could offer no resistance to the avengers.

So perished miserably the last of the noble herd that once roamed over the valley of the Susquehanna. A few stragglers survived; but less than thirteen months later, on January 19, 1801, Colonel John Kelly killed the last Pennsylvania buffalo at Buffalo Cross Roads, some six miles west of the Susquehanna at Lewisburg, above Northumberland. Strangely enough, the last elk in the state was killed less than a dozen miles from this spot, though not until 1878.

Now we turn back to Snyder County, from which the pursuit of the buffalo herd led away too soon. This is one of the smallest counties in the state, containing only about two hundred square miles. But from Jack's Mountain on the north to Shade Mountain on the south it contains more scenery of real grandeur than many counties several times its size.

Selinsgrove has a sightly location opposite a number of fine islands in the river. These islands must have attracted the attention of Anthony Selin, a Swiss captain in the Revolution, who laid out the town. At least one of them, the Isle of Que, lured Conrad Weiser also, according to an old story of his dealings with Shikellimy, the Indian chief. One day—so the story goes—Shikellimy said to Weiser, "I dreamed that Tarachawagon had presented me with a rifle." Weiser had no choice, and the coveted rifle became the property of the wily Indian. But a few days later Tarachawagon said to Shikellimy, "I dreamed that Shikellimy presented me with the large and beautiful island situated in the Susquehanna river." The island in question—the Isle of Que—was a favorite possession of Shikellimy's; yet he gave it to his friend, though as he did so, he said "Tarachawagon, let us never dream again."

Why should any searcher after truth delve deeper

into the story than the record that Conrad Weiser and his descendants were once owners of the island?

Another good story is told in connection with Selinsgrove. One of the early residents of the town was Simon Snyder, for whom the county was named. Snyder was governor of the state from 1808 to 1817. Incidentally it might be said that his service was notable because of his advocacy of free public schools. It was also notable because of his efforts to introduce coffee into the wilds of Snyder County. At one time he brought a supply of coffee from Harrisburg and distributed it to a number of his friends. Most people liked the new substitute for rye. But there was one woman who complained bitterly; she said, "That man Snyder is not fit to be governor." Asked her reason, she explained that she had put into the pot, unground, the bag of coffee he gave her, and the mixture that resulted was unfit to drink.

The attractions of the surroundings of Selinsgrove are great, as will be found by those who take the short road to Middleburg, the county seat, along the Middle Creek Valley, past Fort Hendricks, the blockhouse that rendered such good service in days before the Revolution when the Indians from the north delighted to come to this region for the hunting and the fishing. To the north of Middleburg a road crosses Jack's Mountain to Mifflinburg in Union County. Of the many attractions of the road, perhaps the first is the Indian mound, nearly one hundred feet high. Ten miles to the west of Middleburg—whose original name, by the way, was Swinefordstown—is the settlement of Beaver Springs. Once the name accepted by the village was Adamsburg, but fortunately there was a change because of the historic beaver dam that once stood not far from the site of the modern dam, perhaps a mile from the mouth of Beaver Creek.

One of the finest stands of hemlock timber still standing in the state is in Jack's Mountain forest, a state forest reservation, to the north of Beaver Springs. There the closely crowded monster trees rise like monarchs from the valley, as if they would run a race with the mountain in piercing the sky. Here is the forest primeval. Here one catches himself repeating the nature-loving Bryant's words:

> "Stranger, if thou hast learned a truth which needs
> No school of long experience, that the world
> Is full of guilt and misery, and hath seen
> Enough of all the sorrows, crimes and cares
> To tire thee of it, enter this wildwood,
> And view the haunts of Nature. The calm shade
> Shall bring a kindred calm, and the moist breeze
> That makes the green leaves dance, shall waft a balm
> To thy sick heart. Thou wilt find nothing here
> Of all that pained thee in the haunts of men,
> And made thee loathe thy life . . .
>   . . . These shades
> Are still the abode of gladness; the thick roof
> Of green and stirring branches is alive
> And musical with birds . . .
>   . . . The cool wind
> That stirs the stream in play, shall come to thee
> Like one that loves thee . . . . "

Beyond Beaver Springs and the beckoning hemlock forest is a pass through the mountains, where the prospect is wonderfully pleasant. And then, to end the tale of the sights within reach of Middleburg, let it be said that a short walk of five or six miles north leads to New Berlin, over the line in Union County, a town notable because every street affords a view of the overshadowing Jack's Mountain.

THE PENNSYLVANIA HIGHLANDS

In the Middle Creek Valley there was, until a few years ago, a curious narrow-gauge railroad. This was three miles long, and it led from Beaver Springs to Shawversville and the Shade Mountain. During the thirty-five years of the road's history steam engines, horses, and mules were used to transport the iron ore and lumber from the mountains. In 1913 the rails were taken up, since the road was no longer needed.

The Middle Creek Valley Railroad was opened in 1871. The people rejoiced for three years. Then it failed, and was shut down. Not until 1876 was it repaired and reopened.

Perhaps the anxiety of Snyder County people to have a railroad was made stronger by the fact that they had a road once and lost it. Port Trevorton, seven miles below Selinsgrove, was the terminus. This town was named for J. B. Trevor, of Philadelphia, who backed the railroad, the Trevorton, Mahanoy and Susquehanna. Fifteen miles of rails were laid through primeval forests and a rough wilderness. The grade was sometimes as great as ninety-eight feet to the mile. At Port Trevorton a wooden bridge was built across the Susquehanna, of timber found on the Isle of Que at Selinsgrove and floated down stream. The structure was 3460 feet long, and there was a trestle of 1400 feet more.

The bridge was made profitable by adapting it to highway use as well as for the railroad, though, curiously, there was no partition between the railroad and the footway.

In 1855 it was prophesied that here was sure to be "the main crossing for all the travel to Pottsville, Reading, &c." For a time it looked as if the prophecy was to be fulfilled, when it was used not only by travelers, but by immense droves of cattle. Frequently there were so many cattle wanting to cross that the fields about Port Trevorton were filled with them.

The continual passage of the cattle endangered the bridge, already weakened by the chemical action of acid in the bark on the pine timbers. Fearing a repetition of the disaster by which the rhythmic motion of fifteen hundred cattle had caused a bridge not far away to fall into the river, the Reading Company, the purchasers of the railroad, took down the structure. For many years the piers stood in the stream; traces of them may still be discovered. These are the last relics of the pioneer road of Snyder County, whose rails were removed soon after the destruction of the bridge.

The Port Trevorton bridge led across to Northumberland County, one of the strangest in contour of the many oddly shaped counties in Pennsylvania. The Susquehanna not only forms the entire western boundary, but the North Branch cuts across the middle of the county in a graceful series of curves between hills whose summits provide sweeping prospects that remind one of the Tennessee mountaineer who offered to take John Muir to a ridge from which he could see both ways. "You will have a view of all the world on one side of the mountain, and all creation on the other," was his inviting assurance.

A visitor who appreciated the beauty of this panorama was Abijah Hall, who came this way on horseback in 1799. He spoke feelingly of "the slow, majestic crystal stream, with monstrous mountains and banks on each side, and a level road on a flat not more than a hundred or two yards wide, covered in general by lofty maples and beeches . . . calculated to please lovers, not farmers." In speaking more particularly of the Susquehanna, he said, "What a pity, several rapids and falls below should prevent this being as useful as 'tis pretty."

Hall would not have been so disdainful of the lands of this section if he had explored the valleys whose fertility has made them much sought after since the days of the first settlers who came this way in time to learn pioneer ways and to respond heartily to the call of Washington for soldiers of the Revolution. Northumberland County has the proud record of being one of the strongest supporters of the conflict.

Sunbury, the thriving railway town where the highway from Reading joins the road up the Susquehanna, was built about old Fort Augusta, one of the dozen or more outposts between the Delaware River and the Maryland line established as a barrier against unfriendly Indians. Here had long been a town of the Delawares called Shamokin, or the abode of the chief. Shackamaxon, the residence of the chief on the Delaware when Penn came to America, is thought to be another form of the name Shamokin. This, the most populous Indian town on the Susquehanna, was a favorite stopping place for the war parties of the Six Nations when on the way to fight the Catawbas.

Life at the fort was full of interest and danger. In 1757 conditions were at their worst, for that year a party of eight hundred French and Indians descended the West Branch to attack its stronghold, but when they saw how well defended the place was they were afraid to attack and stole away as quietly as they came.

Throughout that year of alarms vigilance was never relaxed. Colonel James Burd, the commander, wrote in his diary of an instance of the care exercised for the safety of the valley. He told of a woman who "hallowed for help from the west side of the river."

He sent "a party of 50 men and two officers in four Battoes." Provision was made for the safety of the party, "lest an ambuscade should be framed and the woman prove a decoy." The commander's decision to investigate was due to the pleading of a man who had escaped to the fort from the Indians, his captors; he was grieving for his wife, who was still in the hands of the Indians, and he could not bear to think of anyone in trouble going without rescue. To his joy the woman proved to be his own wife, who had wandered eight days after her escape from those who had captured her "upon Swetarrow" (Swatara).

The road from Sunbury to Reading was laid out in 1770. To it was given the name "the Great Road." It was a popular track with those who came in great numbers from New Jersey and the region about Philadelphia to take up lands in the New Purchase of 1768. Later it became a thoroughfare for the transportation of farm products to Philadelphia, and an avenue of travel even for sight-seers.

From Sunbury the road up the West Branch was laid out in 1775. The first town on the route was Northumberland, at the junction of the West and North Branches of the Susquehanna—famous in early days because of its connection with Chief Shikellimy of the Iroquois and his son, Captain Logan, friends of the settlers; later as the home of Dr. Joseph Priestley, the discoverer of oxygen, and always, to lovers of the far look, for the vision presented on a clear day from the summit of Blue Hill.

To the northeast are the Montour Ridge, the Shamokin Hills, and the stream where, in the stormy days of the Revolution, some survivors of the Wyoming Massacre floated down on rafts, flatboats, and canoes.

THE PENNSYLVANIA HIGHLANDS

The southern sweep of the eyes takes in the beautiful island between Northumberland and Sunbury (where two hundred and fifty acres were bought in 1788 for $1600), the town of Sunbury, nestling along the river, and, beyond the enticing bends, the blue waters and the precipitous banks of the Susquehanna. The northern vista is made up of a delightful mixture of river, mountains, and fertile farms.

Blue Hill was a frequent resort of Shikellimy, who lived on what is now one of the best kept farms in the neighborhood, on the west bank of the Susquehanna, four miles from Lewisburg and less than fifteen miles from Northumberland. Within a short distance of his home he had a number of routes he liked to take when he was in the mood to wander in this vast hunting ground of the Iroquois. Not far away, across the river, was the mouth of Chillisquaque Creek, whose name is a variation of Chillicothe, one of the tribes of the Shawnees. On the boundary line between Union and Snyder counties, in the White Mountains, is the Devil's Den, a sink on the top of a mountain where the last bison herd was annihilated. Farther along, in the "tight end" of Buffalo Valley, is the beginning of the gorge of the Karoondinha, whose glorious scenery continues as far as Coburn in Center County. At the beginning of the gorge the Paddy Mountains and the White Mountains come so near to each other that one is apt to think he might almost throw a stone across the valley.

This is one of the spots where it is well to go alone and revel in beauty and peace. The visitor to the valley may be alone, but he need not be lonely. Everywhere there may be silence, but the silence should not be oppressive. For the friendly mountains speak in a language that makes loneliness impossible. What do they say? Go and hear for yourself. Take your troubles there, and note how marvelously they melt away. In contact with the majestic mountains there you may gain peace for tumult, repose for weariness, strength for weakness, courage for faintheartedness.

But the mountain lover can find solitude without going farther from the river bank than Lewisburg. He can be alone on a number of heights near the town, and can still feel that he is in touch with the throbbing life of the valley spread out before him. Some of those who settled the town in the days when the Indians were yet in the valley made what others thought were wild prophecies of the future development of the surrounding country.

The future did not look promising in 1777. Then the dread of the Indian came to a head at the time of what became known as "the Great Runaway." Ever since the Fort Stanwix treaty of 1768 hardy frontiersmen had been building their cabins and clearing their fields along the river in what is now Lycoming County. They scorned to give way to the terrors of earlier years; but in 1777 the dread of the Indians, who, they learned, were coming down the river, became so great that they fled in a panic, bound for Fort Augusta. A vivid picture of this "runaway" was written in days when the Indians were still more than a tradition in the valley:

"Boats, canoes, long-troughs, rafts hastily made of dry sticks, every sort of floating article had been put in requisition, and were crowded with women and children and 'plunder.' There were several hundred people in all. Whenever any obstruction occurred at a shoal or a riffle, the women would leap out and put their shoulder to the flatboat or raft, and launch it again

THE PENNSYLVANIA HIGHLANDS

into deep water. The men of the settlement came down in single file on each side of the river to guard the women and children."

The strange flotilla proceeded along the river past the site of the present city of Williamsport, around the mountain whose presence obstructs the passage of the river, turning then to the south and on down by Fort Muncy and Milton and Northumberland to Sunbury. The Indians pursued as far as Fort Muncy, but, after destroying the blockhouse there, they gave up the chase. Probably Fort Augusta's strength was so great that they were afraid to venture against it.

Eleven months after the "Great Runaway," two hundred Indians and one hundred British regulars surrounded and captured Fort Freeland, eight miles northeast of Milton, located on Warrior's Run, in a beautiful region frequently called Paradise.

From Milton to Muncy, even by the winding river road, is only about eighteen miles. One of the sights of the town at this great bend of the Susquehanna is the monument to Captain John Brady who, was sent in 1778 to protect the settlers on the West Branch. His faithful service encouraged many to renew the fight with the wilderness.

Muncy is the point of departure for Eaglesmere. The road leads along winding Muncy Creek, through a valley bordered by mountains whose forest-covered slopes seem but a continuation of the green fields that lead up to them. Sometimes the mountains approach the road closely, as at Picture Rocks, where is the rugged cliff used for centuries by the chiefs of the Loyalsock and Muncy valleys to tell vividly the story of great events in the life of the tribe. There are no pictures there now, for the soft rocks have lost their surface. But the bold precipice is still there.

Near Tivoli the valley seems to be shut in by the mountains, but the highway winds among the encircling hills until it finds a path on into Sullivan County.

Steadily upward mounts the road until, after miles of scenery that no one should miss, though most travelers do miss it, because it is in a section where the turnpikes are not at their best, beautiful Eaglesmere is reached, at an altitude of more than two thousand feet. Rocks and hills surround this gem of the mountains; forest and glen and waterfall vie with each other to make the region attractive. It is said that some of the depths of this spring-fed lake have never been sounded.

Once the six hundred acres of blue water now known as Eaglesmere bore the name of the Englishman Lewis who built glassworks to take advantage of the fine glass sand on the west shore of the lake. The war of 1812 and poor transportation facilities combined to drive him out of business.

Of course Eaglesmere has its legend. It is said that once there was no lake here, but only a great chasm. In the chasm was an entrance to the underworld, where the spirit of the Indian who had wronged his neighbors, or had failed to do the work expected of him when he was alive, was confined until he should make everything right.

The Indians believed that six hundred armed spirits stood at the entrance to the underworld, to keep out those who had no right to enter. Fear of these spirits deterred most people; but Stormy Torrent, a powerful chief, resolved to make the attempt. His purpose became known. Efforts to dissuade him were in vain. Finally thousands of Indians gathered to see him brave the anger of the spirits. The instant he stepped into the gorge, they were awed by the breaking of a great storm. When this was over the chasm was filled as it is to-day. Next day "a cloudless sky looked down on the waters of a beautiful, tranquil lake, clear as crystal."

Somehow it has not been thought necessary to devise a tale to account for Hunter's Lake, a body of water half as large as Eaglesmere, and but four miles distant. This was long a favorite resort for fishermen.

A third notable lake in Sullivan County, Lake Ganoga, is less than fifteen miles southeast of Eaglesmere, but by the roundabout road made necessary by the difficulties of this highland region the distance is more than twice as great. This road leads through La Porte, the county seat, whose altitude is about nineteen hundred feet. Ganoga Lake is near the summit of the main range of the Allegheny Mountains, and is 2235 feet above the sea—the highest body of fresh water east of the Rocky Mountains. The altitude of the lake can be appreciated by those who climb to it through the wild glen where are thirty-three cascades, several of them more than one hundred feet high.

All about Lake Ganoga is a vast forest, reminder of the day when practically the entire county was covered with trees. Scores of square miles of these were felled and the logs were sent to the mill by way of Muncy Creek or Loyalsock Creek. By a series of dams these waterways were made to do the bidding of the lumbermen.

Soon after Loyalsock Creek crosses into Lycoming County, it flows through Loyalsock forest, another of the state forest reservations where tremendous strides have been made in the conservation of the timber resources that once seemed doomed to utter destruction.

SEEING PENNSYLVANIA

Two more of the plunging creeks of this well-watered country had a prominent part in early history—Lycoming Creek and Tiadaghton or Pine Creek. When the region was first opened for settlement there were so many applicants for each three hundred acres of land which a settler might own that it became necessary to have a lottery. Scores of allotments were made east of Lycoming Creek. Many wished to go west toward what is now known as Pine Creek. But the authorities were uncertain whether the treaty made with the Indians allowed settlement farther west; the limit of its purchase was Tiadaghton Creek, and they could not tell whether the creek that enters the Susquehanna at the present site of Williamsport or that which comes from the north beyond Jersey Shore was Tiadaghton. Accordingly it was announced that those who settled beyond what is now known as Lycoming Creek must do so at their own risk; they could not count on the protection of the law.

The pioneers beyond Lycoming thereupon decided to be a law unto themselves. Every year they elected three men, who were charged with the settlement of all disputes. These were called "fair-play men." From their decision there was no appeal, and all were bound to enforce it. Anyone who refused to obey was set adrift on the Susquehanna in a canoe, at the north of the Lycoming.

Of the stories told of the "fair-play men" the best is the narrative of their interest in the discussion of Congress at Philadelphia in the days of 1776. This culminated in a public meeting, held on Pine Creek, when they declared themselves independent of Great Britain. This meeting was held on July 4, 1776!

The rule of the fair-play men lasted until 1784,

when it was learned that the Tiadaghton Creek of the treaty was really Pine Creek, not Lycoming. Accordingly the settlers between the creeks who had persevered were given title to three hundred acres each.

The place on the Susquehanna where the fair-play men set afloat recalcitrants became the site of Williamsport, long famous as the healthiest city in Pennsylvania and the fourth city for health in the United States. Perhaps one of the reasons for this fine record is a situation so beautiful that those who live there have no excuse for being dull or dispirited. The long straightaway of the river is displayed from Bald Eagle Mountain south of the city, while the foothills of the Alleghenies to the north are a restful sight to the weary and an inspiration always. In fact, the city has one of the choice locations of a county of which men have said that here the handiwork of Nature is as prominently displayed as in any county in the state.

Williamsport did not begin to grow rapidly until James H. Perkins, a New Hampshire man, had the daring vision of an immense log boom by means of which the logs floated down the Susquehanna and its tributaries could be collected for later transport to sawmills down the river. He did not see why the logs of pine and hemlock should be built into rafts before being sent to market, when a boom such as he had in mind would solve all difficulties. Accordingly he built the boom, whose capacity was 300,000,000 feet of timber.

The sending of single logs instead of rafts down the tributary creeks led to trouble. As always when a labor saving plan is adopted, there was an outcry from those who thought their occupation was endangered. The raftsman organized. Public meetings were held to denounce the log floaters. One such meeting, held on November 1, 1853, determined that "at all hazards to our person and property the floating of logs in the Moshannon Creek shall from this night cease." Before the meeting adjourned a committee was appointed to devise means of ending the abuse, "peaceably, if they can, forcibly if they must." Another meeting at Clearfield insisted that log floating would have a ruinous effect on "the development and prosperity of our now flourishing and interesting country." At this meeting also it was decided to fight, if need arose, to save "our ancient system of lumbering."

Not many years elapsed, however, before even the most bitter opponent of the new system was compelled to own that the anticipated curse was proving a blessing—a blessing that might have been immensely greater if steps had been taken to replant the forests or to protect the young trees from forest fires. Not until the State Forestry Department began work were the necessary reforms undertaken.

The city is the center of one of the Forestry Department's greatest activities. The Bald Eagle forest, south of Williamsport, and Gray's Run forest, to the north, are object lessons of what can be done for the scientific care of trees. But the care of these and other forests was begun too late to save the vast resources of pine timber. In 1910 the last log was floated down the West Branch, and in 1911 the Williamsport boom was removed.

No one who has the opportunity to revel in the ever-changing vistas provided so generously by the Susquehanna can afford to miss the stretch between Williamsport and Jersey Shore. But it is just as difficult to think of failure to pass through the rare section of country south of the river, between these points. The memo-

THE PENNSYLVANIA HIGHLANDS

ries of a leisurely jaunt over the twenty miles, more or less, of hill and valley road will be a perennial joy. The very names of the townships passed through whet the appetite: Susquehanna, Bastress, Limestone, Nippenose. Bastress township takes its name from the town, situated in a valley noted for beauty and fertility. A little to the south of Bastress the highway joins the valley road that leads northwest back to the Susquehanna and Jersey Shore. It will be hard to resist the temptation to turn to the left, and pass on to the lovely White Deer Hole Valley, just over the mountains. But the road to the right through the Nippenose Valley leads to Jersey Shore—unless one yields to other allurements of this richly dowered region. The valley, with its seven surrounding mountains and its Oriole Cave, which dates back only to 1896, when it startled the residents by its sudden appearance, should satisfy any normal appetite for the beautiful. But will it, when one learns that it is only necessary to turn aside along Rauch's Creek, through Rauch's Gap, to Rauchtown, and that "there is no finer or wilder rocky gorge in the eastern states except perhaps Crawford Notch and the Old Man of the Mountain in the White Mountains of New England?" On the gorge's bill of fare are "castellated crags, lofty precipices, dim caverns, winding defiles, dizzy peaks." Readers of these descriptions will be able to enter into the feelings of their author, who, when speaking to the writer of this volume of the wonders of his native Pennsylvania Highlands, said he was living in the memory of the grandeur of the mountains and the loveliness of the valleys, and was longingly waiting for the chance for another soul-satisfying pilgrimage thither.

It is a simple matter to turn aside once for a side trip.

SEEING PENNSYLVANIA

But what if one side trip leads to a second, and the second to a third? For as surely as the unwary pilgrim yields to the mute invitation of southern Lycoming until he reaches the gorge of Rauch's Creek, just so surely will he wish to forget schedules (those mortal enemies of vacation joys) long enough to follow the old lumber road up Gotschall Run, whose wild beauty will prove all the justification needed for schedule murder. The penalty for taking this added bit of enjoyment will be nothing more than the extension of the tour in the back country to McElhattan, in Clinton County, on the Susquehanna. From there the way will be easy along the winding Susquehanna east to Jersey Shore.

Yes, there will be a second item in the penalty—the necessity of pausing at Jersey Shore at least long enough to take the road to the south and look at what might have been seen if the scheduled course had been followed toward the river, when the invitation came to go aside to Rauchtown. Within a few miles we find the spring which is the source of Antes Creek (marked by one of the pillars from the old state capitol at Harrisburg, erected here in 1900 to commemorate the two hundredth anniversary of Penn's treaty with Chief Widaagh, who in 1700 granted the territory for settlement), the gorge of Antes Valley, Widaagh's Spring (at the foot of Bald Eagle Mountain), and the site of Antes Fort, the stronghold of Indian days, with its commemorative tablet erected by the Daughters of the American Revolution.

Jersey Shore was named by settlers whose loyalty to the old home in New Jersey persisted in spite of the allurements of the ever changing glories of the new home. There was little in the new situation to make them think of the state between the Delaware and the sea; so they satisfied homesickness in an easy and commendable fashion.

One of the features of the country that lured the pioneers of Jersey Shore was the Tiadaghton or Pine Creek, famous in early days because of Indian raids, prominent in later years because of the dozen billion feet of white pine timber floated on its surface to the boom at Williamsport and to the mills beyond, and notable always by reason of its passage through what has been called "the great Pennsylvania canyon." So what if the scheduled route does call now for a speedy return to Williamsport? Who could pass by Pine Creek if there is any possibility of exploring for a few miles the rugged stream that leads through the Black Forest reservation and waters the base of ridges once covered with noble trees, but which now are barren because of forest fires and unscientific lumbering operations?

A railroad follows Pine Creek. But why take a train through such a gorge as this, if it is possible to ride in a slow-moving machine, or, better, to clamber along on foot? Of course the rear car of the train affords a good view of the country after it has gone by. But why not be where there is no one to say nay when the desire comes to linger in a specially attractive spot? And isn't it much better to be able to touch the water of the stream at will than, riding by, to think how good that water would feel? It is good to crane the neck from the car window for a view of the rocky sides of the canyon; but far more satisfying is the upward look that takes in both walls at once, and a section of the blue sky above. The passenger can appreciate the engineering difficulties surmounted by those who built the old Pine Creek and Jersey Shore Railway, through mountains long thought insurmountable; but in ten minutes the pedestrian can see more of engineering triumphs than the passenger can discover in an hour.

A second creek road leads directly north from Jersey Shore. It is possible to follow this to Steam Valley, there joining the road which in due time the writer proposes to take from Williamsport. But the creek road is worth a round trip, if only to see how a stream can really meander if it takes a notion. Eleven times in seven miles the creek is crossed by the highway, whose course is comparatively straight for a Lycoming County road.

After the creek of many crossings comes the opportunity for the neglected stretch of Susquehanna's waters between Jersey Shore and Williamsport. Touch with half a dozen brawling creeks, tossing through their narrow courses, will give renewed appetite for the miles in the valley of the river that pushes patiently onward in its search for an opening leading to the point of union with its sister river from the northeast.

Williamsport is the gateway to another of the turbulent streams of Lycoming, the creek which gives its name to the county. In its valley may be seen mountains in profusion, gorges, waterfalls, and tributary runs without number rushing down from the uplands. Here was the route of the Indian to central New York, traces of their Sheshequin trail still being visible. Here lumbermen by the thousand floated rafts and single logs from the forests of Tioga and Bradford counties to Williamsport. Up the creek rollicking crews toiled on their return to the camps, following Lycoming as far as Trout Run, then ascending that creek, crossing the mountain, and pushing on to the head of Tioga Valley—jolly, shouting, singing companies whose progress demanded the attention of everybody within reach of voices that carried far in the mountain air.

But the lower reaches of the Lycoming are best known because here was the beginning of the old Williamson Road, otherwise called the Blockhouse Road, whose story is one of the romances of the central Pennsylvania country.

The first chapter of the story was written in 1792, when Charles Williamson, whose principals were in England, bought more than a million acres of land in Pennsylvania and New York from Robert Morris. He was in Northumberland when a message came to him that a large company of emigrants was on the way, and that he was to lead them through the Pennsylvania wilderness.

He had a choice of routes. He might take them up the Susquehanna to Tioga Point, and from there by land; or he might take them directly north. The former route was long and there would be grave dangers of many kinds, and the latter route did not exist.

He did not hesitate long. If there was no road through the wild country, it should be built, even if the distance was more than one hundred miles. In response to his appeal for help the Pennsylvania Assembly granted him one hundred pounds. Undiscouraged by this pitifully small appropriation, he began work as soon as the emigrants were ready to make the journey.

His plan was to direct the men in the party as they broke a section of the wilderness. When the way was open for a short distance, a log house was built for shelter. Here provisions were left for the women and children, who were brought to the end of the first stage. Then the road makers continued their toil until there was need for a second shelter, and the women and children could advance another stage. The temporary shelter, or blockhouse, gave the first name to the road.

The provisions were brought from Northumberland by pack horses, until that point was too far in the rear; then other sources of supplies had to be sought. Once, when the company was almost out of food, a messenger was sent from Canoe Camp across to Tioga Point (now Athens), on the North Branch of the Susquehanna. On his return to the emigrants there was a great feast.

The road followed the Sheshequin trail up the Loyalsock to Trout Run, then on to Blossburg and Canoe Camp. Here canoes were built and the party floated down stream to Painted Post, New York. The final stage of the journey was to the site of the town of Bath, which was then founded.

When the completion of the road was announced, in 1796, there was great excitement. This was the first highway in all this section, and it shortened the distance from Northumberland to Painted Post about one hundred miles, opening to settlement a wide territory.

Williamson's next step was a triumph of advertising genius. He sent announcements of the completion of the road to Harrisburg, as well as to Washington, and these were read to the lawmakers assembled there. Coupled with the announcements was an invitation to all who would to come through the wilderness, over the Blockhouse Road, and be the guests of its builders during a two weeks' program of theatrical performances, races, and other amusements. Promise was made that guides would be waiting at Philadelphia, Easton, Lancaster, Carlisle, Harrisburg, and Northumberland, to give safe conduct to prospective guests.

The invitation was accepted by hundreds. It is recorded that for weeks the road through the wilderness

THE PENNSYLVANIA HIGHLANDS

was traversed by a procession almost unbroken. Sometimes the old blockhouses were used at night. Again a camp would be made by the roadside. Probably the travelers stopped one night with the keeper of a tavern who, later on, made unrighteous profits by driving into a hidden forest pen the cattle of emigrants who stopped with him, and, as a result always had large quantities of what he called elk meat!

For thirty years after the triumphal pilgrimage of the invited guests of the proprietor, the Williamson Road was the recognized highway for emigrants bound to north-central Pennsylvania and southern New York.

Travelers to-day will find this a thoroughfare of marvelous interest. It is difficult to compare the scenery of one section with that of another; the best possible statement is that from Williamsport to Blossburg there is such satisfying variety of all the best and richest in landscape that one is eager at once to turn round and go back over the road. Near Trout Run, fourteen miles from Williamsport, is Crescent Gap, where the Lycoming makes a crescent-shaped sweep in breaking through the main chain of the Alleghenies. From Trout Run to Liberty views of the valley and the distant mountains rejoice the heart. From Liberty to Blossburg there is such a profusion of beauty that many who have lingered over this bit of the road declare they have seen nothing in the Rockies so fine.

At Blossburg—the road builders called the place Peters's Camp—coal was discovered in October, 1792. While many years passed before the value of the discovery was recognized, the district was among the first to have railroad transportation for the promotion of the coal trade. By 1840 the road to the Chemung River and canal was opened.

SEEING PENNSYLVANIA

From Blossburg to Wellsboro, by way of Canoe Camp, there are prospects so fine that an appetite is created for the side trip from Wellsboro to Antrim. The route of the railroad leads into the heart of the finest of the country, though the highway which runs at some distance from the railroad also offers pleasing variety of striking landscape. The view into the valley where Wellsboro has its seat is best from Round Top on the railroad, while all the way to Brownlee there is a prospect to Pine Creek and the mountain ridge beyond. The end of the line is at Antrim, a coal center developed since 1866 in what was till then a wilderness, and still boasts surroundings inviting in their wildness. Blackwell's forest, which stretches to the north of Antrim, will preserve for future generations some of the wild scenes of former days.

Wellsboro, Tioga's county seat, is in Delmar township. There is a story behind that name. The first settlers, being from Virginia, Delaware, and Maryland, were unable to agree on a name for the locality; each wanted to honor his own state. So there was a compromise, Vir-del-mar being the strange result. Fortunately, on the organization of the township in 1808, the first syllable was omitted.

The highway from Wellsboro across the center of Tioga County to Galeton and Coudersport in Potter County has well been called by travelers the scenic route. Almost all the way the valleys of creeks are followed closely, with mountains about them on either hand. To the north, soon after leaving Wellsboro, is the Chatham forest, whose Asaph nursery for seedling trees makes easy a first-hand study of an important part of the work of the State Department of Forestry. Millions of seedlings of pine, spruce, and other trees are

IN THE HEMLOCK FOREST
Photo by State Department of Forestry

VALLEY VIEW TOWARD TIVOLI
Photo by J. Horace McFarland Company

ASAPH NURSERY
Photo by State Department of Forestry

RUINS OF OLE BULL'S CASTLE, NEAR OLEONA
Photo by State Department of Forestry

THE PENNSYLVANIA HIGHLANDS

shipped each year from this nursery, both to private individuals and to other state forests.

Almost directly south of Galeton is another of the most celebrated of the forest reserves, but it is best to postpone a visit to this until a road can be taken southeast from Coudersport. The road leads over the ridge of the Allegheny basin, whose height is at least four hundred feet greater than the Susquehanna basin, and the outlook on valley and mountain is correspondingly delightful. This is the county where the Allegheny, the Genesee, and the Sinnemahoning have their source —streams that flow to the St. Lawrence, the Gulf of Mexico, and Chesapeake Bay. This fact is a guarantee of worth-while scenery.

But the Coudersport and Jersey Shore turnpike is noted for something more than fine scenery, or the state forest in the southeast corner of the county, or the observation tower at Cherry Springs where rangers watch for signs of forest fires and where tourists may climb and on a clear day see south to Lock Haven and north to the New York state line. Not the least of its claims to distinction is that it runs through the valley where, in 1852, Ole Bull, the Norwegian violinist, made his ill-starred attempt to colonize a company of fellow-Norwegians. Oleona and Cartee Camp, villages on the line of the road, are reminders of the historic failure.

The impulse that led to the purchase of thousands of acres of land on and near Little Kettle Creek came when his countrymen who had settled in the South told him of their privations, hardships, and poor health. He made up his mind to have for them a home in Potter County, to "found a new Norway, consecrated to liberty, baptized with independence, and protected by the Union's mighty flag."

Some eight hundred settlers took possession of the three hundred houses built. There were also a store and a church. The founder built for himself a castle of feudal proportions, on a bluff overlooking Little Kettle Creek, not far from the village now known as Oleona.

For some months all went well. On February 6, 1853, Ole Bull wrote to his brother:

"Of my activity as leader and controller of my little state in Pennsylvania, you can have a conception only when you know that I am engaged simultaneously in laying out five villages, and contracting with the government for the casting of cannon, some two thousand in all . . .

"Philadelphia has subscribed two millions to the Sunbury and Erie road, which goes near the colony on the south; New York has also given two millions to a branch of the Erie and New York road from Elmira to Oleona, the northern line of the colony.

"So many have applied for land that I have been obliged to look out for more; I have bought 20,000 acres to the west, and in the adjoining county (McKean) I have the refusal of 112,000 acres. In Wyoming County I am contracting for an old deserted foundry with forest, water-power, work-shop, and dwellings, and am taking out patents in Washington for a new smelting furnace for cannon."

In intervals between concert tours the great violinist liked to go among his people and live in the old castle. It is still a tradition of the neighborhood that he found his greatest delight in playing his violin on the ramparts of the castle or on the banks of Kettle Creek. There he would "reproduce the rush and roar of rapid streams, the frolic of the winds through the rocky glens, and the tempest's crash on the mountain top."

But disaster came. One night when he was entertaining guests at dinner a man brought word from a

THE PENNSYLVANIA HIGHLANDS

merchant of Philadelphia that the agents who had sold him the lands on which the colony was built were scoundrels; that the merchant was the real owner of the forest acres whose wildness had attracted the violinist.

Ole Bull hurried that night to Lock Haven, on his favorite Norwegian horse, and was soon in Philadelphia. The owner told him how he had tried in vain to overtake him with legal notice, as soon as recovery from an attack of yellow fever enabled him to learn the facts.

The owner expressed hearty sympathy with Ole Bull and offered to give him a good title to the land for a price that was merely nominal. The artist, however, was unable to do more than protect the residents already on the land. In vain the head of the colony pressed charges against the malefactors. For a long time he was unable to secure justice, and he became the victim of their relentless pursuit and persecution. For five years he fought them, earning the costs of the suit by giving concerts, and at the end of that time he received small damages.

During these years of trial Harriet Beecher Stowe and James Gordon Bennett were among influential friends who came to his help. Once, when his reputation was being assailed, Mr. Bennett offered him the columns of *The New York Herald* to make answer. But Bull replied: "I tink, Mr. Benneett, it is best tey write against me, and I plays against tem."

Most of the colonists found their way to the West. A few remained, among them Ole Bull's secretary, John Andriessen, who was a storekeeper in Oleona for forty years after the collapse of the colony.

To-day there are but two or three buildings left of those so hopefully constructed. Among these is the castle, whose ruins, within the limits of the Ole Bull forest, are carefully preserved by the Department of Forestry. The walls look down on "a sheer descent of three hundred feet to where Kettle Creek winds about like a thread of silver. Across the ravine is another mountain, as steep but not as high as the one on which the castle is located."

The Coudersport and Jersey Shore turnpike makes easy access to the wildest part of Potter County. This road was begun in 1829, but was not in good condition for many years, until the State Highway Department took it in hand. It is a route that appeals to the sportsman as well as to the lover of the beauty of the primitive forests. A writer in *In the Open*, a Pittsburgh sportsman's magazine, once said of the thoroughfare and its surroundings:

"It traverses and borders state forest land for a distance of fifty miles. It passes through some of the best fishing and hunting sections of the state. The route is unique in that it traverses an uninhabited region and one may travel sixteen miles without passing a dwelling. The bear, deer, and elk are free to roam where they please, and occupy a vast, unbroken domain of 150,000 acres."

No wonder sportsmen talk of Potter County as the greatest outing spot in Pennsylvania. Its two hundred miles of attractive roads, its numerous fine streams, its seven hundred thousand acres of wild land fit only for timber and game, and the thousands of acres of state forest land combine to make a sportsman's paradise.

Once it was thought that oil might be discovered in this section of the state, but the wells driven near Coudersport and elsewhere in 1885 and 1886 remained dry. The search for mineral wealth brought to light numerous

THE PENNSYLVANIA HIGHLANDS

treasures of the sort that procure profit not of the material kind. Of these one is known as the "Sweden Valley Ice mine," a few miles from Coudersport, on the road to Oleona. Here was found the entrance to a cave, perhaps fifteen feet deep, where in midsummer the water from the rocks becomes ice. On the walls icicles form, and on the floor there is a sheet of ice that becomes thicker until fall. Then it disappears, and in winter there is no ice in the cave.

This natural ice house would have been a convenience to the early settlers of the county if they had known of its existence. Yet the lack of ice in summer was far from being their greatest privation. In 1811 a pioneer who was out of flour went to Jersey Shore with two yoke of oxen. On the way down he crossed Pine Creek eighty times. The time required for the round trip was eighteen days. The breaking of two axle trees, two upsets, and the loss of a wheel in crossing Pine Creek at one point were incidents of the trip. For sixty miles the road was without a house.

Coudersport, one of the towns where some of the early settlers congregated, has the distinction of being the first of the hundreds of towns and cities in the great Ohio Valley; the Allegheny River rises less than five miles away. Thence the road west toward McKean County follows closely the windings of the river as far as Port Allegany. Thence the stream turns northward for a taste of New York state before making up its mind to pursue its devious course toward the Gulf of Mexico. It is a curious phenomenon that the North Branch of the Susquehanna enters New York in a similar manner, only to leave it after as brief an acquaintance with Pennsylvania's northern neighbor as the Allegheny makes. Because of the vagaries of these two streams, two New York cities, Olean and Binghamton (near the border), are situated on rivers that belong to Pennsylvania.

Port Allegany once boasted a name much more picturesque. As Canoe Place the site was known both to Indians and emigrants, who, after ascending the West Branch of the Susquehanna as far as Emporium, would cross the divide to the Allegheny, build canoes here, and float down the latter stream.

This gateway to the upper Allegheny country gives a pleasant foretaste of the rich series of exquisite landscapes to be observed by those who know the lower waters. From the hills that limit the valley where the town is built there is a wide-spreading outlook up stream and down stream as well as toward Smethport, the county seat.

The high lands about Smethport, east to Port Allegany and northwest to Bradford, became a fertile field for oil promoters. In 1861 the first producing well in the county was sunk at Smethport. Later there were hundreds of wells in the county.

To Prospect Hill, two miles west of Smethport, one of the highest points in the state, a pilgrimage should be made for the sake of a comprehensive look at the surface of a county whose distinguishing features are tablelands near the center some two thousand feet above sea level, and valleys of streams, at least four hundred feet lower. The result is an extremely broken surface that makes landscapes entirely different from those provided in most other parts of the state.

Ceres, in the northeast corner of the county, shares with Smethport the honor of being among the earliest settlements in McKean. A number of the oldest roads in the region radiated from Ceres, among these being

LUMBERING IN POTTER COUNTY
Photo supplied by Boyd S. Rothrock, Curator Pennsylvania State Museum

THE CHEMUNG RIVER, NEAR ATHENS
Photo from Lehigh Valley Railroad

THE PENNSYLVANIA HIGHLANDS

one to the south, and one into New York state, to a junction with the Hamilton Road, the route of emigrants from the East to the Allegheny River at Olean. From Smethport also there is a road north to Olean. This follows the Allegheny to the point where the Hamilton Road emigrants took skiff or canoe or flatboat for the western counties of Pennsylvania, or for the Ohio River region.

From Olean east to Elmira the searcher for Pennsylvania scenic glories can retrace in a general way the route taken by these emigrants and can feel that he is on a road that is almost as much a part of the highway system of the state to the south as is the National Road in northern Maryland, for it also is closely related to the history of the state. Then the scenery of Allegany, Steuben, and Chemung counties is akin to that of the counties over the line in Pennsylvania.

A few miles west of Elmira the road crosses the route taken by the makers of the Williamson Road from Northumberland in 1792. All the way from Elmira to Wilkes-Barre, it is in the valley of romantic streams, first the Chemung, then the West Branch of the Susquehanna.

Soon after the boundary of Pennsylvania is crossed the attention is attracted by the regular contour of what is called Spanish Hill. From the summit, one thousand feet above the sea, and nearly three hundred feet above the river, there is a view that will repay the trouble of the ascent. The name is a reminder of the tradition that the mound is the work of the Spaniards. With just as much reason it has been attributed to the Scandinavians and the Mound Builders. Yet the geologists say that it is a natural feature, probably the most recent geological formation of the valley. When the continental glaciers passed this way, coming out of the valley of the Susquehanna, this was perhaps a part of the terminal moraine.

Naturally the Indians took advantage of a site so easily fortified, and had here one of their strongholds. Traces of their work have been found on the hill.

Alexander Wilson, when making his trip to Niagara Falls, gave rein to his poetic tendencies when he looked at the eminence:

> "Now to the left the ranging mountains bend
> And level plains before us wide extend;
> When, rising lone, old Spanish Hill appears,
> The post of war in ancient unknown years.
> Its steep and rounding sides with woods embrowned,
> Its level top with old entrenchments crowned;
> Five hundred paces thence we measured o'er,
> Ere all its circling boundaries we explore.
> Now overgrown with woods alone it stands,
> And looks abroad o'er open fertile lands."

Five miles below Spanish Hill is the junction of the Chemung and the Susquehanna rivers. The musical name the Indians gave the place was Diahoga, "where the loving waters meet." There they had a town, the largest in the state north of Shamokin, known as the "south door" of the Long House of the Six Nations. Here, in 1790, Colonel Timothy Pickering held a conference with the Six Nations. One of those present was Thomas Morris, son of Robert Morris, whom the Indians adopted into the Seneca nation, the name given him being Otetiani, "always ready."

The modern name of Tioga Point, Athens, was given to it by the Connecticut Susquehanna Company in 1786. For years before and after that time the place was a center of operations against the settlers from Pennsyl-

THE PENNSYLVANIA HIGHLANDS

vania who opposed the claims of the Connecticut Company. From here the English and Indians assembled for their attack on Wyoming in 1778. And here, in 1787, Colonel John Franklin was arrested and sent in irons to Philadelphia, charged with high treason against the state as leader of those who planned to organize a new state, he being the governor.

The triangle above the meeting point of the rivers presents a remarkable landscape. The rivers are on two sides of the almost equilateral triangle. The third side is marked by hills not far from the state line. Hills beyond the river, from a height of some five hundred feet, overlook the common valley, with its fertile farms. The apex of the triangle is formed by the narrowing of the valley where the rivers start to come together, then seem to change their mind and postpone the meeting until several miles below. "There is no lovelier spot between the Atlantic and the Great Lakes than this spot," has been said. "The place is beautiful as the gates of paradise," another visitor declared.

But perhaps the finest tribute ever paid to this gem of Pennsylvania scenery was written by N. P. Willis in 1849:

" 'A!' Imagine the capital letter laid on its back and pointed south by east, and you have a pretty fair diagram of the junction of the Susquehanna and the Chemung. The note of admiration (exclamation point) describes a superb line of mountains at the back of the Chemung Valley, and the quotation marks express the fine bluffs that overlook the meeting of the waters at Athens. The cross of the letter (say a line of four miles) defines a road from one river to the other, by which travelers up the Chemung save the distance to the point of the triangle, and the area between is a broad plain."

The course of the Susquehanna for some distance is

characterized by a succession of cross valleys, shut in by ranges of hills through which the river flows. Perhaps the loveliest of these is "the sweet vale of Sheshequin," about six miles long by two broad, entirely surrounded by hills except for the gaps that have been made by the river.

At Towanda three valleys converge, so that the situation of the town is remarkably advantageous and picturesque. Perhaps this is why the Nanticokes were attracted to it as a burial place for their dead. The Indian name for the burial site was Tawandee, "at the burial place." Here David Wilmot, the author of the Thirteenth Amendment to the Constitution, was buried.

Below Towanda are many historic sites and noted places—the Narrows of the Susquehanna, Wysox Valley and Wysox town, with the boulder and tablet erected by the Daughters of the American Revolution to General Sullivan, whose expedition marched along these banks in 1779, and Standing Stone, opposite a high rock across the river, long a landmark of the Indians and the pioneers.

Asylum, a romantic location on the right bank of the river, is the memorial of one of the numerous vain attempts of enthusiasts to plant colonies in Pennsylvania. In 1791 the Duc de Noailles decided to open here an asylum for unfortunate Frenchmen who had been driven from home to Santo Domingo by the Revolution, and later had fled from Santo Domingo because of a rebellion of the blacks. In partnership with Marquis Antoine Omer Talon, Noailles bought 2400 acres of land from Robert Morris. The plan called for the later purchase of 200,000 acres of wild land, to be cleared and cultivated by the colonists. The Asylum Company

THE PENNSYLVANIA HIGHLANDS

was formed, and in this Robert Morris was for a time a partner. More than a score of houses were built for the use of Frenchmen who came to the valley, but they had not been in them long when disaster overtook the venture. Financial difficulties led to the reorganization of the company. Then the plans for the cultivation of the land by the colonists did not work out. Among the emigrants there were comparatively few laborers, the majority being made up of men of noble birth, many of whom had been members of the king's household. They understood the luxuries of city life far better than the stern demands of a frontier civilization. The result might have been foreseen.

But, while the colony failed, its short life gave a legacy of permanent value to the county. A taste for improved modes of living had been brought into a rough community, better roads were demanded, and in numerous other ways the influence of colonists of a high type of intelligence and training made itself felt. The results can be seen to-day.

It is remarkable that at the time of the Asylum experiment a notable company of English authors was thinking seriously of emigrating to America and founding a colony on the banks of the Susquehanna. Samuel Taylor Coleridge and Robert Southey were leaders in the movement. They had worked out a new scheme of living which they called Pantisocracy. In the words of Coleridge, the idea was "to remove the selfish principle from ourselves, and prevent it in our children, by an abolition of property; or, in whatever respects this might be impracticable, by such similarity of property as would amount to a moral sameness, and answer all the purposes of abolition."

The scheme was still under discussion when a land

agent from America persuaded Coleridge that the twenty-six adventurers who were to regenerate society should settle on the banks of the Susquehanna, because of its excessive beauty and security from hostile Indians. He told them that £2000 would suffice; that land would be cheap; that the twelve men in the party could easily clear three hundred acres in four or five months, and that for six hundred dollars a thousand acres could be cleared and houses built on them!

Fortunately the plan died before the impractical dreamers embarked on what would surely have been a disastrous enterprise.

A colonizing experiment that was successful, at least for a time, was made a few miles farther down stream, at Wyalusing. There, about 1765, the Moravians built a mission station where there were perhaps forty houses. To this they gave the name Friedenshütten, or "tents of peace." The land they occupied was granted to the Christian Indians by the Cayugas, but the Fort Stanwix treaty of 1768, in transferring the Susquehanna lands to the Penns, failed to make mention of the previous grant. For this reason the Moravians thought it would be wiser to secure another location, though surveyors had been ordered by the governor not to operate within five miles of the mission.

Accordingly, in 1772, a pilgrimage was made across trackless areas to western Pennsylvania. The journey made by the "241 individuals, of all ages, with cattle and horses, from the North Branch across the Allegheny Mountains, to the Ohio, would be even in these days of locomotive facilities, a most arduous undertaking."

Loskiel, the historian of the mission, has left a record of the epic journey. Some, he said, went by land, and some by water. "The land travelers had to care for

HOMET'S FERRY, NEAR WYALUSING
Photo from Lehigh Valley Railroad

ON THE SUSQUEHANNA, WEST OF FALLS
Photo from Lehigh Valley Railroad

THE PENNSYLVANIA HIGHLANDS

seventy head of oxen, and a still greater number of horses, and they sustained incredible hardships in forcing a way for themselves and the beasts through the very thick woods and swamps of very great extent, being directed only by a small path, and that hardly discernible in some places." In the Great Swamp the undergrowth was so dense that many times it was impossible to see one another at the distance of six feet. The swamp was sixty miles across. One winding stream was crossed thirty-six times.

The party that went by river had difficulties as great, but of a different kind. Yet they managed to get to the appointed meeting place, and go on to the chosen site for the new mission station at Friedenshütten in Beaver County.

The roundabout water route from Wyalusing to western Pennsylvania is for a long distance by the North Branch. Soon after Wyalusing has been left behind this cuts across Wyoming County from northwest to southeast. At the time of the historic journey much of the county was covered by forests, one remnant of which is the Wyoming forest, to the south of the river soon after it enters Wyoming County.

Tunkhannock, the county seat of Wyoming, has a most eligible location between two hills. One of these rises 650 feet above the river, while the other is 1150 feet high. Tunkhannock Creek, entering the Susquehanna here, adds features of note to the landscape. The valley of the creek gives opportunity for a memorable vacation ramble. The climax of this ramble would be the passage under the great Tunkhannock viaduct, at Nicholson, by means of which the Delaware, Lackawanna and Western Railway crosses from mountain to mountain 240 feet above the stream.

Tunkhannock may be made a starting point for side trips to three of the mountain lakes whose beds probably were made by the glacial ice cap that is responsible for many of the beautiful features of northeastern Pennsylvania. To the east is dainty Lake Winola, whose outlet, Falls Creek, reaches the Susquehanna at Falls Station, after making a series of fascinating cascades, Buttermilk Falls being the best known of these. To the north is Lake Carey, one thousand feet above sea level. The road leading to it is an attraction equal to the lake. To the south, and just over the line, in Luzerne County, is Harvey's Lake, the largest of the Pennsylvania lakes, whose basin is more than twelve hundred feet above sea level.

Between Tunkhannock and the mouth of the Lackawanna the Susquehanna breaks through North Mountain, which forms the rim of the Wyoming Valley, in a wide gorge above Pittston. Description of this famous valley must be reserved for a later chapter, when the entire region from Wilkes-Barre to Scranton will be under discussion.

The Pittston gorge has seen tens of thousands of great rafts descend the river to Wilkes-Barre and beyond. The movement began as early as 1796, when thirty rafts were floated. In 1804 there were 552 rafts. By 1827 the traffic had increased to such an extent that, during five weeks of a single freshet, 1030 rafts and arks passed Wilkes-Barre. In four weeks in 1849 the total increased to 2243 rafts and 268 arks. Then, gradually, the numbers decreased, until to-day even a small raft is a curiosity.

In following the route of the lumber rafts from Wilkes-Barre one is attracted by the ridge just below the city that rises somewhat abruptly from the north bank, the

THE PENNSYLVANIA HIGHLANDS

low-lying islands scattered here and there in the shallow river, and the farm lands on the more gentle slope of the south bank.

The ridge on the right bank is of peculiar beauty nearly opposite Nanticoke, where the river forms an acute double bend. The feature on this side of the stream is a mountain 865 feet high. On the opposite bank Kingston Mount slopes down to the water. The highway follows the ridge on the right bank, now near the level of the river, again rising high enough to afford a welcome study of water and valley.

At times the hills are a mass of verdure, but there are enough clearings to show what a loss in scenic beauty would be caused by the cessation of the conservation work of the State Department of Forestry.

Below Shickshinny the right bank is much more broken and open, but on the left bank the hills rise almost from the water, and the wanderer by the highway has a better opportunity to view them than the passenger on the railway that follows the left bank, often on a narrow ledge blasted from the rock.

Wapwallopen, at the southern end of a long, sharp turn in the river, is distinguished by the rugged front of Wapwallopen Hill. For a time this will seem to shut off the stream like a great dam, but an unexpected turn leads on to reaches that would make the observer hold his breath if he had not learned that the Susquehanna teaches the necessity of expecting the unexpected.

In the neighborhood of Berwick the river and its surroundings are at their best. Here is the introduction to Columbia County, whose advantageous location between the anthracite regions and the Allegheny Mountains gives it some of the finest scenery in the state.

Two early travelers who passed this way did not have the pleasure of using such satisfactory roads as are now provided by the State Highway Department. Colonel Thomas Proctor, in 1791, after crossing the river from the east side at Berwick, said that he proceeded up the west side about twelve miles, and, in endeavoring to go through the Narrows, the river being exceedingly high and rapid, had a narrow escape from drowning:

"With great difficulty we surmounted the summit of a steep precipice, being unable to return by the same defile we had attempted to pass through. From this I endeavored to go around the mountain, which lay along the river; and, after having traveled an hour and a half, over the most rugged ground, and seeing no end to the ridge of mountains, we shaped our course through the woods, to the place from where we departed in the morning."

It was four years later when the Duc de la Rochefoucauld-Liancourt had his troubles with the roads out of Berwick. Learning of a new road, shorter than the old, he was ferried across the river to reach it. The ferry boat, rowed by a man of seventy, was too small. The baggage was sent first, with two horses. Two men and two horses followed. One horse stepped over the low rail into the water. The boat heeled and filled. Fortunately the horse was pulled in from the river by one of the passengers, and the boat righted just in time.

When the land was reached there were further difficulties. The road could not be found. "We had to travel eighteen miles over felled trees, deep morasses, rocks, and loose stones," the Frenchman said. His girth broke, and his saddle loosened. Twice he fell from the horse's back. Finally the horse ran away.

At the time this wanderer floundered on the banks of

the Susquehanna, there were still visible reminders of the old Shawanese Indian villages between Bloomsburg and the mouth of a near by stream whose winding course adds a pleasant touch to the landscape spread out from the summit of one of the heights near the town.

Below Bloomsburg the river makes another of its sharp turns, then receives the waters of Catawissa Creek near the site of what is probably the oldest village in Columbia County, called Catawissa as early as 1728. Up the valley of the creek leads the Catawissa Railroad, from early days one of the most celebrated of the scenic railways in eastern Pennsylvania. To-day it is a part of the Reading system. From the river far back into the interior it leads the way to wild gorges, mountain precipices, and sylvan chasms almost without number. Possibly the most notable feature on the line is Mainville Gap. This, though of course less grand than either the Lehigh Gap or the Delaware Gap, is notable among the mountain passes of the state.

Catawissa has its Lover's Leap—a striking ledge of rock, where it is said Minnetunkee, daughter of the Delaware chief, Lapackpicton, met her death. Her father caught her there with a lover whom he did not favor. He fell over the precipice into the river, and she threw herself after him. But if every story of a "lover's leap" along the Susquehanna is to be accepted, leaping precipices must have been an industry that seriously interfered with the growth of the Indian residents.

Indian legends also cluster about the streams and hills of Montour County, Columbia's small but beautiful and fertile western neighbor. Lapackpicton is the hero of some of these. His name is preserved through its association with a bold cliff on the right bank, near

Danville, which bears a fancied resemblance to a stern Indian face.

The county itself bears the name of an Indian who was one of the most picturesque characters of colonial days, Andrew Montour. Madame Montour, his French mother, was three-quarters white, but after her marriage to Carondowana, an Iroquois chief, she preferred to live with the Indians. Though a relative of Queen Esther, whose conduct at Forty Fort was so bloodthirsty, she was a friend of the whites, for whom she was able to perform many services, since she was influential with the Indians.

Andrew Montour, her son, frequently went with Conrad Weiser to Indian conferences, and he was one of the few natives who fought on the side of Braddock at Turtle Creek. Later descendants of Madame Montour lived at the foot of Montour's Ridge, and one of them was honored by the county when it was organized out of the neighboring Northumberland County.

Danville, Montour's county seat, was one of the earliest iron centers of the state. Montour's Ridge, back of the town, is full of iron. But it is just as notable for its quiet beauty—beauty that was appreciated by the Indians of more than a century ago as much as by their successors to-day. How they enjoyed their periodical excursions down the valley from the north! How they must have lingered over the ever changing glories of land and sky and water. How much pleasure they must have taken in looking at the triple reflection so often seen in the waters of the Susquehanna—the deep green of the verdure on the islands, the lighter green of the hills, the blue of the sky deepened and emphasized by clouds.

And as later lovers of beauty wander down from

ON THE WAY TO EAGLESMERE, IN COLUMBIA COUNTY
Photo by J. Horace McFarland Company

ON THE SUSQUEHANNA, NEAR DANVILLE
Photo copyrighted by Detroit Publishing Co.

THE PENNSYLVANIA HIGHLANDS

Wilkes-Barre and Danville to Northumberland and Harrisburg, they gaze in wordless satisfaction, rejoicing to behold those bountiful gifts of Nature of which Henry van Dyke sang:

> "These are the things I prize
> And hold of dearest worth:
> Light of the sapphire skies,
> Peace of the silent hills,
> Shelter of forests, comfort of the grass,
> Music of birds, murmur of little rills,
> Shadows of clouds that swiftly pass,
> And, after showers,
> The smell of flowers
> And of the good brown earth."

ROUTE V

ALONG EASTERN WATERWAYS
THE ANTHRACITE COUNTRY AND THE POCONO PLATEAU
ABOUT 580 MILES

> "Straight mine eye hath caught new pleasures
> Whilst the landscape round it measures;
> Russet lawns and fallows gray,
> Where the nibbling flocks do stray,—
> Mountains on whose barren breast
> The laboring clouds do often rest,—
> Meadows trim with daisies pied,
> Shallow brooks, and rivers wide . . . "

EVEN though it was of an English landscape Milton sang in ecstasy, his words may well come to the lips of one who climbs the nine hundred feet above the Schuylkill at Reading to the summit of Mount Penn. Except that the mountains are not barren, every feature of the English landscape described is reproduced in the Schuylkill and Lebanon valleys, four hundred square miles of whose surface are open on a favorable day to the gaze from this summit. Neversink Mountain, near by, provides a different view; but both of these mountains, alike favorites of the Penns when they set aside for a manor the country about what is now Reading, look out on green forests and fertile farms, on tree-clad mountains and winding rivers, on creeks whose waters are lost in the lime-stone formations and on streams that persist in their course to the winding river.

Berks County has a remarkable series of waterways. From all sides these tributaries come to the central Schuylkill, "the hidden creek" of the Dutch, whose waters were the fishing ground, or Navesink, of the

Indians, where shad were caught in profusion until the canal was built. Most of the creeks rise within the borders of the mountain-walled county; some that rise within the county flow to neighboring counties, but the fruitful valleys depend for irrigation almost entirely on native resources.

And what cooling, appealing names some of these waterways bear!—Monocacy, Ontelaunee, Manatawny, Tulpehocken, Cacoosing, Wyomissing. There is poetry in every one of them. Antietam is also here—to the gratification of Reading people. Here is the source of the city's water supply, two hundred acres having been set aside some years ago as a watershed. School children from the city have planted these acres with seedlings supplied by the State Department of Forestry, so that the day is coming when the cool forest will throw its protecting arms about the springs for their children's children.

A number of these tributaries of the Schuylkill are crossed at their mouths by the road that leads north toward the Kittatinny or Blue Mountains, on the border between Berks and Schuylkill counties. This is the old Center Road, begun in 1808 and completed to the Susquehanna River at Sunbury in 1812. For the most part it follows the east bank of the river, though it cuts across some of the bends of the stream. These bends are a notable feature of the landscape of northern Berks, though none of them is as remarkable as the double bend below Reading, which describes an "S," as the observer from Neversink's heights may note.

The river and the highway have for companion the canal, begun in 1816, completed as far as Schuylkill Haven in 1817, opened to Port Carbon in 1823, and in operation to Philadelphia in 1824. Until the tow paths for mules were constructed the first primitive rafts and scows were drawn by men who, in single file, bent against the breast-sticks fastened at intervals in the tow line. These human horses shared public interest with the tunnel built for the canal at Auburn, over the line in Schuylkill County, the first tunnel on the continent. Modern engineers smile at the idea of that tunnel, for it was built largely that it might be the first tunnel; a slight detour would have made it unnecessary. Not many years later it was changed to an open cut in the rock.

As was the case with some of the early railroads, anyone was permitted to use the canal facilities who could pay the tolls. These were low, considering the cost of the waterway (about three million dollars). In 1818 $233 was collected. By 1824 this amount had increased to $635, and next year to $15,775, nearly two thirds of the payments being for coal. The rapid development of the coal industry made the canal a fair investment for a time; but the day of railroads soon arrived, and the canal gradually lost its usefulness.

As the mountains are approached the rugged country becomes still more beautiful. Perhaps the best view awaits those who leave the highway at Hamburg, turning to the right towards Lenhartsville and continuing a few miles up the road to Pine Creek. The drive along the Ontelaunee, the view of the Pinnacle, the highest peak of the Blue Ridge in the state, and the vision of the amphitheater, where the mountains form a circle, combine to make imperative this variation in the program. Back near the main road, in the vicinity of Hamburg, are the Blue Rocks, many acres of them, beneath which is a subterranean stream whose sound may be plainly heard. Point Lookout, above the rocks, is a convenient place

LOOKING TOWARD MOUNT PENN, READING
Photo by State Department of Forestry

NEAR BERNE, BERKS COUNTY
Photo from Philadelphia & Reading Railroad

for studying the country before passing on, in the company of river, canal, and highway, into the Schuylkill Gap at Port Clinton, the fourth in the remarkable series of gaps in the Kittatinny Range. In 104 miles there are five of these gaps, each of them used by a river (the Delaware, the Lehigh, the Schuylkill, the Swatara, and the Susquehanna), at almost equal intervals. Within the Schuylkill Gap the two branches of the Schuylkill unite to form the main stream.

After keeping close to the river for many miles, it seems a pity to leave its banks for a time, beyond Port Clinton, but the quiet beauty of the valley road is so great that the river is not missed. Orwigsburg, once the county seat, is located in this stretch away from the river, yet its situation is delightful; the distant view of hillside and mountain is a variation in the landscape.

The basin at Schuylkill Haven was one of the important parts of the canal slack-water navigation scheme. If this basin could only tell of the tremendous coal traffic that passed this way from Pottsville and the regions beyond, bound for the gap at Port Clinton and the Philadelphia markets! In the early mining days a larger amount of coal passed down the canal than was shipped from the Lehigh and Lackawanna fields combined.

Four miles beyond Schuylkill Haven, above the gorge by which the river breaks through Sharp Mountain, is Pottsville, the metropolis of the south anthracite fields. Here, in 1812, coal was loaded into nine wagons by Colonel Shoemaker, the discoverer, and taken to Philadelphia. The effort to introduce it was vain; the man who made the attempt was called an impostor, because he tried to sell stone for coal. Two loads were sold at a nominal price, and seven were given away. The proprietor of a Delaware County rolling mill promised Colonel Shoemaker to try it, but the foreman would have nothing to do with it. Early the morning after delivery the owner, assisted by the Colonel, started a fire, then went to breakfast. On their return the men found the coals in a glow. The skeptical foreman was converted when he saw iron go through the rolls "like lead." He apologized, and began to talk coal.

Yet not until 1824 did anthracite give Pottsville a name. Then a boom started that was responsible for great changes in the beautiful valley of the Schuylkill. Values increased rapidly. Land bought for $9000 in 1824 sold in 1829 for $42,000. In 1823 four hundred and fifty acres were bought for $190, and in 1829 one-fourth of the tract was sold for $9000. Earlier in the same year a man who bought a bit of land for $1000 sold it, after nine months, for $16,000.

The story of the influx of fortune-seekers from Philadelphia and Reading by the Ridge Road and the Center Road sounds like a bit of California description in the days of the gold excitement:

"Fortune kept her court in the mountains of Schuylkill County, and all who paid their respects to her in person found her as kind as their wildest hopes could imagine. The Ridge Road was well traveled. Reading stared to see the lengthened column of emigrants, and her astounded inhabitants looked with wonder upon the groaning stage-coaches, the hundreds of horsemen, and the thousands of footmen, who streamed through that ancient and respectable borough, and on for *Ultima Thule,* Orwigsburg . . . Eight miles further brought the army to the land of milk and honey, and then the sport began—the town was far from large enough to accommodate the new accessions. New towns were laid out in the pathless forests, many of which never went beyond the paper stage."

Stephen Girard was among the investors who turned to lands in Schuylkill and adjacent counties at this period. For $30,100 he bought seventy-three tracts of coal lands, sixty-eight of these having been at one time in possession of Robert Morris and his partner John Nicholson. A corps of surveyors was sent out from Philadelphia to run lines on the property; but they found the work most difficult, not only because much of the ground was covered "to the height of above eighteen feet, on an average, with dense undergrowth," but because supplies for the surveyors were not at hand. A representative of the Philadelphia financier wrote that "the number of persons engaged in surveying is so considerable, and their appetite from labor and keen air so good, that the provisions furnished vanish very fast; in my opinion if you could send from your farm two or three barrels of potatoes, a barrel or two of beets and turnips, radishes, a keg of white beans, great good would be done."

A letter from one of the surveyors told more particularly of the work:

"I have run lines where no human being ever trod, over mountains as steep—nay, steeper in many instances than the roof of any house, and from 60 to 150 perches ascent or descent, embodied in which must be immense quantities of coal. At one place in the vicinity of our first encampment, Mr. Allen had a vein opened to ascertain the quality as well as its extent. The coal turned out to be of an excellent quality, the vein uncommonly extensive, running directly into a high mountain apparently inexhaustible."

For the immediate improvement of the property Girard planned sawmills, to be operated by some of the splendid water power of Schuylkill County; log houses for workmen; landing piers on the Schuylkill,

SEEING PENNSYLVANIA

and three boats to run from these to Pottsville. That there might be a still more satisfactory outlet for the coal, he decided to have also a railroad from Danville to Pottsville. He himself subscribed for $100,000 of the capital stock, while others quickly made up the balance. As a director of the road he took steps to secure from English manufacturers the iron for the rails. The specifications for these are of interest, as indicating the manner of construction in that day, when parallel wooden stringers were bolted on a double row of spaced stone sills, these stringers being protected from the wear of the flanged wheels by "straps of iron two inches wide and one half an inch thick, cut at the ends at an angle of 45, and 18 feet long from heel to point, or 18 feet and 2 inches long from point to point."

The railroad was to run through some of the Girard coal lands, and a town was to be laid out on his property. On December 20, 1831, instructions went from Philadelphia to the agent at Orwigsburg, which was a central point for dealing with claimants who had been occupying the Catawissa Valley lands. This was one of Girard's last letters; next day he was taken ill, and in five days he was dead. The will directed that none of his lands should be sold.

Those were perhaps Schuylkill County's most exciting days, until the conflict with the Molly Maguires more than forty years later—a conflict incident to the development of the coal lands of which the Girard estate owned a rich section. This excitement was due this time primarily to the emigration of Irishmen. Most of the Irish were good citizens, but some of them banded together and terrorized the county. In the entire county there were less than six hundred members of the order, but these controlled the schools and the township

A BEND IN THE SCHUYLKILL RIVER
Photo from Philadelphia & Reading Railroad

NEAR POTTSVILLE
Photo from Philadelphia & Reading Railroad

ALONG THE SCHUYLKILL CANAL
Photo from Philadelphia & Reading Railroad

government in many sections of a county which then had 116,000 population. After ten years the Maguires were compelled to disband, and in bringing about this result others of the Irish residents were prominent. Pottsville was one of the four or five leading centers of the order's activities.

Tamaqua, too, was a stronghold of the terrorists who made residence unpleasant in the midst of its notable surroundings. The town is in a deep valley, limited by the Sharp and Locust mountains. From the top of Sharp Mountain, in the rear of the town, there is a splendid view of the whole interior coal basin. The Little Schuylkill here flows through a characteristic mountain gorge.

From Tamaqua north into Luzerne County and on to Hazelton and Wilkes-Barre the way is through valleys, among the Nescopeck Mountains, through the Nescopeck Pass, and along ridges that parallel in a general way the Lehigh River in Carbon County, to the east. Wilkes-Barre, the town of Wilkes and Barre, where stone coal was burned first in 1808, is the eastern gateway to Wyoming Valley—that favored spot before which description falters and adjectives are impotent. Waugh-wau-wame, "broad valley," the Indians called this basin surrounded by mountains, twenty-seven miles long, and averaging three miles in breadth. "Few landscapes that I have seen can compare with it," was the verdict of a traveler of 1829. "It was the great natural wonder, the Yosemite of that day," Sydney George Fisher has said. "It aroused the interest and became the talk of everyone in England. It was described as one of the happiest spots of human existence."

Fitz-Greene Halleck, after speaking of his anticipations of the valley, wrote:

> "I then but dreamed: thou art before me now,
> In life, a vision of the brain no more.
> I've stood upon the wooded mountain's brow
> That beetles high thy lovely valley o'er;
> And now, where winds thy river's greenest shore,
> Within a bower of sycamores am laid,
> And winds, as soft and sweet as ever bore
> The fragrance of wild-flowers through sun and shade,
> Are singing in the trees, whose low boughs press my head."

Lydia Huntley Sigourney is another of the poets who have sung the glories of the valley. Her theme is the meeting of the Susquehanna and the Lackawanna, in the Lackawannock Gap in the Blue Ridge:

> "Rush on, glad stream, in thy power and pride,
> To claim the hand of thy promised bride;
> She doth haste from the realm of the darkened mine,
> To mingle her murmured vows with thine;
> Ye have met—ye have met, and the shores prolong
> The liquid notes of your nuptial song.

> "On, on, through the vale where the brave ones sleep,
> Where the waving foliage is rich and deep,
> I have stood on the mountain and roamed through the glen,
> To the beautiful home of the western men;
> Yet naught in that region of glory could see
> So fair as the vale of Wyoming to me."

The best point from which to look out on the meeting of the waters is from a rocky peak near Pittston, known as Campbell's Ledge, because of a bare rock jutting out from the cliff not far from the summit of the six-hundred-foot eminence. This ledge was once called Dial Rock. It faces south, and the Indians learned that when the sun touched the rock it was noon. The settlers in the vicinity soon learned to use the Indian's timepiece. Even if there is doubt as to the story of the poet Campbell's fabled residence in the valley, it is of interest to note that his name has been given to such a notable landmark.

The valley is rich in other eminences, from which it is possible to feast upon the wonders of the region. One of these is Lookout Mountain, back of the village of Wyoming, near West Pittston. This is the highest point in the range on the west of the valley. The road through Schooley's Gap that leads up the mountainside to the spot affords views that should prepare the traveler for what he will see from above; nevertheless, the final outlook that bursts upon him is startling. Far to the north is the Lackawanna Valley, "the sister of Wyoming." Just below are the lower hills, the river banks, the green fields, and the slopes that look as if laid out by a landscape gardener. To the south the valley extends toward the Nanticoke Gap near Shickshinny where the Susquehanna seeks the low lands that open the way to its sister stream at Northumberland.

Prospect Rock is another point of vantage to be sought to-day as it was sought in the early days of the valley. At that time a visitor spoke of the panorama spread out as magnificent:

"The valley, with the beautiful Susquehanna dotted with many a verdant island winding through it; the pleasant old villages that lovingly cling to the banks of the river, and, beyond all these, the three-fold tier of mountain ridges that rise one above the other, along the western sky, one of them near at hand, with its well-defined form, while the other two peer from above with their blue tops, as from some other world."

But the best of all views is obtained from the summit of Wilkes-Barre Mountain. The airline distance to

Wilkes-Barre is but three miles, but the railroad requires eighteen miles to make Mountain Top, first going down into the valley, then circling about the mountain in search of the best grade. Here and there a break in the foliage or a depression in the mountain enables the eye to look into the valley, and to secure fleeting vistas. The traveler soon decides that the train moves too fast for his purpose; he is apt to wish that he might walk or drive up the grade, and so be free to stop and gaze at will, instead of looking for a moment and then straining his eyes for the next gap that will afford a glimpse of distant glory. "Such dissolving views are altogether unsatisfactory," someone has said. "They leave but a wilderness of things, rather than a series of distinct negatives."

The first settlers came to the Wyoming Valley from Connecticut. They thought the lands belonged to that colony, by charter right; the Connecticut claim was that all the territory above a line drawn from Stroudsburg was theirs. From the Indians a company of Connecticut adventurers secured the right to settle in the valley about the Indians' own town Waughwauwame, near the present site of Wilkes-Barre.

In 1762 the Connecticut pioneers arrived. Six years later the proprietors of Pennsylvania, who claimed that the valley was within the borders of that colony, bought from the Six Nations title to much territory, including Wyoming, although chiefs of the same nation had previously disposed of the valley to the Connecticut Susquehannah Company.

Soon a colony from Pennsylvania was on the ground, and took possession of improvements made by Connecticut claimants, who, at the time, were absent, having been driven away by the Indians. Of course there was trouble. Fortifications were built by both parties, and there were repeated conflicts. Then began the unhappy Pennamite war, which was not ended until a committee of Congress awarded the territory to Pennsylvania in 1782. During the interval the Wyoming Valley was annexed to the county of Litchfield, Connecticut, with the name Westmoreland. But, while the settlers from the two colonies were bitter enemies in local affairs, they joined forces against the British.

The valley's time of sorrow came in June, 1778, when four hundred Tories and seven hundred Indians advanced against Forty Fort, where some four hundred men and boys gathered to resist them. The fort was held until July 3, by what has been called one of the most gallant defenses in American history. But that day it became necessary to meet the enemy in the open. The settlers were defeated. The fort surrendered. Good treatment was promised. But the British were not able to restrain the Indians, who began a massacre from which few but women and children escaped. These fled in terror, with scant provision, over the Pocono Mountains, to Stroudsburg. Of the awful journey an early historian has written:

"What a picture for the pencil! Every pathway through the wilderness thronged with women and children, old men and boys. The able men of middle life and activity were either away in the general service or had fallen. There were few who were not in the engagement; so that in one drove of fugitives consisting of one hundred persons there was only one man with them. Let the painter stand on some eminence commanding a view at once of the valley and the mountain. Let him paint the throng climbing the heights; hurrying on, filled with terror, despair, and sorrow. Take a single group: the affrighted mother, whose husband has fallen; an infant on her bosom; a child by the hand; an aged parent slowly climbing the rugged way, behind her; hunger presses them sorely; in the rustling of every leaf they hear the approaching savage; the Shades of Death before them; the valley all in flames, behind them; the cottages, the barns, the harvests, all swept in the flood of ruin; the star of hope quenched in the blood shower of savage vengeance."

There is a monument at Wyoming to commemorate the battle, in which, as the inscription says, "a small band of patriot Americans, chiefly the undisciplined, the youthful, and the aged, spared by inefficiency from distant ranks of the Republic, led by Colonel Zebulon Butler and Colonel Nathan Denison, with a courage that deserved success, boldly met and bravely fought a combined British and Indian force."

Under the monument lie the bones of many of the brave defenders. Let them speak to us who glory in their bravery:

> "To God the glory! We, who lie
> Humbly beneath the quiet sky,
> Have drawn the water, hewn the wood,
> And made the best of life we could,
> Winning the sweetness born of strength
> And, through much striving, peace at length.
>
> Great were the perils in our way,
> And hard the labors of that day;
> But over all the blue sky bent,
> And winding through the meadows went
> The wide 'Greate River' to the sea,
> Catching the sunlight gloriously.
>
> "Still on the blue horizon sleep
> The curving hill lines; and there sweep
> Cloud shadows over vale and hill,
> Now chased by sunlight, and now still;
> The locusts chant amid the trees;

Above the clover hum the bees;
And crickets chirping in the grass
Make sweet the long days as they pass.

"To God the glory! We, who dwelt
Long in these quiet vales, have felt
All that there is in life to feel—
Its depths of woe, its heights of weal;
And to our children's children leave
Inheritance to joy and grieve,
And fight triumphantly as we!
To God the glory still shall be." [1]

The massacre at Wyoming led, in 1779, to the expedition of General Sullivan, through the trackless wilderness, from Easton, through Nazareth and the Wind Gap, and thence to Wilkes-Barre and beyond, across the Pocono Plateau—a comprehensive name for the highlands of Monroe, Pike, Wayne, and a part of Carbon counties. Near Stroudsburg it took the Wyoming Path from Pechoquealin (Shawnee-on-Delaware) to Wyoming. Much of the route is to-day included in the forty-mile road from Wilkes-Barre to Stroudsburg, and is one of the best of the state highways for which Pennsylvania is famous.

The first section of this marvelous drive leads to Bear Creek and Bear Lake on the Albert Lewis private forest reserve. Bear Creek is a tributary of the Lehigh, and its course from source to mouth is wildly beautiful.

Stoddartsville, on the picturesque Lehigh, is the last town in Luzerne County. Then comes the strange region that caused such travail to the refugees from the Wyoming massacre—the Great Swamp, or the Shades of Death. It is difficult to think of a swamp on an elevated tableland, but the situation is made clear by a modern description:

---
[1] M. E. Buhler.

"This was, and is yet to-day, a marsh upon a mountain top, the vast, wet, marshy plateau of the Pocono and Broad mountains—an area still unreclaimed, included now in three counties and surrounding the headwaters of the romantic Lehigh. Over the greater part of this singular, saturated table-land there was a dense growth of pines and a tangled, almost impenetrable undergrowth, the whole interspersed here and there with expanses of dark, murky water, often concealed by a lush growth of mosses and aquatic plants, and swarming with creeping things, even as the forests abounded with wild beasts."

So much for the Shades of Death to-day. A description, written but ten years after the tragedy at Wyoming, is supplied by Johan David Schoepf. Read his racy description of a trip through these mountains in 1788:

"The Great Swamp extends only fifteen miles across, but no one knows how far it lies to the north and south. Really, the whole of the region is not what is commonly called swamp, several mountains and valleys being included under the name. I do not trust myself to give a picture of the region. The road cut through is nowhere more than six foot wide, and full of everything which can make trouble for the passengers. On both sides the forest is so thick that the trees almost touch by their height and their matted branches, making a dimness cold and fearful even at noon of the clearest day. All beneath is grown up in green and impenetrable bush. Everywhere lie fallen trees, or those half-fallen, despite of their weight not reaching the ground. Thousands of rotten and rotting trunks cover the ground, and make every step uncertain; and between lies a fat bed of the richest mold that sucks up like a sponge all the moisture and so becomes swampy almost everywhere. One can with difficulty penetrate the growth even a little way, and not without danger of coming too near this or that sort of snake lying hidden from the

RINGTOWN, FROM SHENANDOAH MOUNTAIN
Photo from Philadelphia & Reading Railroad

MOUNTAIN STREAM ABOVE BUCK HILL FALLS
Photo from Lehigh Valley Railroad

sharpest eye in the waste of stones, leaves, and roots. Nature shows itself here quite in the original wildness ... A particularly deep valley in the great swamp is the Shades of Death; its steep mountain sides are distinguished by a great number of the tallest and slimmest pines, with white and hemlock spruce, and these are mixed below with a profuse and beautiful growth of rhododendrons and calamus, the roots waxing lustily in deep beds of mold."

That the Shades of Death have disappeared is due to the tanneries and the lumber mills which drew upon these plateaus for their supplies. Perhaps the most famous of the tanneries was at Gouldsboro, north of Pocono Summit. This was Jay Gould's first business venture.

To-day summer hotels are thick where Schoepf and his predecessors found danger and threat of death. For some miles resorts are thickly dotted here and there. The chain of lakes along the course of the Tobyhanna helps to provide vacation joys for the dwellers in the lowlands; these invite to swimming and boating, and the mountain streams are famous as fishing grounds. Henry van Dyke, who has joyfully ranged over these mountains many times, has sung of the sport he found here:

"Do you remember, father,—
It seems so long ago,—
The day we fished together
Along the Pocono?
At dusk I waited for you,
Beside the timber-mill,
And then I heard a hidden bird
That chanted, 'Whip-poor-will,
'Whippoorwill! Whippoorwill!'
Sad and shrill,—'whippoorwill!'"

This poet's favorite stream is the Swiftwater, to the south of Mt. Pocono; of this he has written much in his delightful essays.

The Swiftwater is one of the features in the glorious panorama spread out from the summit of Mount Pocono, two thousand feet high. Down into the valley, between the Pocono and the Kittatinny, and on to the stately slopes of Delaware Water Gap, is a view that makes the fortunate beholder glad to be alive and eager to inspect more closely the slopes and valleys of the landscape so viewed.

But before following in person where the eye has pointed the way it would be well to turn northeast to Cresco, where Buck Hill Falls in Buck Hill Creek are hidden in the mountain forest. There are three of these falls, and the total descent of the water is nearly one hundred feet.

The Pennsylvania Department of Forestry has control of the tree-clad slopes near Cresco and beyond. One of the provisions made for the protection of the forest from fires will prove, incidentally, a help to the sightseer. This is the observation tower about three-quarters of a mile west of Cresco. From this can be seen large portions of Pike and Monroe counties, including the Pocono Plateau and the Delaware Water Gap.

The road through the state forest extends along the ridge to La Anna and South Sterling. At every turn the one who is traveling alone sighs for company in his enjoyment. Yet if two nature-lovers of kindred spirits are together on this route they are more apt to be silent than to exclaim; speech will seem unnecessary, words a profanation.

The journey may be continued along the Wallenpaupack, through Pike County, and on into the wilds of

Wayne. But why go that way now when the route laid out approaches the Wallenpaupack from another direction?

So back through the forest to Cresco, and down to Stroudsburg either by the Sullivan Trail from Mount Pocono or by the highway that follows the route of the Delaware, Lackawanna and Western Railway. It is not easy to choose; Sullivan Trail may be better surfaced, but the road farther to the east passes through such wonderful country that little account is taken of a few additional bumps.

Knowledge of the story of the building of the railroad adds to the pleasure taken in the ride to Stroudsburg. This story goes back to the closing years of the eighteenth century, when Henry Drinker, the Philadelphia Quaker, bought from the state some twenty-five thousaid acres of forest land in what are now Lackawanna, Wayne, Pike, and Susquehanna counties. There was no good outlet for this tract until, in 1819, he built what is still known as "Drinker's Road," from New Jersey into the Lackawanna Valley. But the day came when the wagon road did not satisfy the financier. He wondered if a railroad could not be constructed for the marketing of the anthracite coal which was already attracting attention.

His first step was to take an ax and cut a route through the forest from what is now Pittston, across the Pocono Plateau, sixty miles to Delaware Water Gap. Then he planned a road with a series of inclined planes, for which the power was to be supplied by water on the levels, and by horses on the planes.

A road was actually constructed from Scranton to the Erie Railroad. This gave access to New York, but by such a roundabout route that a railroad over the

Pocono Mountains was decided on. Mr. Drinker was no longer connected with the project, but his ideas were carried out by the engineers who surveyed a route from below Stroudsburg to Scranton. The present Pocono division, originally called the Delaware and Cobb's Gap Railroad, extended to the Delaware River, where connection was made for New York. The result was a line to that city at a saving of one hundred miles.

Another result of Henry Drinker's land and railway interests in the Pocono is that ever since the Quakers of Philadelphia have been specially drawn to these spacious mountain regions.

Not far from the Delaware the road passes through Stroudsburg, one of the historic points of eastern Pennsylvania. Stroudsburg was of interest to the lumbermen in the days when the Analomink—whose leafy waters have been followed from near Cresco—carried down logs from the mountains. The place was of interest to the pioneers because of the location here of Fort Hamilton, during the French and Indian War, and of Fort Penn, during the Revolution. The commander of Fort Penn was Colonel Jacob Stroud, later the founder of the town.

In the winter of 1771 Stroudsburg was of interest to the settlers in the Wyoming Valley because they turned in this direction when they were out of provisions. Once nine men were sent to Stroudsburg for flour, and the Lehigh was crossed by wading after a way had been cut through the ice that lined either shore; and a road was cut through the wilderness. When they reached Stroudsburg they were liable to arrest since they belonged to Connecticut. Their danger was great because, on the night of their coming, there was a wedding party at the home of the man whose help they sought. He hid them, however, so saving them from a probable trip to Easton in the custody of the sheriff. Next day they were sent back over the rough mountains, each carrying seventy-five pounds of flour.

There is a tradition that when Teedyuscung, chief of the Leni Lenapes, was living in Stroudsburg, a blacksmith who was not of much account said to him:

"Well, cousin, how do you do?"

"Cousin? How do you make that out?" was the puzzled reply.

"Oh, we all come from Adam!"

"I am glad it is no nearer!" was the Indian's crushing retort.

The scenic features of the country a few miles below Stroudsburg and East Stroudsburg are so commanding that visitors sometimes pass by the beauties of the neighborhood of these twin towns. The time required for a ramble on the heights above or in the valley below will be amply repaid.

Several miles east of Stroudsburg flows the Delaware, the river of which "William Moraly, Gent" wrote so learnedly in 1743, in his "Voyages and Adventures." His physical and natural history were fearfully and wonderfully made:

"The river is supposed to have its rise from a Lake, in the Mountains of Canada, and is believed from its forest Springs to the Cape, in its Windings, to be above 2000 Miles in length. In the Heat of Summer, nothing affords a more pleasant and delightful Prospect than it does ... In the midst of the river are many small islands, some of them two Miles in length ... In the Summer the Cows will Swim to them, and graze till the Evening, when they will return, but sometimes with the loss of a Leg, by the Shirks ... Great numbers of large Sturgeon gamble on the Water."

But the Delaware has greater wonders to offer than cow-destroying Shirks or gambling Sturgeon—the Delaware Water Gap, grand when seen at a distance from the summit of Mount Pocono, sublime when seen from the heights above the double bend in the river, between beetling cliffs, or from the channel within the gap, or from below, first near at hand, then miles down the winding river. A traveler in stagecoach days said that it was worth a journey of five hundred miles to gaze on the precipitous hills that rise on either side of the river to a height of 1500 or 1600 feet.

One geologist calls this great cleft, which divides the Kittatinny to its very base, a "transverse dislocation," and calls attention to the projection of the eastward section to the northward, a characteristic of all such clefts.

There are geologists who declare that the Kittatinny Ridge, in which the gap appears, was once the margin of a vast lake, into which the Chemung, the Chenango, the Delaware, and the Susquehanna rivers flowed. By the action of the water breaks or transverse dislocations were made in the ridge, which to-day are called gaps; and the rivers found an outlet through these. The Indians must have had some such theory, for their name for the gap was Minisink, meaning "the water is gone."

Other geologists have an entirely different theory. Silliman, for instance, says that there is "no reason whatever to believe that the waters have torn asunder the solid strata"; they have simply flowed through the lowest or least obstructed strata.

But however geologists may differ as to the formation of the Delaware Water Gap, there can be no difference of opinion as to the majesty of the spectacle presented by the passage of the river through the vast opening. Like Niagara, this wonder must be observed from many

WITHIN DELAWARE WATER GAP, LOOKING FROM THE RIGHT BANK
Photo by the Kirkton Studios

DELAWARE WATER GAP FROM THE SOUTHEAST
Delaware River, near Manunka Chunk, in foreground
Photo by United States Geological Survey

points, and year after year. It never palls and it is always friendly. On the railroad the entire gap can be seen well only from a distance; within the gap itself the view from the car window is confined to a single cliff. Even this half view has its compensations—for instance, the study of the shadow of the green-clad mountain in the clear water beneath or the great double arrowhead, half of it formed by a bare place on the shore of the river, half by its reflection in the water.

From the river itself the marvel should be seen, with open sky above, and a view first of one side, then of the other, then of both together. This was the view gained by a raftsman who first passed within the portals of the gap in 1862. The sharp bends in the stream and the rapid current made inattention to navigation dangerous, but he found it difficult to keep his eyes on his work. He has since made scores of visits to the spot, and the joy of that first experience increases with each visit.

Then from the height above, on the Pennsylvania side, where the hotel proprietors have taken possession, there is a prospect that differs from all the others. Fortunately a part of the height has been made into Kittatinny Park, which offers attractions of its own. Thus there has been fulfilled the vision of Anthony Dutoit, the French refugee who sought these heights about 1793, bought land where hotels now stand, and laid out the city of Dutoit. He was ahead of the age, and his project failed.

Wonder is increased by a view of the river above the gap; the aspect of everything is so different from that presented below. Angelo Heilprin, in "The Earth and the Sky," speaks of this:

"I wondered why the Delaware, which flows so peacefully down the valley on the opposite side of the gap, should have so suddenly turned and cut a channel through the mountains instead of following their trail. This is a puzzle."

But this is geology once more. More romantic is the poem on the gap by Elizabeth F. Ellett:

> "Our western land can boast no lovelier spot.
> The hills which in their ancient grandeur stand
> Piled to the frowning clouds, the bulwarks seem
> Of this wild scene, resolved that none but Heaven
> Shall look upon its beauty. Round their breast
> A curtained frieze depends, of golden mist,
> Touched by the slanting sunbeams; while below
> The silent river, with majestic sweep,
> Pursues her shadowed way,—her glassy face
> Unbroken, save where stoops the lone wild swan
> To float in pride, or dip her ruffled wing.
> Talk ye of solitude? It is not here,
> Nor silence. Low, deep murmurs are abroad.
> Those towering hills hold converse with the sky
> That smiles upon the summits; and the wind,
> Which stirs their wooded sides, whispers of life
> And bears the burden sweet from leaf to leaf,
> Bidding the stately forest-boughs look bright
> And nod to greet his coming! And the brook,
> That with its silvery gleam comes leaping down
> From the hillside, has, too, a tale to tell;
> The wild bird's music mingles with its chime
> And gay young flowers, that blossom in its path,
> Send forth their perfume as an added gift."

If possible, that curious half break in the mountain range about twelve miles to the southwest should be seen in connection with the Delaware Water Gap. This is called the Wind Gap. No water flows through it, but from time immemorial it has been a helpful passage for travelers. The Indians came this way; it was on the route of the rascals who outwitted the trusting savages by the Walking Purchase, described later in this chapter;

as has been said, it was the passageway for General Sullivan; and to-day there leads through it a road whose beauty defies description.

Of course there are all sorts of theories about the Wind Gap also. Once upon a time, some say, the Water Gap outlet from the lake beyond the Kittatinny rim was stopped up by ice. The lake formed once more, and a secondary outlet was cut through at the Wind Gap. The day came when the ice in the Water Gap broke away, and the river resumed its wonted course.

Charles Thomson, Secretary of Congress during the Revolution, had an idea slightly different. It was his notion that the Wind Gap, about one hundred feet higher than the Water Gap, was the original outlet for the river. He called attention to the fact that the stones in the Wind Gap seem to have been washed for ages by water running over them.

Once more let the poet have the final word. In 1804 Alexander Wilson passed through the Wind Gap, on his way from Easton toward Niagara. The account of the journey was written in verse. Of the gap he said:

"Lo! the Blue Mountain now in front appears,
And high o'er all its lengthened ridge uprears;
Th' inspiring sight redoubled vigor lends,
And soon its steeps each traveler ascends.
Panting we wind aloft, begloomed in shade,
Mid rocks and moldering logs tumultuous laid
In wild confusion; till the startled eye
Through the cleft mountain meets the pale blue sky
And distant forests; while sublimely wild,
Tow'rs each tall cliff to heaven's own portals piled.
Enormous gap! if Indian tale be true,
Here ancient Delaware once thunder'd through,
And rolled for ages; till some earthquake dread,
In high convulsion, shook him from his bed."

SEEING PENNSYLVANIA

In this region so rich in Indian legend there is a third notable spot, several miles up the Delaware from the Water Gap. This is Shawnee, the site of the Shawnee village Pechoquealin, to which was given the name applied by the Leni Lenapes to the Delaware Water Gap, "a mountain with holes in it." On the site of the village there is now a summer resort, while golf links occupy the ground where once the Shawnees hunted. The river at this point widens to make room for a long, low-lying island. The quiet beauty of island, river, valley, and mountain beyond can be seen best from the New Jersey side.

One of the favorite resorts of the Indians who lived at Shawnee was Marshall's Falls, several miles from the river, on the state highway from Stroudsburg to Port Jervis. This stretch of road, said to be one of the finest highways in the state, both from the physical and the scenic points of view, keeps at a little distance from the river until Bushkill is reached. From there to Port Jervis it skirts the river, crossing creeks, picking a track among the hills that often seem as if they propose to close its passage, and passing within sight of gorges and cascades of wondrous beauty.

This was the road traveled for many years by Judge John Coolbaugh, Revolutionary soldier, pioneer of the valley, whose house was built on the road where the owner could see the passing stagecoach. For this old settler a township, a lake, a railroad station, a post office, and a church have been named.

Just beyond Coolbaugh post office the road passes for half a mile between rows of graceful sugar-maple trees, which give grateful shade as well as abounding beauty. The avenue is an object lesson in the possibilities of tree culture. In the fall of 1876 seedlings twelve

LOOKING UP THE RIVER, DELAWARE WATER GAP

SUGAR MAPLE AVENUE ON STATE ROAD, NEAR ECHO LAKE
Photo by State Department of Forestry

PECK'S DAM, PIKE COUNTY
Photo by State Department of Forestry

FALLS ON DINGMAN'S CREEK IN CHILDS' PARK
Photo by State Highway Department

feet high and two inches in diameter were planted by the roadside, and after more than a generation the trees in double row stand forth in all their dignity.

Within a mile of the maple avenue, on an upland ridge, lies Echo Lake, embowered in trees. This is one of the series of the Kettlehole lakelets of the Monroe Highlands, as the geologists name them. Echo Lake has no visible outlet, but there is a subterranean outlet to Coolbaugh Lake and from Coolbaugh to Marshall's Creek and the Delaware.

At Bushkill the road along the Delaware enters Pike County, the most sparsely populated county in Pennsylvania, and one of the most notable for its great beauty. Pike and Wayne counties together have been called a natural park. Back from the river are broken spurs of the Poconos, where many streams have their source. These flow serenely along through the rather poor soil of the county until they approach the slate and shale formations near the Delaware. Then they leap over rocky ledges, making a series of waterfalls that are the admiration of beholders.

Bushkill is at the junction of two tumbling streams, the Big and Little Bushkill. Of the several cascades in the neighborhood the falls of the Little Bushkill are the finest in the state. The Delaware at Bushkill is worthy of special note because of the famous Wallpack Bend, where the stream makes a well-defined "S."

From Bushkill to Port Jervis the highway is at the base of a cliff, by the side of the river. Frequent gorges break the cliff, and variety is given to the road by glimpses of river, hill, and forest.

Dingman's Ferry is distinguished by Dingman's Creek, whose seven-mile course has numerous gorges, cataracts, and ravines. At High Falls the water leaps

130 feet. Liberty Falls, Charming Falls, Kelpy Falls, Deer Leap Falls, Fulmer Falls, and Factory Falls are also near by. The Silver Thread enters Dingman's Creek after passing through the Soap Trough, described as "an inclined plane descending one hundred feet, always filled with foam."

Reynoldskill, one more of the tumultuous trout streams of the neighborhood, has the distinguishing "kill" in its name, evidence of the fact that the first settlers in this region along the Delaware were the Dutch, some of whom came from New York before William Penn came to Philadelphia.

From the heights above Dingman's there is a remarkable view up and down the Delaware and back into the interior, where are many of the club houses of Philadelphia sportsmen attracted there by the fishing for pickerel, black bass, and trout.

Milford, the county seat of Pike County, has a notable site on a high bluff above the Delaware, from which there is an advantageous view of many mountains. N. P. Willis chose an unusual way to speak of the town's situation; he said that Milford looks "like a town that all the mountains around have dismissed and kicked into the middle." Picking its way among the mountains to a resting place in the Delaware is another of the Dutch kills—Sawkill, with its fine private collection of waterfalls and its rocky gorge below.

Milford is the home of the Yale School of Forestry's experiment station, as well as of Gifford Pinchot, the famous friend of Theodore Roosevelt, and his partner in the fight for the conservation of natural resources, including forests. The experiment station is an evidence of this Pinchot interest in conservation, for its endowment came from the family.

One of the interesting sights near Milford is the monument to Thomas Quick, pioneer, whose son is said to have slain ninety-nine Indians because of their treacherous murder of his father. One of the stories told of the Indian-killing son is that one day, while splitting a log in which his wedge was sunk, he was surprised by Indians. He agreed to go with them if they would first help him to split the log. Their part was to take hold of the halves of the log and pull it apart while he drove the wedge farther in. Of course, when their fingers were well in, he knocked the wedge out, and caught them all!

The traveler who has taken the ride from Milford to Port Jervis along the Delaware is not apt to forget the experience. Fortunately the trip must be made on the highway; no railroad breaks the quiet of the county, except as the little thirteen-mile-long Delaware Valley line from Stroudsburg steps over the border at Bushkill.

The right-angled bend in the Delaware at Tri-State Park, near Port Jervis, marks the dividing line between two sections of the stream, which are so different that it is not easy to think of them as parts of the same river. In the ninety miles above the bend it is a rapid, tumbling stream; the water descends 570 feet, whereas in the forty-three miles to the Water Gap it is quiet and placid; the descent is but 127 feet.

It is not enough to skirt the border of Pike along the Delaware; one should certainly cross the county, touching the Wallenpaupack and the Lackawaxen, entering Wayne County, and thence going over the mountains to Scranton. The first section of the route follows an old Indian trail from the Delaware to the Susquehanna, "and in many respects it still resembles an

Indian trail," says the Blue Book. The route is apt to prove lonely; once, for a space of ten miles, no house is seen. This is where the road passes through Blooming Grove Park, a state reservation.

Once more the streams are centers of attraction. Shohola Creek is reached about fifteen miles from Milford. If one has the opportunity, he would do well to follow this stream to the Delaware, perhaps fifteen miles above Port Jervis. At Shohola Falls there are four cascades. Then comes "the glen," a cleft in the rocks some two hundred feet deep where the creek is fifty feet wide. From the glen the course to the Delaware is rocky, tumultuous, and strangely beautiful. Some have said that the glen of the Shohola is second only to Watkins' Glen.

Soon after crossing the Shohola the road turns northward toward Hawley and the Lackawaxen, whose entrance to the Delaware is also marked by a wild gorge. At Hawley the Wallenpaupack seeks the Lackawaxen. In its eagerness to join the Wayne County creek it forms a series of cataracts and rapids, descending some two hundred and fifty feet in about two miles. The Paupack cataract descends sixty-one feet. Wallenpaupack means "dead water," and for the first twenty miles of its course the stream is true to its name. Not on the last miles of its course, however.

Lackawaxen Creek has a place in history for at least two reasons. On July 22, 1779, the battle of Lackawaxen, or the Minisink, was fought, though on the New York side of the Delaware, and in 1842, on its banks, not far from the mouth, Horace Greeley began his colonizing experiment. Desiring to have a community similar to Alcott's Brook Farm, he organized the Sylvania Society with a capital of $10,000. This colony was based on "the common ownership of property and the equal division of labor." The shares were sold for twenty-five dollars each. One share was a membership fee. Seven thousand acres of wild land were bought, watered by Shohola Creek and several small lakes.

Greeley himself furnished most of the money required. The colonists sought their new home by way of Milford, to the number of three or four hundred. A large common building was erected for their accommodation, and shops were provided for communal activities. The board of directors found difficulty as soon as they began to assign the colonists to their tasks. There were those who did not wish to do rough work; they did not see why they should not be employed in the shops.

To add to the difficulties, the soil was poor and the crops failed. Finally, in 1844, there was frost on July 4. This was the final blow, and the experiment was abandoned. Greeley was disgusted with a country that, as he said, could raise only snakes and stones.

Later visitors, however, have been able to see many things more pleasing in Pike. There is the glorious Lackawaxen Creek, for instance, with its quiet stretches and its foaming, rocky reaches where the man with an artist soul delights to go. Zane Gray went there, and on his return home he wrote to *Outing* a message about the creek that served not only to tell his own keen pleasures, but has awakened curiosity in the minds of hundreds, many of whom have visited the waters for themselves, only to learn that much more might have been said:

"It is a little river hidden away under gray cliffs and hills black with rugged pines. It is full of mossy stones and ragged riffles. All its tributaries, dashing white-sheeted over ferny cliffs, wine-brown where the whirling pools suck the stain from the hemlock roots, harbor the speckled trout. A mile or more from its mouth the Lackawaxen leaves the shelter of the hills and seeks the open sunlight and slows down to widen into long lanes that glide reluctantly over the few last restraining barriers to the Delaware."

The Lackawaxen has had an important place in the transportation history of the northeastern country. In the early days coal was taken by sled from Carbondale, twenty miles through Rix's Gap, to the river at White Mills, in Wayne County, above Hawley, and was then loaded on rafts and sent by the Lackawaxen and the Delaware to Philadelphia. The trip was so dangerous and the desire to reach New York instead of Philadelphia was so urgent that a canal from Honesdale to the Hudson River was begun in 1826. Connection was made with Carbondale by a railroad sixteen and a half miles long, which climbed about nine hundred feet to the summit of the Moosic range. On this route to the summit there were eight inclined planes, while the descent from Carbondale to Olyphant was made by two planes. Stationary steam engines furnished the power on the up grades, while gravity and horses were also employed. This, the second railroad in Pennsylvania, built in 1829, was at first intended for coal traffic only; passengers were a later consideration.

The first locomotive in the United States was tested on this road by Horatio Allen, whom the Delaware and Hudson Canal Company, builders of the gravity line, sent to England to buy four locomotives. One of these, the Stourbridge Lion, was brought from New York to Honesdale by river and canal. The trial was made on August 8, 1829. Business was at a standstill; everybody took a holiday because of the great event. Years later Mr. Allen told the story of the day:

"The road had been built in the summer; the structure was of hemlock timber with rails of large dimensions notched on caps placed far apart. . . .

"After about three hundred feet of straight line the road crossed Lackawaxen Creek on trestlework about thirty feet high, and with a curve of about one hundred and fifty to four hundred feet radius. The impression was very general that the iron monster would break down the road, or that it would leave the track at the curve and plunge into the creek. My reply to such apprehension was that it was too late to consider the possibility of such occurrences; that there was no other course but to have a trial made of the strange animal which had been brought there at great expense, but that it was not necessary that more than one should be involved in its fate; that I would take the first ride alone, and the time would come when I should look back to the incident with great interest.

"As I placed my hand on the handle I was undecided whether I should move slowly or with a fair degree of speed, but holding that the road would prove safe, and proposing, if we had to go down, to go handsomely, and without any evidence of timidity, I started with considerable velocity, passed the curve over the creek safely, and was soon out of hearing of the vast assemblage present. At the end of two or three miles I reversed the valve and returned without accident to the place of starting, having made the first locomotive trip on the western hemisphere."

The engineer and directors were convinced that if the power for the cars was to be supplied by a locomotive, the wooden rails then in use would have to be replaced by iron rails. Since they could not afford to make the exchange, they turned again to mules and horses. The Stourbridge Lion was run off the rails near the canal lock, and there remained for fourteen years, an object of dread to the children of the neighborhood. Then the boiler was taken to the Carbondale shops, to supply steam for a stationary engine. Finally the boiler went to the scrap heap, but was later rescued, and the restored engine may now be seen in the Smithsonian Institute at Washington.

Later a gravity road was built from Scranton direct to Hawley, with twenty-two planes. "No two miles of the journey are alike," an early passenger wrote:

"Now a rush through a narrow cut in the solid rock, now a wide vision on either hand, a view across the valley, of stream and upland losing itself in the far distance in another range of hills, until the misty outlines of others still beyond blend in with the faint blue of the sky; then a rushing waterfall or quiet stretch of the forest."

This second route over the Moosic range is now a part of the Erie Railroad. A highway keeps fairly close to the road so vividly described. The upper road, from Honesdale to Carbondale, is also paralleled by a highway which enables the traveler to study the panorama of hills, valleys, and rich farm lands, so different from the scene presented by the southern road.

The pedestrian along such a road in Wayne County will experience the freedom of which Hamlin Garland writes:

"What have I gained by the toil of the trail?
I know and know well.
I have found once again the lore I had lost
In the loud city's hell. . . .

"I have threaded the wild with the stealth of the deer,
No eagle is freer than I;
No mountain can thwart me, no torrent appall,
I defy the stern sky.
So long as I live these joys will remain,
I have touched the most primitive wildness again."

VALLEY VIEW, NORTH OF HONESDALE
Photo by State Highway Department

ABINGDON HILLS, LACKAWANNA COUNTY
Photo by Horgan

ALONG EASTERN WATERWAYS

But road-wandering in Wayne County should not be confined to the journey from Hawley to the Moosic Mountains. There should be also a tour of the fourscore lakes that nestle in the highlands of the county that has more such bodies of water than any other county in Pennsylvania; there is at least one lake in every township but one. On the lower road Lake Ariel will have been seen already. But many other lakes are amid much rougher country; many of them are kept as hunting and fishing preserves, for to these wilds of Wayne sportsmen resort for trout and pickerel and bass, as well as for deer and bear.

Many of the lakes can be seen from High Knob, whose elevation is 2010 feet, or from North Knob, which enables the visitor to look down on the surrounding country from a height of 1900 feet. Two of them are within reach from the road from Honesdale to Scranton. Beach Lake is northeast of Honesdale, while Lake Lodore is near the western boundary. While the area of this lake is but three hundred acres, the shore line is more than five miles long. A part of the shore is a cliff whose summit affords a prospect twenty miles to the north and fifteen miles to the south.

This county also has its tale of an early land experiment that failed. In 1792 there was formed in Philadelphia by Henry Drinker a company whose title was so long that it is advisable to take a long breath before reading it: "The Union Society for Promoting the Manufacture of Sugar from the Maple Tree and Furthering the Interests of Agriculture in Pennsylvania, the Society's attention to be principally confined to that purpose and to the Manufacturing of Pot and Pearl Ashes."

Three thousand acres were bought in Wayne County,

at ten shillings per acre. There were sixty shares, the par value being £5 per share. Dr. Benjamin Rush, William Sansom, Timothy Pickering, Elliston Perot, Richard Peters, and Robert Morris were associated with Mr. Drinker.

One of the purposes of the company in preparing maple sugar for the market was to enter into competition with the sugar of the South and the West Indies in the hope that the company might be able to supplant it, and so, perhaps, help in the solution of the vexed problem of slave labor.

Some acres of land were cleared, a sawmill was built, as well as a house, a stable, and a blacksmith shop. Then there was made the disconcerting discovery that they could not count on more than three or four weeks in the year during which the sap would flow, so that sugar could be made from it.

Not until November 9, 1795, was the announcement finally made to the stockholders that it was no longer expedient to prosecute the work: £1400 more than the capital had been expended; the lands were later sold for $1125.

Wayne County, with its lakes and legends, is left behind by the road that leads over the Moosic Mountains to Carbondale. From there a delightful tour can be arranged twice across Susquehanna County, distinguished for lakes and mountains, as well as for railroads in whose construction there have been remarkable engineering feats.

Northwest of Carbondale, and over the line in Susquehanna County, is Dundaff, a town mentioned in a pioneer's diary on January 1, 1824. A new line of tri-weekly stages had been put on the Owego and Milford turnpike, to run to New York. "Huzza! huzza! the new stage!" he wrote. "It was forty-one hours coming from the city, but might have got in in less than forty hours, but stayed at Dundaff unnecessarily."

A roundabout road, not of the best as to surface, but wonderful as to scenery, leads east to a point close to the boundary of the county, then north along the line of the Erie Railroad to Ararat township, called "the observatory of Susquehanna County." The summit of the railroad is more than two thousand feet high, while Mount Ararat and Sugar Loaf are higher still. From the summit the eye sweeps the horizon from the hills beyond the first dip of the Susquehanna into Pennsylvania, to Bald Mountain at Pittston. To the west the hills of Bradford County are visible.

The railroad points the way to Starucca, where, near the mouth of Starucca Creek, the great eighteen-arch bridge, 110 feet high, was built. The cost was $325,000, a sum that seems small in comparison with the cost of the Tunkhannock viaduct in Wyoming County; but it was a large sum for such work fifty years ago.

Another advantage of the meandering course suggested here is the approach to Cascade Creek, a tributary of the Susquehanna not far from the boundary line of the state, with its sixty-foot cascade half a mile from the mouth. At this point the Susquehanna is but ten miles from the Delaware.

There is a fascinating road along the Great Bend, where the first settlement was made in 1787. Within the Great Bend, Quaquaga, one of the two highest mountains in the county, lifts its head.

Henry Drinker, whose maple sugar speculation in Wayne County failed so signally, owned, with others, 500,000 acres in Susquehanna County. One day in 1815, when Mr. and Mrs. Drinker were on their way to inspect these lands, he had trouble on the road near Great Bend. At one point it became necessary to abandon the wagon, in which was the Drinker trunk, and to proceed with the hind wheels only. To these the trunk was fastened. "Then, jumping the horse over the logs plentifully scattered in the path, and lifting the wheels, the journey was continued." At a stream two canoes were put together and covered with planks. On these trunk, horse, and passengers passed safely over.

The Drinkers, after reaching Great Bend, must have returned to the southern end of the county by the Snake Creek road, through Montrose, toward Meshoppen Creek. This was a wildly beautiful route then, and the scenery is marvelous to-day. Some miles to the west, soon after turning south, is Silver Lake, the home in early days of Dr. Robert H. Rose, owner of 100,000 acres in the county and agent for the Pennsylvania claimants against the settlers from Connecticut.

The name of Dr. Rose is perpetuated in the county seat, Montrose, the center of some of the finest scenery in the county. The town is about eighteen hundred feet high, and on all sides the country slopes rapidly to the valleys below. The view from some parts of the town is glorious, especially in the neighborhood of the Montrose Assembly grounds, with the attractive Lake Montrose.

The approach to Montrose from the railroad is impressive. The Lackawanna climbs from Alford, and the Lehigh Valley makes the ascent from Tunkhannock. The latter road is but twenty-seven miles long, but it is 1045 feet higher at Montrose than at Tunkhannock. On the way there are six distinct summits. The same general route is followed by the electric line to Lake

NEAR MONTROSE
Photo by Horgan

NICHOLSON VIADUCT, WYOMING COUNTY
Photo by State Highway Department

SALT LICK ON WHARTON CREEK, LACKAWANNA COUNTY
Photo by State Highway Department

Winola, where connection is made for Scranton. This will be found one of the finest trolley rides in the East.

The best highway route from Montrose to Scranton is across country to the Lackawanna, then along the railroad and Martin's Creek, across Tunkhannock Creek at Nicholson viaduct, and south to the city of the Lackawanna Valley.

In every direction from beautiful Scranton most attractive trips can be made. Lake Winola, Clark's Summit, Carbondale, Mount Cobb, and the Nay Aug Valley, are among the glorious surroundings that lure and satisfy the searcher for the picturesque.

A roundabout trip to Wilkes-Barre may be made through the Nay Aug Valley, but while this should not be missed, the ride over the Laurel line through the Lackawanna and Wyoming valleys should also be taken. The adjoining valleys have been likened to two outspread wings, balanced on a pivotal point at Pittston, half way between Scranton and Wilkes-Barre.

There are those who say that the beauty of these valleys is marred by the culm banks and the coal breakers. Yet this is a matter of opinion. Once an Englishman asked an American wheelman who was riding from Liverpool, by way of Birmingham, to London, "Why do you go through the Black Country?" He gave the very reason that sensible travelers are apt to give for lingering in these Pennsylvania valleys; they are not marred, but their beauty is enhanced, by the ever-present indications of underground activity, even by the distressing cave-ins above the mine workings. Really the breakers and the culm banks are so few, comparatively, and the valleys are so gloriously ample, that even those who wish to complain find slight reason.

No wonder Connecticut did not wish to give up these

valleys, that Penn wanted to keep them, that the Indian resented the white man's intrusion, and that settlers persisted in returning in spite of repeated massacres.

The few miles below Scranton, through the ridge that frames the Lackawanna Valley on the north, are a preparation for the more open lands toward Pittston, and then for the Vale of Wyoming below.

Mountain Top, overlooking Wilkes-Barre, is well worth a second visit. From here the Lackawanna and Wyoming valleys are spread out like a map. For twenty miles the towns and villages and the shining river may be seen in all their beauty. The scene changes every moment, only to become more attractive until it is shut out entirely by intervening ridges.

Glen Summit is the next vantage point on the Lehigh Valley Railroad and the highway that keeps it close company, for a distance, at least. To the west lies the valley of the Wapwallopen and the mountains beyond. Here is a place to stand and drink in the grandeur of the wild surroundings, while saying a hearty amen to Henry Timrod's exclamation:

> "At last, beloved Nature! I have met
> Thee face to face upon thy breezy hills,
> And boldly, where thy inmost bowers are set,
> Gazed on thee naked in thy mountain rills."

The rapid down-grade rush from Glen Summit discloses ridge beyond ridge to the far horizon, the first green, the next blue, the last so hazy that it might almost be a cloud, and all showing the continuously undulating sky line so characteristic of Pennsylvania mountain scenery. Now and then there is the sharp descent in a ridge that suggests a gap. Sometimes there is a compensating opposing descent, and it may be there

HORSESHOE CURVE, NAY AUG VALLEY
Photo by Horgan

WILKES-BARRE COLLIERY, PITTSTON
Photo from Lehigh Valley Railroad Company

is an overlapping ridge whose complementary slope is hidden from view.

Soon the Lehigh is reached at White Haven Junction. Here the view up stream is a delight, while down stream it keeps up its charm in a most alluring manner.

White Haven offers a side trip up the Nescopeck Valley, whose revelations are cumulative, until Prospect Rock is reached, nine miles away. Across a deep ravine, to which has been given the name Glen Thomas, Cloud Point gives assurance that it can provide a view as magnificent as Prospect Rock.

Back to the swirling Lehigh, and the encircling mountains. The channel is not more than three hundred feet or so wide; and it turns suddenly, irregularly and often. This is said to be the most irregular and rugged mountain region in the state, and the fall of the river is especially rapid here. From White Haven to Mauch Chunk the total fall is 642 feet. In this twenty-five mile stretch the stream cuts through at least seven distinct mountains. It is a pity that the river is not followed closely by a good road; but it is possible to keep within reach of the stream much of the way, though often by indifferent roads.

In the days of the canal packets the route between White Haven and Mauch Chunk was most popular because of its grand scenery. So there was much sorrow when the flood of 1862, with the river thirty feet above low water mark, did so much damage to the canal that transit was interrupted and never resumed its former proportions. More than one hundred and fifty lives were lost in the flood, as many canal boats were destroyed, and thirty million feet of lumber.

From the river there are fascinating glimpses of the stratified rocks, whose departure from the perpendicular tells the story of the great upheavals by which these mountains were formed. Roads do not always give opportunity to see these bits of river scenery, for they have a disagreeable fashion—from the standpoint of the sightseer—of cutting across bends which the railroad follows faithfully.

Toward Glen Onoko the river and the railroad seem to dispute the narrow passage between the rocky tree-clad slopes which rise almost perpendicularly. The road is on the heights above the stream.

At a point where the river makes a sharp turn about a beetling crag, a picturesque foot suspension bridge, wide enough for one passenger to cross in comfort—when he becomes used to the height and the swinging structure—leads with abrupt descent across the stream to a sheltered house on the left bank. Not far away is Glen Onoko, which, in the opinion of some, vies with Switzerland in its mountain scenery, its glens and waterfalls. Onoko Falls is ninety feet high. At one point can be seen not only Onoko Falls, but also Chameleon Falls, 150 feet high, and the cascade.

Mauch Chunk also has been called "the Switzerland of America." It is "a town of two main streets, one along the mountain wall above the river, the other reaching back into a gap in the mountain." A visitor in 1852 gave a description of it that is not untrue to-day:

"It is a bird's nest of a place, hemmed in by high and steep mountains on all sides, some gracefully curving around it, while others terminate abruptly in its midst, and seemingly frown down upon it."

The town, whose name is Indian for Bear Mountain, was settled in 1815, for the development of its coal resources, whose discovery dates from 1791. On the summit of Sharp Mountain, where is to-day the town of

GLEN SUMMIT SPRINGS
Photo from Lehigh Valley Railroad Company

VIEW FROM FLAGSTAFF MOUNTAIN, MAUCH CHUNK
Photo from Philadelphia & Reading Railroad Company

ALONG EASTERN WATERWAYS

Summit Hill, a hunter found the first coal. He took samples to Philadelphia, and a company was organized in 1792 to develop the mine. Little was done, however, until after the war of 1812, and the attempts made then were unpromising. In Philadelphia permission was given to try the new fuel under the boiler of the new water works at Center Square. The engineer said it put the fire out, so what remained from the trial was broken up and used instead of gravel.

Two new companies were formed in 1818—the Lehigh Coal Company and the Lehigh Navigation Company. These two companies later became the Lehigh Coal and Navigation Company. But progress was slow. In 1820 but 385 tons were mined from the fifty-three-foot vein on top of Mauch Chunk Mountain. At as late a date as 1824 there was great distrust of the coal. This was illustrated by the passage in Abijah Hall's notes of travel when he said:

"My father procured a lump of Lehigh coal about as large as his two fists, and tried it on his wood fire in an open Franklin stove. After two days he concluded that if the world should take fire, the Lehigh Coal mine would be the safest retreat, the last place to burn."

Until 1827 wagons were used to transport the coal from the top of the mountain to the Lehigh. Then the daring project was made to build the gravity road to Summit Hill, on Mount Pisgah, nine hundred feet above the river. The work was done in rapid time, and by May 1, 1827, the road was in operation. The short road at Quincy, Massachusetts, and the section of the Baltimore and Ohio from Baltimore to Ellicott's Mills, are the only older roads on the continent.

The trip up the gravity road soon became one of the wonders of travel. Its fame has been world-wide. Not only is the method of transportation attractive, but the view from Mount Pisgah is sublime. Below lies Mauch Chunk with its typical oxbow bend, in the shadow of the mountains. At their base winds the Lehigh. Mountain ranges stretch away in succession. Lehigh Gap is seen to the southeast, while Schooley's Mountain also appears, though this is distant by rail sixty-five miles.

For many years coal-carrying activities ceased at the Switchback. During the European War there was talk of using it again for coal-carrying, as well as for sightseeing, but the proposal to adopt it for this emergency use was not carried out.

Far older than Mauch Chunk is the first settlement on the site of Lehighton, several miles down the river. At the foot of the hill on which is the old Moravian graveyard is the site of Gnadenhütten, where the Moravians came in 1746. Here, where the Warrior's Path crossed over the Lehigh Mountains, David Brainerd appeared when the mission was in its glory, and visited among the Indians with the customary eagerness of one who, as he wrote in his Journal, was always eager to afford them "frequent Opportunities of attending divine service, which seems, under God, a great means of keeping the Impression of divine things alive in their Minds."

In 1754 the mission moved bodily to what is now Weissport, then called New Gnadenhütten. Soon after the removal the Indians destroyed the mission. Later Benjamin Franklin arranged for the building of Fort Allen here, to be one of the frontier defenses in the French and Indian War.

All the way from Lehighton to Lehigh Gap the rare combinations of river and mountain vistas become more pleasing. The road is always twisting and turning, and each turn brings fresh delights—now a dam, above whose breast the deepened waters invite the swimmer, again a jutting headland or a glimpse of well-kept farm land, a ridge whose summit disappears in a bank of low-lying clouds, or a mysteriously dark glen that lures one from the road to search out the secrets of the mountains.

At Lehigh Gap the Lehigh forces its way through the Kittatinny Range, one more of the great mountain-disdaining feats of the torrent that rises more than two thousand feet above the sea, and descends fifteen hundred feet in the ninety-mile course to the Delaware. The towering cliffs on either side of the river can be appreciated by the passenger who leaves the train, not merely for a hasty glance, but for a walk up the creek whose entry into the river at this point adds to the picturesqueness of the surroundings. From one point of observation there is a smaller mountain that seems to close the gap. But between the obstructing mountain and Mauch Chunk another passage appears, and the way is open for the river to pass into Northampton County and begin its further descent to the nearby Delaware and its triumphant exit at Easton between two more mountains.

Professor Silliman, the geologist, was greatly stirred by the grandeur of the gap and its surroundings. "As we approached the gap," he wrote, "the view became very beautiful, and as we entered it by the side of the Lehigh and of the fine canal upon the left of the bank, the mountain ridge, here cleft from top to bottom, and rising apparently a thousand feet, presented on either hand a promontory of rocks and forest, rising abruptly and forming a combination both grand and beautiful."

From this point there are reaches where the waters

eddy and whirl, yet the greater part of the journey is conducted so circumspectly that Augusta Moore was led to sing:

> "Lehigh, I dream that in thy voice
> I catch a tone of gladness,
> That yearning love is in thy touch,
> That thou wouldst soothe my sadness.
> Only in dreams for thirty years
> Have I beheld thee flowing,—
> Whither away so fast, dear stream?
> Why dost thou moan in going?"

Now every town along the way tells a story or invites the eye. There is Slatington, from whose quarries has come some of the best of the country's slate; Laury's, where, just opposite, a rock projecting sixty or seventy feet above the river was called by the Indians Opekassett; Amenton, near Coplay, where, in 1740, a Philadelphian built a shooting box for himself and his friends which he called Grouse Hall, though, because it was painted white, it became known as White Hall; Cementon and Catasauqua, where roads, trees, houses bear witness to the fact that here is the center of the cement industry of eastern Pennsylvania, though, just beyond, the green trees and the hillsides are once more reflected in the waters alongside of which the slow-moving canal boats speak eloquently of the days of leisurely travel.

Allentown is the center from which the cement towns may be explored with ease. Within twelve miles to the northeast of the city is produced at least one-fourth of all the Portland cement used in the United States.

But Allentown and its neighborhood have much more than cement to offer to visitors. At the confluence of the Lehigh, the Little Lehigh, and Jordan Creek, it is one of the most beautiful cities in the state.

GLEN ONOKO
Photo from Lehigh Valley Railroad Company

ALONG THE LEHIGH, NEAR ALLENTOWN
Photo by the Kirkton Studios

There may have been a little indecision as to its name—Northampton was the title chosen before 1800 and again between 1811 and 1838—but there could not well be two thoughts about the unusual setting. It is built on a height, where the slope is to the river on the east and to the creek on the north. From Bauer's Rock, on South Mountain, three miles southeast, the view of the surroundings is superb.

There are in reality two rocks on the summit of the mountain. The southern rock looks out upon the Saucon Valley, the mountains, and the country to the southeast. The northern rock looks toward Allentown, the Lehigh Gap, the Blue Hills, the Wind Gap, and the entire country to the west and the north, including the Trexler deer and buffalo parks, nine miles north.

Allentown had its loyal part during the Revolution. One evidence of this is the bronze tablet on Zion Reformed Church, telling that here was a place of the concealment of the Liberty Bell when the occupation of Philadelphia by the British in 1779 led to the hasty removal of the historic relic from its place in Independence Hall.

A memorial of the recent European War also has been left in the Fair Grounds whose use, under the name of Camp Crane, resulted in the training of thousands of surgeons and their staffs for their mission of healing the wounds of the battlefield.

Bethlehem also has its memorials of the Revolution, as well as indications that it had a large part in the European War. Here Lafayette's wounds were tended after the battle of Brandywine. Here Congress remained several days in 1777. The Sisters' House was used as a hospital for some time, as a tablet records. Gun and ammunition were made for the army, as they were manufactured in immense quantities during the European War by the Bethlehem Steel Works—a plant that employed 700 men in 1863, 9000 men before the recent War, and increased its plant tremendously at the call of the nation and of the allied world.

Yet this is the city of the Moravians, the abode of peace. However, the people realize that sometimes the best way to have peace is to compel peace. The quieter message of the place is given in part through its music, an inspiring feature of its worship that attracts visitors from far and near. There is the picturesque custom of announcing a death at sunrise, when the trombone choir plays from the church cupola, one member facing north, one south, one east, one west. And, among other musical festivals, there is the great Bach Festival, the modern development of the old service of song first given in 1742, when Zinzendorf gathered the Moravians of his day on the hillside, across the river from the place where the church stands to-day. And because of this observance, as well as because of the life of the singers, "Bethlehem is Christianity set to music."

In the days of old Bethlehem was an oasis in the desert, a place of beauty in the midst of wild desolation. In 1784 Johan Shoepf wrote of coming the last half of the way from Philadelphia "through the tedious sameness of bush and forest," and was relieved and gladdened by the unexpected appearance of "lofty buildings in this presumptive wilderness." The Marquis de Chastellux told of his pleasant impressions more fully:

"After travelling two days through a country alternately diversified with savage scenes and cultivated spots, on issuing out of the woods at the close of the evening, in the month of May, found myself on a beautiful extensive plain, with the vast eastern branch of the

Delaware, richly interspersed with wooded islands, and at a distance of a mile in front of the town of Bethlehem rearing its large stone edifices out of a forest, situated on a majestic but gradually rising eminence, the background formed by the setting sun. So novel and unexpected a transition filled the mind with a thousand singular and sublime ideas, and made an impression on me never to be effaced. The romantic and picturesque effect of this glorious display of natural beauties gave way to the still more noble and interesting sensation arising from a reflection on the progress of the arts and sciences, and the sublime anticipation of the 'populous cities' and 'busy hum of men,' which are one day to occupy, and to civilize the vast wilderness of the New World."

The modern visitor will not find surrounding desolation, but he will find a beautiful city by a pleasant river, with a hill in South Bethlehem that gives a wide prospect from the Delaware Water Gap to the disappearing Blue Ridge in the southwest.

Nazareth, famous as the educational center of the Moravians, is within easy reach of Bethlehem, on the road that leads to the Wind Gap.

Both Nazareth and the Wind Gap were landmarks in the Walking Purchase contest of 1737, while the Lehigh was crossed between Bethlehem and Freemansburg. The Indians had calculated that the Lehigh would be the limit of the primitive surveying expedition; they did not dream that it would be crossed before the trip was much more than begun.

The Leni Lenapes, accustomed to William Penn's honorable method of dealing with them, made a treaty ceding additional lands to the "proprietor of Pennsylvania," extending from the Delaware in lower Bucks County to the most westerly branch of the Neshaminy, thence "as far as a man can go in a day and a half," and from the point so indicated to the river Delaware once more.

In 1682, when William Penn had bought land under similar conditions, he walked leisurely, in company with Indians and friends. After the Indian fashion they would sit down frequently, to smoke or to eat. In a day and a half a distance less than thirty miles had been traversed.

But Thomas and John Penn had a different idea. They advertised for fast walkers, and promised a rich prize to the one who should reach the farthest point in the stipulated time. Three men volunteered their services, Solomon Jennings, James Yates, and Edward Marshall. These men practiced walking for the occasion. The way was cleared for them through the wilderness far beyond the Lehigh.

The start was made from Wrightstown in Bucks County. The men took their station at a spot marked to-day by an obelisk. Edward Marshall was determined to outwalk the others, and carried a hatchet in his hands, that he might swing it from side to side, and so balance the action of his legs. As he hoped to do, he succeeded in passing both of his companions by the time he crossed the Lehigh. There was a halt of fifteen minutes for dinner, which was carried by a man on horseback. At the Wind Gap he was given a compass, since from that point the trail had not been blazed for him.

Progress was continued the second day until two o'clock in the afternoon. By this time Marshall having passed to the right of the Pocono Mountains, reached the limit of his progress, completely exhausted. The Indian who followed him the second day found it difficult to keep him in sight. When the tree was marked to indicate the spot reached, the Indian sadly witnessed the mark.

The distance covered was more than one hundred and ten miles. This sounds like an impossibility, but another record tells of the journey from Mauch Chunk to Philadelphia, in 1832, of a dispatch bearer who walked ninety-six miles between five in the morning and midnight.

But the cunning of the purchasers of the Indian lands was not yet at an end. Instead of running a line to the Delaware at the nearest point, they ran it at right angles to the line of walk. This reached the Delaware at the mouth of Lackawaxen Creek in Pike County. Thus the Indians were called upon to yield practically all of their lands on the Delaware within the boundary of Pennsylvania.

When later the surveyor general and others passed over the ground, they were four days in covering Marshall's route. No wonder the Indians were enraged. It is said that their treatment on this occasion led to their siding against the English in the French and Indian war. Their feelings were indicated by one of their number who said of the "walk," "No sit down to smoke, no shoot a squirrel, but lun, lun, lun all day long."

West of Freemansburg, and within a short distance of the place where Marshall crossed the Lehigh, is a commanding ledge from whose summit may be seen a large section of the territory covered that first day of the walk.

Easton, the point where the trusting Indian thought the line drawn from the end of the walk would reach the Delaware, is at the junction of the Delaware, the Lehigh, and the Bushkill. The Indians called the region "the forks of the Delaware." In later days the raftsmen spoke of the place as "Little Water Gap," because of the passage here of the Delaware through Weygadt Mountain. They dreaded the spot because it was the approach to Foul Rift, where great boulders in the stream impeded their progress. Geologists say these were left by the great glacial terminal moraine, which crossed the Delaware at this point.

In colonial times Easton was a town of great importance. Here, from 1754 to 1761, Indian conferences were held. At one of these gatherings Teedyuscung succeeded in inducing the Delawares to take a stand against the Six Nations, to whom they had been so subservient that they swallowed the insulting message from the northern Indians, "We conquered you, we made women of you; you know you are women, and can no more sell land than women."

In the early days of the nineteenth century, Easton's chief importance was as a canal center. Artificial waterways led to Mauch Chunk, to Bristol, and to New York. The canals to Bristol and to Mauch Chunk are today the only canals in regular use within the state of Pennsylvania.

From a number of heights above the Delaware in and about the city there are wide prospects of valley, river, and mountain. One of the best vantage points is on the campus of Lafayette College, whose grounds were long tended by the once famous Ik Marvel. Lafayette College is but twelve miles from Lehigh University at Bethlehem. It is a curious fact that these schools had for their benefactors, respectively, Ario Pardee and Asa Packer, once closely associated in the early days of the region. Packer was a boatman when the Lehigh canal was in its infancy, and he frequently carried goods to

DELAWARE RIVER AND CANAL.
Photo from Philadelphia & Reading Railroad

DELAWARE RIVER, NEAR EASTON
Photo from Philadelphia & Reading Railroad

Pardee, who kept a store at Hazleton. Both men made fortunes in the coal trade.

On another of the heights above the city the Marquis de Chastellux stood in 1782, "to view the noble and enchanting prospect, with which it is impossible to satiate the eye." Probably he was writing of the outlook from the top of Weygadt Mountain, spoken of as one of the finest prospects in eastern Pennsylvania. From here Northampton County can be seen to the Kittatinny Mountains. The range is sharply outlined to the eye, without break except for the Wind Gap and the Water Gap.

Before the days of the Bristol canal communication with Philadelphia was by the highway, or the excuse for a highway that sufficed for a long time. The route of the first stage driver was along the river for a few miles, then south by way of Doylestown.

A variation of the route was indicated in an advertisement of 1776:

"This is to let all Gentlemen and others know, that by the Incouragement I have from Several Gentlemen, That I, Jacob Abel of Philipsburg in Wessex County, West New Jersey, have resolve to Ride Post for the good of the Public. Intended to begin on the 5th day of February next on Monday in every Fournight till the 5 day of April, and from the 5 day of April to the 5 day of December next, ensuring every Monday in a Week.

"Take therefore myself the Liberty to recommend myself in the favor of the Publick. Advising them that on my return to Philadelphia shall Ride to German Town at the turn off on York Road, Cross the River at Darram and propose to Lieve my Packet at the following Person . . .

"Any Passel or Letters What any Gentleman Person or Persons will be pleased to trust to the Rider care, may depend they shall be safely delivered; and, if it should be required, are willing (as able) to give security. Any Person or Persons that is willing to give incouragement to the Rider are desire to sign their worthy Names on the Superscription paper left in several Hands . . ."

"Darram" was probably Durham, eight miles below Easton, at the mouth of Durham Creek. Here at one time was an Indian town named Pechoquealin, some forty miles below the town of the same name near the Water Gap.

Less than two miles from the mouth of the creek was the famous Durham iron furnace, built in 1726, where shot and shell were made for Washington's army. James Logan was one of the owners; andirons made at the furnace may be seen to-day in his old home, Stenton, in Philadelphia. Near the furnace was a blacksmith's shop where were built the first Durham boats used for transportation on the Susquehanna and the Delaware. Washington used boats of this pattern in his historic crossing of the Delaware; there is a bronze relief of one of them on the Trenton Battle monument.

Durham furnace was a popular stopping place for curious visitors. Alexander Wilson was there in 1804, when making his pedestrian journey to the north. Of his visit he wrote:

"Light beat our hearts with changing prospects gay,
As down through Durham vale we bend our way,
And pause, the furnace curious to explore,
Where flames and bellows lately wont to roar
Now waste and roofless; as its walls we pass
The massive shells lie rusting in the grass.
There let them rest, fell messengers of death,
Till injured liberty be roused to wrath,
In whose right hand may they, though hosts oppose,
Be blasting thunderbolts to all her foes."

A little to the west of the site of Durham furnace, Buckwampum Hill, the highest eminence in Bucks County, lifts its head. A beautiful rural country is spread out in all directions from the foot of the hill. Numerous watercourses diversify the landscape, Durham Creek being one of the pleasantest of these. It is related that into this creek one of Edward Marshall's companions fell exhausted during the "walk" of 1737, and that he was blind when he recovered consciousness.

The road leaves the Delaware River at Kintnersville, just a mile above the Nockamixon Rocks, an almost perpendicular cliff of red sandstone. Prospect Rock, the highest point, is 360 feet above the water. One of the most attractive drives in Pennsylvania is at the foot of the cliff. In 1832 a stage line from Easton to New Hope ran at the base of the rocks, and the enterprising proprietor said in his advertisement, "The towering rocks of Nockamixon are of themselves so grand and majestic as amply to repay the stranger for a ride of pleasure to see them."

For three miles the river passes through what is known as the Narrows, between Rock Hill in Pennsylvania and Musconetcong Mountain in New Jersey. Travelers know the cliffs on the Pennsylvania side as the Palisades of the Delaware. They may be seen to best advantage from the trains of the Pennsylvania Railroad from Trenton to Philipsburg.

Perhaps twenty miles south of the Palisades, Doylestown, the county seat of Bucks County, is seated on high lands which command a wide prospect of some of the finest farming land in the state. To the east, toward New Hope, is the vale of Lahaska, with its great spring, Hollikonk, and its outlet basin, Aquetong, where, according to the Indians, a deer pursued by an

Indian escaped, while the Indian broke through the limestone crust, from which the spring burst forth. There, the story goes, he ever pleads for release.

To the south is the Neshaminy, always numbered among the most beautiful streams of the state. On its banks stands the church from which John Fitch was walking when the idea of the steamboat first came to him.

Farther down the stream Washington had his headquarters when Lafayette came to him first. And on the same creek, only three miles from Doylestown, is said to be the site of the grave of Tamanend, Indian chief, the original of New York City's St. Tammany, who, according to the story, was burned to death near the spot of his burial. The sad manner of his passing was celebrated in 1783 by the Tammany brotherhood of Philadelphia as they sang:

"At last, growing old and quite worn out with years,
 As history doth truly proclaim,
His wigwam was fired, he nobly expired,
 And flew to the skies in a flame."

From Doylestown a pleasing road leads northwest over hill and dale back to Lehigh County, passing on the way, in Milford township, the home of John Fries, the man who, in 1798 and 1799, led the people in rebellion against the government, because of the imposition of an insignificant but unpopular dwelling tax. The rebellion reached such proportions that President Adams issued a warning to the insurgents. Troops were sent out along the Bethlehem road. After capturing Fries, the soldiers marched from Quakertown to Allentown, and then back to Philadelphia by way of Reading. Fries was convicted of treason, but was later pardoned by the President.

The road followed by the troops from Allentown to

NESHAMINY FALLS
Photo from Philadelphia & Reading Railroad

SIX MILES EAST OF DOYLESTOWN
Photo by the Clay Studio

Reading dates from 1753. It crosses over into Berks County at Maxatawny, the center of a district so loved by the Indians that they remained there long after they had left other parts of the country. All the way to Reading, and several miles below the road, is a range of fine hills whose summits limit the view to the south, while gently sloping ground between rests the traveler's eye.

Where the road turns south along the Schuylkill toward Reading is the little town of Berkley. The name was given to it because its situation in the valley, with reference to Reading, is similar to that of Berkley in England to its neighbor, Reading.

From the early days of the colony, visitors who knew England have said that the valley of the Schuylkill in Berks County is like the best of rural England. But those who have learned to love these hills and vales are unwilling to think that there is anywhere a country that can be compared to the lands that lie in the shadow of Penn and Neversink, the guardian mountains of the manor of Penn at Reading.

ROUTE VI
FROM PITTSBURGH TO LAKE ERIE AND BACK
ABOUT 300 MILES

"FORT du Quesne will be the most considerable and important place of any, perhaps, in North America, and by its situation and many conveniences the most proper of any place to become the capital of that whole continent and give laws to it.'

The loyal Pittsburgher will appreciate that quotation from the *Universal Magazine of Knowledge and Pleasure*, published in London in July, 1757, and, while agreeing that the prophecy has not been fulfilled in its entirety, he can console himself by the reflection that the city is filling a place far more important in the nation than the writer dreamed would be possible, and also in the assurance that he was just as wild in many other assertions made in the article. For instance there was the odd statement that "the Ohio runs through a great part of our colonies of Pennsylvania and Carolina, and waters a country near five hundred miles square." He insisted that the Ohio was "not less than ten or twelve thousand miles long, from its source near the habitation of the Six Nations to its confluence with the Mississippi."

Fort du Quesne was said to be "about midway between Canada and Louisiana, the most convenient of all places, . . . a place of consequence and importance, and the rendezvous of all the people of North America."

In the desire to take advantage of the highway nature had generously provided for the use of the people of the continent who made "rendezvous" there, many efforts were made to provide for the navigation of the

PITTSBURGH TO LAKE ERIE AND BACK

Ohio. One of the most curious of these attempts was described by James Kenny, a trader at Fort Pitt, the successor of Fort du Quesne. The quotation is from his diary.

"1761, 4th mo: 4, A young man called Wm. Ramsey, has made two little boats, being squair at ye sterns, and joined together at ye sterns by a swivel, make ye two in form of one boate, but will turn around shorter than a boat of ye same length, or raise with more safety in falls and in case of striking rocks; he has also made an engine that goes with wheels enclosed in a box, to be worked by one man, by sitting on ye end of ye box, and tredding on treddles at bottom with his feet, sets ye wheels agoing which work sculles or short paddles fixed over ye gunnels turning them round; ye under one always laying hold in ye water, will make ye boate goe as if two men rowed; and he can steer at ye same time by lines like plow lines."

Unfortunately history tells nothing more of this contrivance whose inventor had in mind a thought that might have been developed into a regular steamboat, many years ahead of Robert Fulton or even of John Fitch.

More startling still was the effort made in 1801 by a Frenchman named Louis Anastasius Tarasçon. He had the vision of Pittsburgh not merely at the head of navigation on the Ohio, but as a seaport laying tribute on foreign commerce. The first year's shipbuilding program included one vessel of 120 tons and another of 250 tons. These were loaded with flour, one for St. Thomas, the other for Philadelphia. At Philadelphia the latter vessel loaded for Bordeaux and returned with a cargo that was sent on to Pittsburgh by wagon, across Pennsylvania. The ships could sail down the river, but they could not return!

Henry Clay told in Congress of an experience of the captain of one of the Tarasçon-built vessels. At Leghorn "the Master presented his papers to the customhouse officer, who said to him, 'Sir, your papers are forged; there is no such port as Pittsburgh in the world; your vessel must be confiscated.' But the captain took a map of the United States, directed him to the Gulf of Mexico, pointed out the mouth of the Mississippi; led him a thousand miles up to the mouth of the Ohio, and then another thousand up to Pittsburgh. 'There, sir, is the port from which my vessel cleared out,' he said, in triumph."

Keelboats and barges were used for transport between Pittsburgh and Louisville until 1811, when Nicholas J. Roosevelt, Chancellor Livingston, and Robert Fulton planned for the construction of the first steamboat in western waters.

Mr. Roosevelt was the builder. Men were sent to the forests to cut timber for ribs, keels, and beams. These were rafted down the Monongahela to the shipyard. Planking was cut from white pine logs in the old-fashioned saw-pits. A shipbuilder and the mechanics required were brought from New York.

At last the boat, one hundred and sixteen feet long, was ready, and was christened the *New Orleans*. There was a ladies' cabin containing four berths. One of these Mrs. Roosevelt announced her intention of occupying. Friends in Pittsburgh appealed to her to give up the dangerous project; but she insisted that there was no danger; she believed in her husband.

Eager watchers at Pittsburgh saw the vessel swing into the stream and disappear around the first headlands; the prophecies of disaster at the very start had not been fulfilled. The pilot, the captain, and the crew had their misgivings, but these were soon set at rest by the behavior of the boat.

PITTSBURGH TO LAKE ERIE AND BACK

The route taken by the first Ohio River steamboat is also, for more than twenty-five miles, the route of the traveler who would go north to Erie, for the Ohio flows to the northwest before turning west and then south.

Fourteen miles from Pittsburgh, and just over the line in Beaver County, was located Logstown, an Indian village in colonial days, where the English gathered for the making of treaties, even when the French were in the stronghold at Fort du Quesne, and though Logstown was one of the places where, in 1742, Celeron de Bienville had planted a leaden plate, claiming the Ohio Valley for France.

Conrad Weiser, who was a visitor there in 1748, was accompanied by William Franklin, the son of whom Benjamin Franklin was so proud until he grieved his father by becoming a Tory during the Revolution. Christopher Gist arrived at the river outpost on November 25, 1750. Major George Washington followed in November, 1753, and held a conference with Chief Tanacharison, the Indian who, at a later date, said sadly, "The French claim the land on one side of the Ohio, and the English on the other: where does the Indian land lie?" Five years later Christian Frederick Post, Moravian missionary, found here "about thirty houses." In 1764 Colonel Bouquet stopped at the trading post when on his expedition against the Ohio Indians. At that time he said:

"The lower town extended about sixty perches over a rich bottom to the foot of a low, steep ridge, on the summit of which, commanding a most agreeable prospect over the lower and across the Ohio, which is quite 500 yards wide here, and by its majestic, easy current adds much to the beauty of the place."

Not far above the site of old Logstown George

Rapp founded his celebrated community town, Economy, erected substantial buildings, of which many are still standing, and began the development of the village. Of this place a traveler of 1826 said, after a visit:

"The articles for the use of the society are kept by themselves, as the members have no private possessions, and everything is in common. The clothing and food they make use of is the best quality; of the latter, flour, salt meat, and all long-keeping articles are served out monthly; fresh meat, on the contrary, and whatever spoils readily, is distributed whenever it is killed, according to the size of the family."

The five hundred Economists of 1843 were reduced to 250 in 1890, and since then they have gradually dwindled. But while their activity in the town is now only a matter of history, their helpful influence in the county and, in fact, the entire country can be easily traced.

Two towns near the great bend of the Ohio are closely connected by history as well as by tradition. Monaca, or Philipsburg, as it was called once, was a boat-building town, until a seceding company of two hundred and fifty people from Economy bought the place, and for eighteen months tried to build up a rival town. The boatyards were then removed to Freedom, whose situation on the flats and in the hills has been spoken of as one of the most picturesque on the Ohio River. On the heights there is afforded a splendid view of the river, the valley, and the majestic bend where the stream turns toward the Gulf of Mexico.

At the point where the entrance of the Beaver River from the north completes the triangular division of Beaver county, so similar to that of Allegheny and several other counties in the state, the "Tuscarawas trail," the local name of Nemacolin's Path, crossed the

PITTSBURGH TO LAKE ERIE AND BACK

Beaver River and led on through what is now the city of Beaver. On the site of Rochester was Mingo Village, and from here another trail led to Lake Erie.

The Beaver River itself was one of the pathways of Indian travel for those who sought Presque Isle and Lake Erie. Later it became the route for the Beaver division of the canal toward Lake Erie, included in the scheme of Pennsylvania internal improvements. It is of interest that the stream was named for the beaver, whose activities along the bank were noteworthy. The little animal gave its name to Beavertown also, and then to Beaver County.

When Washington paid his second visit to Beaver County he admired the country at the confluence of the rivers. On October 21, 1770, he wrote that land in the neighborhood could be bought for £5 for one hundred acres, in ten thousand acre lots. This might seem an attractive price, until the added words of Washington are remembered, "At present the unsettled state of the country renders any purchase dangerous."

Within five miles of the mouth of the Beaver there are many bustling towns, all in a setting unusually attractive. As long ago as 1840 it was said of them:

"Beaver is not, properly, one town, but a little cluster of towns, a sort of United States in miniature, situated around the mouth of the river and four or five miles up that stream."

Rudyard Kipling grew enthusiastic on the occasion of his visit to this region. Witness his words:

"Imagine a rolling, wooded English landscape, with the softest of blue skies, dotted at three-mile intervals with foothills, quaint little villages, and a generous manufacturing town."

The prosperity of this cluster of communities, as well

as part of their picturesque character, is accounted for by the falls of the Beaver, five miles above its mouth, whose water power is supplemented by the stretch of stream below. There, within five miles, the fall is sixty-nine feet.

Bridgewater and New Brighton, two more of the towns whose industries are fed by the water power from the falls, were chosen by Aaron Burr in 1805 for the building of boats for the transportation of his expedition to establish an empire in the southwest. The boats, called Orleans boats, differed from the old keel boats in being covered over for protection from the weather.

An earlier expedition of an entirely different character disembarked not far from the spot where Aaron Burr's boats started on their journey. In 1770 David Zeisberger brought sixteen canoe loads of Indians down the Allegheny from Venango County to Pittsburgh, then up the Ohio to Beaver, and up the Beaver to Beaver Falls. There the canoes were left behind and the possessions of the emigrants were taken by land to Kaskaskunk, not far from the site of Darlington, in the northwestern part of Beaver County. Mission work was carried on at this place for three years, when it was necessary to give it up because of increasing danger.

One of the picturesque river junctions so characteristic of Pennsylvania is at New Castle, the county seat of Lawrence County. Here, near the center of the county named for Perry's flagship in the battle of Lake Erie, the Mahoning and Shenango Rivers come together to form the Beaver.

The quiet, peaceful surroundings of beautiful Lawrence County are so satisfying that the thoughtful traveler responds quickly to Bishop Spaulding's characteristic definition of education:

BEAVER
Photo by John C. Bragdon

JORDAN RUN, ERIE COUNTY
Photo by State Department of Forestry

PENETRATION ROAD IN MERCER COUNTY
Photo by State Highway Department

PITTSBURGH TO LAKE ERIE AND BACK

"To run, to jump, to ride, to swim, to sit in the shade of trees by flowing waters, to look on orchards blooming, to dream in the silence that lies amid the hills, to feel the solemn loneliness of the deep woods, to follow cattle as they crop the sweet-scented clover, to learn, too, as one knows a mother's face, every change that comes over the heavens from the dewy freshness of the early morn to the restful calm of evening, from the overpowering mystery of the starlit sky to the look with which the moon smiles upon the earth; all this is education of a higher and more real kind than it is possible to receive within the walls of a school; and, lacking this, nothing shall have power to develop the faculties of the soul in symmetry and completeness."

When the way leads to New Wilmington, in the northern part of the county, the impression is deepened. For, in the neighborhood of the town, Neshannock Creek comes down from the north; Neshannock Falls are just outside, and there are heights from which to view the fertile valley to the north, the south, and the east.

From New Wilmington there is opportunity to go across the southwest corner of Mercer County, through the valley of the Shenango to Sharon, one of the most attractive towns of western Pennsylvania, and from Sharon it is possible to approach Lake Erie by a road that just avoids the state line, then crosses it and trespasses on Ohio to Conneaut on the lake. Another road, however, though perhaps not so good, leads north from Sharon, through some of the most interesting country in Mercer and Crawford counties, and comes within reach of Lake Erie halfway between Conneaut and Erie. For many miles this road passes through the valley of the Shenango, then turns toward Conneaut Lake in Crawford County. This, the largest lake in the state, is three miles long and one mile wide. The Indians called it Kon-ne-yaut, "snow place," because the snow and ice remained here long after they had disappeared from the surrounding country. From the clear water of the lake the Beaver and Erie canal was supplied in part, the surface of the lake being raised ten feet by a dam across the southern outlet. When the canal was abandoned, the dam was removed, and the lake was restored to its former state, making the place more than ever a joy to those who go there for a brief time or remain in the hotels or cottages that have been built on the shore.

Crawford County owes much of its singular beauty to the fact that it is on the summit of the watershed that separates the valley of the Mississippi from that of the St. Lawrence. The ridge between Pine Creek and Conneaut, immediately north of the lake, is the point of division. From this ridge the ground slopes from the five hundred feet elevation of Conneaut to the five hundred and seventy-three feet of Lake Erie, and from it as from the shore of the lake, there are waiting for the visitor vistas of rare beauty.

"Nowhere is the landscape more picturesque and charming," is the verdict of one who yielded gladly to the lure of Conneaut scenery. "The distant line of blue hills is hardly distinguishable from the clouds of heaven. Not infrequently in winding along the bold headlands, one comes upon a hidden cascade as enchanting in its appointments as the cunningly devised imitation, planned with studied elegance for the gratification of an oriental monarch. A valley may stretch away for a score of miles, through which a stream lazily pursues its tortuous course; the bold hills close in at its mouth almost to the very margin, leaving scarcely room for the smaller to make its way to the larger body. The traveler never ceases to admire the varying line of the hori-

ON THE ROAD IN CRAWFORD COUNTY
Photo by State Highway Department

AFTER A FRESHET IN LAWRENCE COUNTY
Photo by State Highway Department

OVER THE HILLS AND FAR AWAY
Photo by J. Horace McFarland Company

IN THE RAVINE, NEAR PITTSBURGH
Photo by State Highway Department

zon, cut by the summits of remote ridges, sometimes jagged by a relentless peak, at others rounded out by a comely slope."

A short detour to the west of the lake leads to famous Pymatuning Swamp, the source of the Shenango, whose nine thousand acres are thought to have been at one time the bed of a lake. One reason for the conjecture is that Indian canoes have been found beneath the surface. In the days before much of the land was made available for agriculture a local historian said of it:

"Though there are portions of the surface sufficiently elevated to support forest vegetation, yet it cannot be entered with teams for removing logs, except in winter time, when it is frozen over. In a part of the swamp is a growth of tamaracks, where in the fall of the year vast flocks of wild pigeons from Canada made their roosting ground. In the hot summer nights the constant flapping of their wings, produced by being crowded from their perches, gave forth a sound not unlike the distant roar of Niagara. Hunters would enter the swamp in the drouth of summer, and, aiming up at a limb bending down with the weight of the birds, would fire, and, having struck a light and picked up as many as could be discovered in the tall grass, would pass on for another shot."

On now to the north, following the direct route taken by the pigeons from Pymatuning when returning to Canada; on to the road that leads not far from the southern shore of Lake Erie.

At Presque Isle is the only break in the elevated barriers of sand and clay that stretch between the water and the land. Here Erie looks out from the bluff on the bay and the peninsula. The harbor, four miles long by half a mile wide, is one of the best on the lake.

At this point, in 1742, Celeron de Bienville built a fort of logs as one of the series of forts planned to hold the region west of the Alleghenies against the English traders. Later the stronghold came into the hands of the English and the colonists. General Wayne had a garrison here, in 1794, when on his way to the Maumees. His death occurred on his return to the fort in 1796. His body was buried near the lake, but was removed to Old St. David's at Radnor, near Philadelphia, in 1809.

Presque Isle next came into prominence in 1812. In July of that year Captain Daniel Dobbins lost his vessel to the British at Mackinac Island. By way of Erie he went to Washington, and at a meeting of the Cabinet he gave the first information of the surrender of Mackinac Island and Detroit. At the same time he urged the establishment of a naval depot at Erie. Not only was his suggestion adopted, but he was given a commission in the navy, and was instructed to proceed to Erie and begin to build a number of gunboats. Three months after the capture of his vessel he was at work. Six months later, when he had brought ship carpenters from Black Rock, iron from Pittsburgh, and timber from the forests near by, and had completed three gunboats, Commodore Perry arrived. More ship carpenters were brought from the east, the work was speeded up, and in August, ten months after the beginning of operations, the fleet was ready for sailing. During the process of lifting the vessels over the bar the British fleet was in sight, but when the gunboats were ready the hostile vessels had disappeared. Perry sought them. Finally, on September 10, 1813, he came up with them, gave battle, and spoke the memorable words, "Don't give up the ship."

Pennsylvania might have missed the honor of having the fleet built within her borders, and it was due to the farsightedness of General William Irwin, whom Washington sent to northwestern Pennsylvania to examine and report on the land, that the valuable frontage on Lake Erie became a part of the state. Noting that Pennsylvania had no harbor on the lake, and only a meager frontage of several miles, he resolved to tell others of the need of securing the Triangle that now forms nearly half of Erie County. Congress arranged matters by persuading New York, Massachusetts, and Connecticut to release their claim. Then the 202,187 acre tract was sold to Pennsylvania for $151,640.25, or seventy-five cents per acre. The patent was signed by George Washington as President and Thomas Jefferson as Secretary of State.

The first step in the procedure was taken when Pennsylvania bought from the Six Nations who had not included the Triangle in earlier sales, the Indian rights to the land by the payment of $12,000. The treaty, made in 1789, was signed by more than twenty chiefs, who had picturesque names like the Big Bale of a Kettle, the Broken Twig, Twenty Canoes, Tearing Asunder, the Dancing Feather, Bandy Legs, and Throw Into the Water.

Several years passed before the Indians were satisfied to let go the territory they had sold. In 1791 a second treaty was made, $800 additional was paid, and the land was open to settlement.

The value of the acreage transferred was appreciated not only because of the lake frontage, but because of the fact that, unlike other parts of Pennsylvania, it was a level plain, separated by a low ridge some eight or ten miles back from the shore, from the higher land to the south.

A picturesquely worded opinion of the quality of the land was given by Colonel Andrew Porter in 1788:

"The soil will come under the description Tolarable good. The country is clear of mountains and but very little broke with Hills. In many parts of it are very rich Tracts of land, and some parts are rather wet and swampy. It abounds with a great variety of Timber."

Erie, the metropolis of the Triangle, is notable in railroad history as well as in naval history. When the first railroads were constructed the gauge of the road from the East was four feet ten inches; of that from the West six feet. Through trains could not be run; passengers had to transfer at Erie. Usually it was necessary to remain in the town for a part of a day, or for the night.

In 1846 the Erie Railroad talked of changing the gauge from six feet to standard width. The merchants and the city officials protested; why should they approve a change that would deprive them of much of their income? It was better, they felt, to be at the terminus of two roads than to have trains pass through the town. As an expression of dissent they tore up portions of seven miles of the Erie's tracks, and passengers had to be transferred across the gap in the dead of winter. This trip, called "crossing the isthmus," was much dreaded by the passengers, many of whom had feet, hands, and faces frost-bitten. Horace Greeley, one of the victims, said in the *New York Tribune*, "Let Erie be avoided by all travellers until grass shall grow in her streets."

Of course a compromise was reached before many years, and "the isthmus" became history.

Long before the days of railroads, wagon roads crossed the easy, level stretches of Erie County. In 1742 Celeron de Bienville cut a road fifteen miles to the

PITTSBURGH TO LAKE ERIE AND BACK

River aux Bœufs at what is now Waterford, where there was another of the series of French forts.

Eighty-five years later the stretch of road was improved and operated as a turnpike. A stage coach company quarreled with the turnpike company over the tolls and built a new road from Waterford to Erie which became known as the "shunpike." A portion of this old road is still in use as a township highway.

From Waterford to the south is the road over which Commodore Perry's powder supply was brought in 1813. The ammunition came by wagons from Wilmington, Delaware, by way of Bedford, Pittsburgh, Butler, and Mercer. When the centennial celebration of Perry's victory was held in 1913, a feature was the passage over the same route of an old Conestoga wagon, loaded with powder.

Along the eastern bank of French Creek, where the turnpike shows the way as far south as Meadville, was the old Indian path from Fort Venango to Fort Le Bœuf. Washington followed this path in 1753, though on his return journey he floated down the stream in a boat. Later visitors to the north followed Washington's route up the Allegheny, then up French Creek to Meadville and Waterford. To this fact was due the settlement of Venango and Crawford Counties long before the Indians' possession of what is now Mercer County was disputed by the pioneers.

Many of the pioneers who ascended French Creek were attracted by the beautiful country in Crawford County, and were led to stop and make their homes —some at Cambridge Springs, where the later discovery of chalybeate water brought prosperity to the community; others in the region south where the valley broadens and the hills and valleys on either side are most inviting. Many who had resisted the temptation farther down the river yielded, at Saegertown, to the lure of the beautiful land.

Meadville, too, has an unusual setting, the valley of Watson's Run, westward, speaking an eloquent message to those who have learned to hear nature's voice. To such travelers it will be almost impossible to resist the road from Meadville to Conneaut Lake, directly through the valley.

Meadville is credited with the accidental discovery of the possibility of making paper from straw, and that in days long before straw paper was made elsewhere. A man who had put straw at the bottom of a barrel, with leached ashes above, noted that when the ashes were removed the straw was soft. Always ready to make experiments, he placed some of the straw in his mouth, chewed it, flattened it on a board, then left it to be dried in the sun. The result was so successful that a patent for the process was secured, and to the industries of the town a mill for the manufacture of straw paper was soon added. The first shipment of the product, 300 reams, was sent to Pittsburgh by canal November, 1828.

At one time Meadville was on navigable water, for Congress made many appropriations for the improvement of French Creek. Boats of twenty tons burden many times passed by the town, successors of the lumber rafts and flatboats of an earlier time.

There enters French Creek at Meadville another stream, one more of the numerous Pennsylvania creeks with an Indian name beginning with C—the Cussewago. The valley is remarkably beautiful, but this was not what the Indian who named it remarked. The story goes that he saw a big black snake on the bank, with body distended, perhaps after a meal on a rabbit. "Kossawausge!" he said to his companion. The exclamation was more musical than its English meaning, "big belly."

Not far from the Cussewago, Cornelius Van Horn had the beginning of a trying experience with a later party of Indians. He was plowing in his field one day in May, 1791, when he was captured, taken to a hill above the town, then on to Conneaut Lake. On the shore of the lake he was compelled to sit by a tree, and then, with arms pinioned behind him, he was fastened to the tree by a deer-skin thong. After a time, in response to repeated tugging, the thong loosened a little. The Indian stretched it tight by pushing it at an angle up the trunk. After a while, when his exhausted captors were asleep, it was easy for him to loosen the thong once more, enough at least to permit him to reach with his teeth a knife he had hidden in his cuff at the time of his capture. With this he managed to sever the thong that bound him to the tree, though he was of course unable to free his arms until he was once more among his friends at Meadville, who had despaired of seeing him again.

The waters of French Creek bore a heavy traffic to Pittsburgh during the late twenties and the early thirties of the nineteenth century. On April 1, 1830, the *Crawford Messenger* said that in a distance of twenty-two miles on the river there were from ninety to one hundred flat-bottomed boats started or about to start for Pittsburgh, laden with produce. Each boat could carry from twenty to twenty-seven tons.

More than thirty years later Meadville was the center of traffic of a different character. In 1866, when the Atlantic and Great Western Railway was building, the general offices were here. The plan was to connect New York and St. Louis by a series of railroads. The route from New York was to be to Salamanca, thence to Meadville, next to Cincinnati, and from there by the Ohio and Mississippi Railway. Meadville, as the outlet for the oil country, was thought to be the future great city of western Pennsylvania, and the logical center of activities on the great through road.

One of the most famous visitors Meadville has had came to the town before the days of railroads. His name was John James Audubon, and he came by the turnpike road from Erie. Though far from famous then, he was making preparation for the fame that came when he completed his wonderful drawings of American birds.

He was almost penniless, and found it necessary to earn his way by his brush. A companion was with him when he reached Meadville. Their joint capital was precisely one dollar and fifty cents. On this occasion the empty pocketbook was filled by the payments of eager customers who flocked to him for portraits at bargain prices, attracted by the drawings of birds and people which he showed them. A merchant agreed to let the artist have space in his store. In his journal Audubon told what followed:

"Next day I entered the artist's room by crazy steps of the store-garret; four windows faced each other at right angles; in a corner was a cat nursing, among rags for a paper mill; hogsheads of oats, Dutch toys on the floor, a large drum, a bassoon, fur caps along the walls, a hammock and rolls of leather. Closing the extra windows with blankets, I procured a painter's light.

"A young man sat to try my skill; his painting was approved; then the merchant; the room became crowded . . . The next day was spent as yesterday. Our pockets replenished, we walked to Pittsburgh in two days."

Soon after leaving Meadville Audubon and his companion were in Mercer County, following the road that was built in 1816. The necessity for a road was impressed on the citizens of the county during the War of 1812, when those fit for military service were subject to call from Erie. That call was sent out whenever an English invasion was thought to be imminent. On its receipt the farmers were expected to drop everything and rush to the north. One call came to Mercer during a church service. The pastor brought his sermon to a hasty conclusion, and within a few minutes the men were on the march. On another occasion farmers in the harvest field heard the insistent summons to arm themselves.

A few years before the war, a curious visitor from England traveled through these valleys. His name was Thomas Ashe, and the tour in the United States, of which a part was through western Pennsylvania, was made in 1806. Among other things, he told of a man who built his house by a salt spring, unaware of the fact that this was a favorite gathering place for herds of buffalo. Once a drove of about three hundred came to the spring, and stopped to rub against the log house. In a few hours "they rubbed the house completely down, taking delight in turning the logs off with their horns. In the meantime, the proprietor of the house escaped with his family.

Another writer of early days called the buffalo "wild oxen." He said the creatures were larger than oxen, "with a fleece like a sheep, of which several manufactures have been made little inferior to silk."

On the way from Mercer to Pittsburgh two more picturesque streams are crossed, Slippery Rock Creek, near the border of Butler County, and the Conoquonessing, "for a long way straight," whose deep gorges and rocky bed make it notable.

The beauty and fertility of the Conoquonessing Valley attracted George Rapp, when he was looking for a location for his community village. In 1805 he selected a site, built mills, began to raise sheep, and started to grow grapes. Because neither the sheep nor the grapes did well he sold the community possessions at Harmony, floated down the Ohio, ascended the Wabash and built a new town in Indiana. The climate there was not what he desired, so he returned to Pennsylvania, this time to Beaver County, where he chose a new location at Economy.

The community experiment started at Harmony was doomed to failure, but unfortunately the town saw the birth of another idea that has not yet failed. For a time Joseph Smith was a resident here, and here he laid his plans for the Mormon church. Next he went to New York, and, after digging up the plates of the Book of Mormon, he was ready to play the game that has led so many people astray.

A pleasanter story is told in connection with the neighboring town of Zelienople. The founder of the town, Deemer Basse, owner of ten thousand acres in the neighborhood, had a daughter Zelie, whom he loved so devotedly that he felt there was but one possible name for the new town. The great wooden castle built by him was burned in 1842. But the name remains, a memorial of fatherly love.

ON THE SHENANGO, NEAR GREENVILLE
Photo by State Highway Department

THE CONOQUONESSING, NEAR FRISCO, BEAVER COUNTY

ROUTE VII

THROUGH THE OIL REGIONS AND SKIRTING THE FOREST COUNTRY

A ROUND TRIP FROM PITTSBURGH
ABOUT 331 MILES

NO traveler who wishes to see historic sites should finally leave Pittsburgh without paying a visit to the Second Avenue Panhandle Crossing. There is nothing special in the surroundings to give inspiration, until it is recalled that on the stretch of track between this corner and the mouth of the tunnel through Grant Hill, nearer the Union Station, occurred one of the epoch-making incidents in the development of the railroads.

Until long after the Civil War all trains, both passenger and freight, were equipped only with the clumsy, difficult, and slow chain hand-brakes. To bring a train to a stop within a reasonable distance was impossible; to prevent fearful wear and tear on the rolling stock, the roadbed, and the passengers was equally impossible. Many railroad officials had ceased to hope for anything much better, until a young man named George Westinghouse overcame their reluctance and their disbelief by making an unanswerable test of the compressed air brake.

For a long time the inventor, then at the beginning of his brilliant career, had been mulling over the problem; he did not see why two freight trains, approaching each other on a single track, could not be stopped in time to prevent a collision in much less than a mile. Various plans occurred to him, but all were rejected. Then came the day when he read an article telling of the building of the great Mount Cenis tunnel by the agency of compressed air. At once he had a vision of the necessary apparatus.

When he was ready for a test, he finally—and that "finally" hides a long chapter of discouragements—persuaded Panhandle officials to permit him to equip a train of five cars to be run from the Pittsburgh station to Steubenville. This was done in 1869. Attached to the rear of the train was a coach which carried the anxious inventor and the interested, but doubtful, officials.

The engineer, who had been carefully instructed in the use of the new brakes, was startled when he emerged from the tunnel to see a teamster approaching the crossing at Second avenue. There was a station between the tunnel and the crossing, but no stop was to be made there; it was thought that precautions had been taken for the guarding of the tracks. The warning whistle was sounded, and the teamster urged on his horses. The frightened animals jerked the driver from his seat and threw him across the rails. The engineer acted instantly; he threw on the Westinghouse brakes with emergency speed, and with a tremendous jar the engine came to a stop within four feet of the prostrate man. Angry officials, whose bruises made them all the more ready to say "I told you so," and the young inventor, who thought that something had gone wrong, stepped to the roadway and walked hurriedly to the engine, only to learn that accident had afforded opportunity for the best possible test of the air brakes. There was an instant change in the atmosphere. Men who had been doubtful before urged that the trip be given up; there was no need for further test, now that they had had such a tremendous object lesson of what the appliance could do. However, the journey was completed to Steubenville, and the Westinghouse air brake that has helped to bring fame to Pittsburgh and Pennsylvania began its career.

Years elapsed before all passenger trains were equipped with the new device, and more years before the law required that every freight train as well should pay tribute to the genius of Westinghouse. It was soon realized that the clamor for the improvement must be heeded, not only by railroads that ran express trains through populous country, but by lines operated in more sparsely settled and difficult territory, like some of that to be covered by the tour outlined in this chapter.

The route begins in Allegheny County and continues through the heart of well populated Butler County, whose rambling streams, sightly hills and fertile farms combine to provide a series of delightful prospects all the way from Cooperstown on the plateau high above Glade Run to the approach to the Allegheny River and the northeastern border.

It is about twelve miles from Cooperstown to Butler, the county seat, whose site was a part of the seventy-thousand-acre tract of land within the present bounds of the county once owned by Robert Morris. In 1802, when plans for the town were first made, investors were told that "the situation is beautiful, being on an eminence which descends in all directions." It was added that "the ridges, all pointing into the little valley, will be convenient for roads from every direction." A visitor in these first days spoke of the howling wilderness that surrounded the embryo city, though he was careful to except "a few scattered settlements as far removed from each other as the kraals in the neighborhood of the Cape of Good Hope." The present-day visitor to bustling Butler and its surroundings finds difficulty in realizing that this description could have been true only a little more than a century ago.

Less than half way between Butler and Franklin, in Venango County, the road crosses Slippery Rock Creek, memorable in connection with an incident of the days before the Indians retired from the country drained by the creek. Captain Samuel Brady, with a number of companions, was surprised by savages who pursued him to the banks of the creek, where they thought they would surely take him; they knew that the stream at that point was quite deep, and the banks were too steep for crossing. But Brady did not hesitate; he jumped, and, to the astonishment of the Indians, succeeded in reaching the opposite bank in safety. "Brady make good jump!" the leading Indian exclaimed in amazement, and so lost his chance to fire on the retreating man, who was zig-zagging in a fashion that confused those who sought his life. It was later found that he had jumped twenty-three feet, and that the water at that place was twenty feet deep.

Not far from the southern line of Venango County, but farther to the eastward, on the Allegheny River, the Indians had a favorite gathering place, and the memorial of their presence is still there—a great rock in the river once covered with inscriptions. Schoolcraft's classic work on the American Indian, published in 1853, gave a fine engraving and a full description of the rock:

"A prominent point of rock, around which the river deflects, rendering this point a very conspicuous object. The rock, which has been lodged there in some geological convulsion, is a species of hard sandstone about twenty feet in length by fourteen in breadth. It has an inclination to the horizon of about fifty degrees. During freshets it is nearly overflowed. The inscription is made upon the inclined face of the rock. The present inhabi-

IN VENANGO COUNTY
Photo by State Highway Department

UNLOADING LOGS FOR THE MILL, FOREST COUNTY
Photo by State Department of Forestry

LITTLE BROKENSTRAW CREEK, WARREN COUNTY
Photo by State Highway Department

ALLEGHENY RIVER, WARREN
Photo by State Department of Forestry

tants of the country call it the 'Indian God.' It is only in low stages of water that it can be examined. . . . The inscription itself appears distinctly to record, in symbols, the triumphs of hunting and war."

In 1742, when Celeron de Bienville was burying his leaden plates, he wrote in his journal that he buried one of these "on the north bank of the Ohio (Allegheny) opposite a bald mountain and near a large stone on which are many figures rudely engraved."

Many years ago there was a project to remove this curiosity to Franklin, but fortunately it is still to be seen in the original location, though the figures have been almost entirely obliterated.

De Bienville buried another plate at the fort near the mouth of French Creek, not far from the site of Franklin. Washington visited this fort in December, 1753. The next year Captain Joncaire, the commander, deciding to abandon the post, went down the Allegheny to Fort du Quesne, his one thousand soldiers and eighteen cannon being carried in sixty batteaux and three hundred canoes. Later they returned, but left again in 1759.

A cunning Indian stratagem succeeded in driving out the English in 1763. The Indians had been accustomed to playing football near the fort. When the ball went over the stockade they would be permitted to enter in search of it. On the day they planned to take the fort, a larger number than usual gathered to play. After a time the ball fell within the enclosure. The gate was opened for those who went after it, and the Indians rushed in, slew the garrison, and burned the fort. A few prisoners were taken, among them a woman who later told the story.

On the site of Franklin, troops from Fort Pitt erected

Fort Franklin in 1787. This fort proved a great protection to the pioneer settlers.

The pioneers of the country learned at least one helpful lesson from the Indians—the virtue of what was called Seneca Oil. This knowledge later enabled them to start an industry that made the county famous, as well as a number of surrounding counties, including Allegheny, Beaver, Butler, Clarion, Forest, Elk, Warren, McKean, and Tioga.

The Seneca oil was gathered from the creeks. A local paper of 1842 spoke of "the Seneca oil from the oil springs or oil creeks, used by the Seneca Indians as an unguent, and in their religious worship. It is almost as celebrated as the naphtha of the Caspian Sea. With it the Senecas mixed their war-paint, which gave them a hideous, glistening appearance, and added great permanency to the paint as it rendered it impervious to water."

The first serious attempt by white men to use the Seneca oil was made by a ferryman on French Creek. Discovering a spring from which the oil issued, he built a dam around it. When water was low, in the summertime, he would collect two or three quarts for use during the next year. Other settlers collected oil from Oil Creek, after building dams. Above a dam the oil would gather to a depth of two inches. This would be soaked into a blanket, and the blanket would be wrung into a barrel. Some of the oil thus secured was peddled over the surrounding country, at twenty-five cents a gill, as a medicine of rare value.

The first great oil well was dug just north of Titusville, over the line in Crawford County. Colonel E. L. Drake, who came to Titusville in 1857, was responsible for the well, and he thus became the real pioneer of the oil industry. When he became a bankrupt a grateful state voted to him and to his wife, should she survive him, a pension of fifteen hundred dollars a year.

The second great well, at Franklin, was so productive that the oil taken from it was worth two thousand dollars a day. Tidings of the new El Dorado flashed all over the country. By 1864 there was a rush of fortune hunters. "The tide of emigration that was poured upon the golden shores of California in 1849 was but a rippling of the waters, compared with the vast billows that rolled over the oil region of northwest Pennsylvania." In 1865, when Venango County was the only oil producer, thirteen thousand barrels a day were shipped. In 1866 it was reported at Franklin, "An incredible amount of business is transacted at the Register's office, reaching $1,000,000 a day in the transfer of leases alone."

During the height of the excitement, C. V. Culver started a bank in Franklin and made plans for a railroad and a new town. The town was to be called Reno, and it was to be the great metropolis of the oil region. "There is not a particle of doubt of the success of the plan," said the glowing prospectus printed in 1866. But the bank failed, and the plan came to nothing. The little town of Reno, on the Allegheny, halfway between Franklin and Oil City, is a reminder of the collapse.

One who was financially involved in this failure was philosophical enough to write:

"I stood beneath the hollow tree,
  The blast it hollow blew;
I thought upon the hollow world
  And all its hollow crew.
Ambition and its hollow schemes,
  The hollow hopes to follow,
Imagination's hollow dreams,
  All hollow, hollow, hollow."

SEEING PENNSYLVANIA

Oil City had its part in the great boom. A newspaper man who came in 1864 to study the situation, wrote a humorous description of what he saw that is appreciated by no one more than by the present residents of the bustling city on the Allegheny:

"Whew! what smells so? Nothing but the gaseous wealth of the oily region. But pigs, mud, no sidewalks! Ah, but you are on the river bank yet. Business can not afford to wash the ways down which oil barrels run nor to scrub their leaky sides. Wait until you reach the main thoroughfare, the grand promenade, the fashionable street of the place. I waited. That is, I walked between walls and oil yards, barns and pens, along the slippery ways, keeping my bearings as I could, and aiming for the Petroleum House first. I found the main street, the promenade, the leading thoroughfare. It was bare of trotting buggies. It was bare of handsome carriages. It was not at all dusty. Upon one side rose a ledge of shale rocks, crowned on top with the primeval forest. At its immediate foot ran the street. No, it didn't run. It couldn't run. Neither could it stand still. It was just too thick for water, and wholly too thin for land. Horses dragging heavy teams with a few barrels of oil sank below this scum and tugged on. Horsemen, booted to the middle, floundered this way and that. The narrowest plank walk filled with hurrying men, muddy and eager, pushed by. A slip of a team horse, and his effort at recovery, sent the liquid, oily, earthy mixture of the street in showers among the walkers. Everybody was used to it."

Andrew Carnegie had his share in the excitement of the day. In 1862 he bought a farm on Oil Creek, above Oil City, and for this he paid forty thousand dollars. The value rose to five millions, judged by the sale of shares on the market. In a single year one million dollars in dividends was paid.

Midway between Oil Creek and Titusville was Petroleum Center, another of the boom towns. At one time it had a population of three thousand, but to-day it is not on the map. An investor who sought the town in February, 1865, told of his experience in a letter characterized by the humor shown by so many who came this way. He began by saying he would not advise the pleasure seeker to select the route from Oil City to Petroleum Center, and continued:

"Let him go through the Dismal Swamp on a flat boat, anywhere rather than here, for anywhere else he will find fewer discomforts than in the dozen miles which separate this place from the mouth of Oil Creek. Without doubt it is a journey full of novelty, and wholly bereft of beauty. Majestic bluffs rise upon either side, almost shutting out the sky and world. In these and the narrow, ragged ribbon of heaven overhead, are much to awaken admiration. But those æsthetic qualities will in no wise compensate for being jolted twelve miles in a lumber wagon, during which operation the stream has to be crossed some half dozen times, either by swimming the horses or venturing them on ice that seems to possess anything but strength. . . . It is along the creek that the richest part of the oil region lies."

The route suggested in this chapter, after leaving Oil Creek, passes through Cornplanter township where—some five miles from the point where Pit Hole Creek joins the Allegheny—Pit Hole City sprang into being almost over night. In May, 1865, a gushing oil well was brought in. In September there were fifteen thousand people in the town. "Thither thousands daily rushed. On every train they came to the land of derricks. From the railroad they scattered on rickety horses, or rickety coaches on rickety roads in search of some spot where the 'grease' should shower upon them untold millions."

At the height of the excitement the farm on which the first well was struck sold for $1,600,000. But after a time the basin under the new location was exhausted, and the buildings were removed.

There were those who prophesied the exhaustion of oil in the country, but they declared that as oil production decreased the flow of gas would increase, since the shallower the deposits of oil the more favorable would be the conditions for the rapid distillation of gas.

The oil product continued to increase until 1891. Seventeen years later there was flowing from the Pennsylvania field less than one-third of the amount produced during the banner year. As the wells failed, pumping was resorted to. It was found to be profitable to pump for one-eighth of a barrel a day. But, according to the prophecy, the failure of the oil saw a proportionate increase in gas production in much of the old oil territory.

Tionesta, on the Allegheny in Forest County, shared in the oil excitement, but not to such an extent as Venango County towns. Here speculation was a little better controlled, though there were many instances of rapid advance in prices. One tract of thirty acres sold for forty thousand dollars; later one-fourth of this tract brought forty-five thousand dollars.

David Zeisberger left in his diary an account of the oil springs on the banks of the Allegheny from which the Indians gathered rheumatism and toothache medicine. His observations were made in 1767, at a point four miles below Tionesta. At this place, which the Indians called Gosgoschunk, he labored for some time with the natives. On the walls of the Historical Society of Pennsylvania there is a painting representing the devoted missionary preaching to the people, of whom he wrote, "I have never found such heathen." In 1769 he removed to Lawunukhannock, "the meeting of the waters," where Hickory Creek enters the Allegheny.

Not far from Lawunukhannock the deer and the bear had a favorite crossing place. In winter wolves were often seen to run the deer on the ice and then kill them. Zeisberger told of seeing two thousand deer killed by the Indians while he was in the neighborhood.

The waters about Tionesta were once freighted with great rafts. Tionesta Creek, especially, brought down to the Allegheny vast quantities of timber. Sawmills were erected near the town as early as 1803.

Tionesta Creek rises in Warren County. It drew on that county for many of the rafts it floated. Warren had great forests of white pine. Brokenstraw Creek, Conewango Creek, and Kinzua Creek were also famous lumbering streams. On them small rafts were floated to the Allegheny, and these were then built into larger rafts, from 250 to 300 feet long and from 60 to 70 feet wide, for floating down the river to Pittsburgh and Cincinnati.

Near the mouth of the Brokenstraw the road passes through Irvineton, a town which the builder, Dr. William Irvine of Philadelphia, tried to name Cornplanter, in honor of the Indian chief who was the friend of all the white settlers in that section. Believing that a railroad would come to the valley, Irvine proposed to be ready. Among other stone buildings he erected the Cornplanter Hotel, "in a style that would do honor to Philadelphia," a wandering writer of the day said. He built stores, bridged the creek, and erected a mill. But his plans for the town miscarried.

At the mouth of the Conewango, near the site of Warren, the county seat, Celeron de Bienville planted one of his six leaden plates. Watchful Indians promptly dug this up as soon as he departed. Warren is a thriving town, advantageously located. It has never been lacking in proper local pride. As long ago as March 20, 1849, the editor of the town paper said:

"Two steamers in to-day; . . . Oh, how we flourish. This is a great town. . . . Think of it! Two steamers in one day; two acres of rafts lying in the eddy, and others passing every moment. Crowds of people thronging the streets and room for more."

One of Warren's reasons for self-gratulation was the provision made in 1861 by the will of Henry R. Rouse, oil operator, for the construction of roads and bridges. The remarkable thing about this will is that it was drawn during the few hours of intense suffering that followed an explosion of gas in one of his own wells. Those who use the county's roads—as well as the poor to whom he left another large portion of his fortune—have had reason to be thankful for this man who felt that his money should remain in the county where he had gained it.

From Warren the road, turning southeast, reaches the Tionesta and follows the creek for a few miles, then crosses once more into Forest County, not far from the entrance into the creek of the small parallel runs called Blue Sheriff and White Sheriff. The man who named the little streams was something of a humorist. In company with the sheriff of Forest County and the sheriff of Warren County, he was on a surveying expedition. The creeks were unnamed, and names were desired. It so happened that one sheriff wore a blue suit that day, while the other wore a light summer suit. What could be easier? The waters were christened forthwith.

There is another water course in the county called

THE START OF A FOREST FIRE
Photo by State Department of Forestry

PINE ROCKS, BETWEEN BEECH CREEK AND RENOVO
Photo by State Department of Forestry

TWO MILES SOUTHEAST OF CLEARFIELD
Photo by C. W. Howard

THROUGH THE OIL REGIONS

Jug Handle. The name was suggested when a pioneer was drinking from a jug, which fell to the ground, leaving the handle only in his fingers.

It is characteristic of the county that the streams flow through gorges, and that they have on their banks hills ranging from five hundred to eight hundred feet high. On the south these hills slope gradually, but on the north they are quite steep.

One of the highest points in the county is at Marienville, once the county seat, a town passed on the highway just before crossing the line into Clarion County. This high point is on Big Level Ridge, a peculiar continuous high summit that stretches from Clearfield County, across Jefferson and Forest, and into McKean County. At Marienville this reaches up 1728 feet.

It is fortunate that a railroad runs through this beautiful country between Marienville and Clarion, a country of hills and forests and valleys where—

"The rounded world is fair to see,
Nine times folded in mystery:
Though baffled seers cannot impart
The secret of the laboring heart,
Throb thine with Nature's throbbing breast,
And all is clear from east to west.
Spirit that lurks each form within
Beckons to spirit of its kin;
Self-kindled every atom glows
And hints the future which it owes."[1]

Bold knobs and undulating uplands are characteristic of the county. The average elevation is about thirteen hundred feet. Once the hills and valleys were covered with primeval forests of pine, hemlock, and oak, but forest fires and careless lumbering have denuded many of the townships of the best timber.

---
[1] Emerson.

The Clarion River cuts diagonally across the county and meets the Allegheny near the western border after a strangely tortuous course whose beginning is at Callensburg. This town is on a height above the stream, overlooking both Clarion and Licking Creeks. The latter stream empties into the river squarely against the current.

A few miles below, at Alum Rock, another stream enters the Clarion from a glen of wild beauty cut from the solid rock. The cliffs, almost perpendicular, are covered with foliage. Scattered here and there are great boulders against which, especially in flood times, the little creek dashes in its passage to the river.

Foxburg, near the junction of the Clarion and the Allegheny, has one of the most advantageous situations in the state, from a scenic point of view. From above the town the view of wooded heights and the deep gorges of both rivers is most effective. One visitor insists that "the mountain grandeur almost equals the scenery of Kittanning Point, with the additional charm of water scenery."

Near Foxburg are some of the best forest lands left in the state. There are eight thousand acres of the finest primeval timber. The richest landscape in the county is spread out before those who go to the southwestern corner, where the Allegheny doubles on itself, making a great horseshoe bend, the distance across the isthmus being less than a mile, while the distance around by water is eight miles. The best view is from the heights, near the junction of the East Brady and Phillipsburg Roads, in what is known as "the neck." This bend was the scene of a battle with the Indians when the savages were defeated.

Back now to Clarion, the county seat. The town is

THROUGH THE OIL REGIONS

built on a level stretch of a turnpike which was frequently used in early days as a racecourse. From points of vantage in and near the town the prospect of river and valley is such as to make one wish to linger. But the pleasant scenes are not gone when Clarion is left behind. Strattonville, two miles distant, is built on a ridge, and here also the reputation of the road for beauty is maintained.

All the way from Clarion, past Strattonville, through Jefferson County, to Du Bois, where the route outlined for this chapter turns aside to the south, the highway followed is that of the Oil City route, famed for its long-distance views from the heights. This was originally known as the Susquehanna and Waterford Turnpike, and it follows much the same route as the Old State Road to Erie, laid out in 1796, which was used in the transport of troops from Franklin County to Erie during the War of 1812. The later road was authorized in 1812, incorporated in 1817, and completed in 1822. Until the days of the railroad this artery of travel always did a rushing business. Stage coaches, conestogas and herds of cattle followed one another in quick succession. Emigrants found it a link in the shortest route between Philadelphia and the West, and in the decade 1840 and 1850 countless prairie schooners passed this way. Frequently there were from fifteen to twenty-five of these in a train, each party having its own leader and guides.

Until this great improvement was completed, those who were compelled to pass through this region felt like voicing some such protest as that of one pioneer:

"How can I e'er the road describe?
'Twould take a far more skillful scribe
Than I; so I will silent be,
Lest some doubt my veracity.

"Enough that 'twas most horrid bad
Than ever I experienced had,
And yet so light our sufferings were
That to complain would not be fair.

"For 'twas as good a road, I see,
As such a road could ever be!
So we take courage and rejoice
Because the weather was most choice."

There is nothing like a sense of humor to lighten the burdens of the road, even burdens like those of the pioneer of 1797 who cleared from the primeval forest a farm on what was to be the site of the turnpike, west of Waterford. His nearest neighbor to the east was at Curwensville, Clearfield County, thirty-three miles away. When he was out of provisions he was accustomed to go to Pittsburgh for them. Once he packed sixty pounds of flour on his back all the way, though more often he used the canoe to transport supplies up the Allegheny and the Red Bank.

To many who pass through this region of rugged hills, with the evidence everywhere that here once was the country of magnificent forests and that the rich vegetation of ages long past underlaid the forests and the hills with rich deposits of coal, the story set down by those who have given their lives to baring the secrets of the formation of these hills and rocks and coal beds is fascinating. How did the rocky ridges come to be as they are? How was the coal formed? Why is the coal here bituminous instead of anthracite?

However geologists may differ in their theories, these theories are alike appealing to the lovers of Nature and of Him who made the hills, "rock ribbed and ancient as the sun," who placed the coal and the oil and the gas where they would supply the needs of His people of yesterday, to-day, and of the generations to come.

The story has never been more appealingly told than in the popular presentation made by Henry M. Alden in *Harper's Magazine* for September, 1863:

"Once America was a long narrow island, reaching from Nova Scotia to the far west; neither Alleghenies nor Rocky Mountains as yet existed, but a great ocean spread away to the north, and another to the south. Gradually, on either side, by the action of the waters, vast deposits of stratified rock were formed, which, accumulating, were at length raised to the surface at numerous points, forming low, marshy islands. These became covered with a luxuriant vegetation, under conditions of atmosphere peculiarly favorable to such growth; generations of this rapid growth quickly succeeded each other, the decay of each forming the basis of that which followed. For ages this process went on; and when the Alleghenies were afterward upheaved in successive ranges to the southward, the reader can easily imagine the great disturbance, the distortion and the dislocation which these stratified deposits must have undergone. He will remember, too, that these ridges, thus suddenly upheaved, must have imprisoned many a large, inlying body of water, which, in proportion to the resistance offered, would the more insistently force various outlets to the open seas beyond, and in its way out would, with its tumultuous current, tear up the already loosened strata—if possible sweeping these entirely away, but otherwise leaving them behind in confused heaps. The ranges of the Alleghenies increase in height as we proceed southward, till in North Carolina they rise more than six thousand feet above the level of the sea. The more southern ranges, being later in their upheaval, and therefore meeting with greater resistance from the continually hardening crust of the earth, were for this reason thrown up to a great height, power in all cases being measured by resistance. These ranges, therefore, offered a proportionally greater resistance to the escape of the waters which they enclosed; hence the greater violence of the escaping waters, which accounts for the fact that, for the most part, the coal measures of the south have been swept away. In regions where there was no violent action of water at all, as in western Pennsylvania, we have the soft bituminous coal, the hydrogen of which has never been permitted to escape; and the reason that we have no bituminous coal in eastern Pennsylvania, as a general thing, is this: The external disturbances which affected the strata, though insufficient to sweep them away, yet so effectually exposed them to the air that the soft coal became in time hardened to anthracite."

Brookville in the midst of the soft coal country, has long been a center of traffic both by land and water. Its situation on the turnpike was a factor that entered into the calculations of those who kept store here as early as 1840. Merchants who ordered their goods from Philadelphia counted on the service of a conestoga freight line that ran through from the city twice each year, Shippensville in Clarion County being the end of the route. When they had to go to Philadelphia themselves, it was necessary to allow two days and a half for the trip on the "limited mail coach" to Lewistown, and one day and a half more, by canal and railroad, to complete the journey.

One of the obstacles that delayed traffic in those days, and hence caused much displeasure, was precisely the feature that to-day is most appreciated in the landscape —the forests. A writer of 1830 gave expression to the common idea when he said, "The scenery around the town would be fine were it not that all the hills, except at the north side, are still clothed by the virginal forests of pine."

One reason for the desire to see the forests disappear

ON THE ROAD FROM TIONESTA TO CLARION
Photo by State Department of Forestry

ON THE PLATEAU BETWEEN CLEARFIELD AND PENFIELD
Photo by State Department of Forestry

was that the falling trees and branches impeded communication by land. An extreme example of the difficulty was recorded when the builders of the turnpike approached Reynoldsville, east of Brookville. Trees were found lying about everywhere. The limbs had completely rotted away and the trunks had nearly disappeared. "They were so thick that it was almost impossible to go a couple of rods without coming across one or more." The trunks were so rotten they would not bear a man's weight. It was thought that they had been blown down by some storm a century or two before, for a forest of gigantic trees was growing above the prostrate trunks.

The first rafts from these great forests of white and yellow pine, hemlock and oak, were started for Pittsburgh on Sandy Lick which enters Red Bank Creek at Brookville. The industry grew rapidly, and was at its height between 1850 and 1860. At this period, during the spring freshets, it is said that one raft would not be out of sight before another appeared around the bend east of the town. Some immense timbers were brought from the forests for these rafts. The largest, probably, was a pine log fifty feet long from a tree one hundred and twenty-five feet tall. Eight oxen had all they could do to take it from the spot where it was cut to Sandy Lick. There it was found to be too large for a raft, and it was sent down the river by itself. A year was required for the journey to Pittsburgh, since it was impossible for a lumberman to accompany it for a through journey; the method adopted was for a passing raftsman to take it on a part of the way, then leave it for some one else.

A second huge log, seventy-five feet long, was made into a canoe. This was hauled to Sandy Lick by a yoke of oxen and was then taken to McKee's Rocks with a cargo of venison and bears' meat. For many years gardeners used it to carry vegetables to Pittsburgh.

At Reynoldsville the turnpike is left behind. But what the road to Punxsutawney lacks in perfection is made up in scenery, since it leads through a section that shows well the character of the rugged country. Near the beginning of the road is an elevation which looks down on the deep valley of Sandy Lick and over toward the valley of Red Bank. These valleys of Jefferson County are from three hundred to five hundred feet deep. In many places the streams are in V-shaped canyons, sometimes with precipitous walls on both banks, again with a slope on one bank, or still again with slopes on both banks. While there are no mountain ridges, there are summits as high as from sixteen hundred to eighteen hundred feet.

Mahoning Creek—the Mohulbucteetan of the Indians, (meaning "where canoe is abandoned"), at Punxsutawney, is a delightful mountain stream on whose banks are many points of great interest. One of these is not far from the town. On the slope of a hill above the creek are numerous large sandstone boulders, remarkable not merely for their size but for the strange kettle-shaped holes in them, evidently the work of men. One of the rocks contains twenty such holes.

Punxsutawney, "the town of the Ponkis" (or gnats), has been spelled in numberless ways. Zeisberger called the place Ponksutenik. Others wrote the word Puncksotownay. Pukeisheno was still another form.

At Punxsutawney are the headquarters of one of the four troops of the famous Pennsylvania Mounted Police, headquarters for the other three troops being at Greensburg, Reading, and Wyoming. Every Pennsylvanian should know and be proud of the story of this splendid body of men, for they have attracted the attention of leaders in many other states, as well as of some who live across the sea.

The story goes back to 1902, the year of the anthracite coal strike. President Roosevelt by timely intervention put an end to the struggle that lasted more than four months, caused endless confusion, and cost perhaps $100,000,000.

The Anthracite Strike Commission, the body appointed by the President to bring peace, strongly recommended the organization of the State Police, "or a proper executive body to enforce the laws with impartial might," in a territory where "the large rural population, the mountainous region, the industrial centers, and foreign immigration" made such a force necessary.[1]

In 1903 Governor Pennypacker recommended the organization of the State Police, and in 1905 he signed the act for the creation of that body whose task it should be to prevent crimes and secure the punishment of criminals in the rural districts of the state.

Captain John C. Groome, Commander of Philadelphia's First City Troop, was made Superintendent, and to him was committed the preparation for and the organization of the State Constabulary. The appointment was justified by his performances, and the performances have been so heartily approved that Colonel Groome, as he is now known, was made head of the military police in that part of France occupied by American armies during the recent war.

Before making definite plans for his new work, Colonel Groome went to Ireland to study the Royal

---

[1] "Justice to All," by Katharine Mayo.

Irish Constabulary. Ireland is about the same in size as Pennsylvania, but ten thousand constables are employed there, while the Pennsylvania act called for only two hundred and twenty-eight men.

When preliminaries had been concluded, and the men honored by appointment had been enrolled, Colonel Groome made known to them his instructions, in part as follows:

"It is possible for a man to be a gentleman as well as a policeman.

"I expect you to treat elderly persons, women and children at all times with the greatest consideration.

"When once you start after a man, *you must get him*.

"In making an arrest you may use no force beyond the uniform necessity.

"One State policeman should be able to handle one hundred foreigners."

The constabulary began work in 1906, and nothing better can be said of them than that they have measured up to the program the commander laid down for them.

Miss Mayo, the Boswell of the body, who, in a fascinating manner, has written of their prowess in a series of difficult though typical cases, has given a brief yet suggestive summary of their activities:

"Here they picked up a country store robber; there a stabber of a night watchman; again a molester of women; a carrier of concealed weapons; a farm thief; a setter of forest fires, and always a little harvest of killers of song birds. . . . Meantime they were dealing constantly with the unassimilated foreign element, teaching it by small but repeated object lessons that a new gospel was abroad in the land."

What a wonderful thing it would have been if Pennsylvania had possessed such a body when the Molly Maguires were abroad in the anthracite region!

THROUGH THE OIL REGIONS

Travelers on the highways should, if possible, visit the barracks at one of the troop headquarters, and should watch for the brawny men, who usually ride alone, each with his horse, his comrade. They will be known by their gentlemanly bearing, their look of determination, and the uniform—a military tunic and riding trousers of dark gray whipcord, black pigskin puttees, black boots, nickel strap spurs, reinforced helmet with black leather strap, and black horsehide gauntlets.

From the Punxsutawney headquarters the members of the constabulary are able to go quickly to any danger point in western Pennsylvania. Frequently they ride toward Pittsburgh, taking the route across the northwest corner of Indiana County and through the heart of Armstrong County as followed in this chapter.

There is water along this road and there are hills—two things that help to make a country interesting. The Little Mahoning stretches across the highway in Indiana County, and in Armstrong County the traveler skirts a tributary of the Allegheny all the way to Kittanning, then follows the river which the Indians called the Ohio to the Kiskiminetas, at the southwest border of the county, and from there on to Pittsburgh.

Kittanning, beautiful for situation, is on the spot where stood the Indian village of that name, the terminus of the Kittanning Path over the mountains from Black Log Valley and Standing Stone (now Huntingdon). Another Indian path led to Le Bœuf from Pine Creek, ten miles north of Kittanning.

The Indian town was destroyed in 1756, when three hundred and seven men marched across the mountain from Fort Shirley, in what is now Huntingdon County, to release eleven prisoners held by the Indians. The savages were surprised at a dance, and the town was destroyed. Colonel Armstrong, who had charge of the rescuing party, was highly commended for his heroism and ability in leading his men through a hostile county, and for the triumphant close of the expedition. The Indians' operations were much hampered by the burning of the village, for from this base operations had been conducted against the frontier during the French and Indian War.

Twelve years later, when the Fort Stanwix treaty transferred to Pennsylvania the Susquehanna lands, Kittanning was a point named on the western boundary. The line led from here to Canoe Place, at the source of the West Branch of the Susquehanna.

One of the red letter occasions in the history of the Kittanning of the early nineteenth century was the day in 1827 when the first steamer ascended the river from Pittsburgh. "Against the rapid current she steamed it majestically at the rate of four miles an hour," read one contemporary account. "She was a beautiful boat of fifty tons," the record concluded.

The coming of a steamer during the next year called out even greater eloquence:

"A sound was heard down the river, 'an unco sugh,' as Burns says, which was soon recognized to be the puffing of a steamboat. The town was immediately in a buzz. All looked to catch a glimpse of the *water-walker*, as she came around the bend below the town. Presently the bright glow of the furnaces burst upon the sight; the report of the swivel resounded among the hills and the boat rushed through the yielding current amid the cheers of the people and was safely moored alongside the wharf. She proved to be the Pittsburgh and Wheeling Packet, of one hundred tons, owned by the Society of Harmonists at Economy—a beautiful vessel, very handsomely furnished with two decks."

Nearly fifty years later, in 1876, Dom Pedro went up the valley, though he went by train instead of by steamer. He was then returning from California, where he had seen the wonders of that state; but he declared that Allegheny Valley was one of the finest he had ever passed through.

Almost all the way from Kittanning to the Kiskiminetas the river flows through a deep, rocky ravine, and is remarkable for rugged scenery, as is the Kiskiminetas, the stream which guided the Pennsylvania canal on its way to the Allegheny and to Pittsburgh.

These deep gorges in the Allegheny have caused many destructive ice jams. One of the worst of these occurred in the winter of 1837 and 1838. A jam that formed below Kittanning backed up the water and the flats below the town were covered. The people escaped to the hills, but in half an hour, relieved by the breaking of the jam, they returned to their homes.

At that period there were twenty-four salt wells in Armstrong County, most of them along the Allegheny and the Kiskiminetas. During one year the product was 65,500 barrels, all secured from wells from five hundred to six hundred and fifty feet deep. The wells were three inches in diameter to a depth of two hundred feet, then two inches. The cost of drilling was two dollars a foot for the first five hundred feet, and three dollars from that point. Yet the cost of a barrel was only two dollars and twelve cents.

An ingenious method was adopted to prevent fresh water from mingling with the salt water in the well. A bag of flaxseed was attached to a copper tube, and this was dropped into a well until the bag reached the salt water. The flaxseed would swell, the hole around the tube would be filled, and the fresh water above could not reach the salt water below.

Not many miles below the mouth of the Kiskiminetas, on the Westmoreland County side, between Logan's Ferry, Allegheny County, and Parnassus, Westmoreland County, is a bridge over Big Pucketa Creek worth looking at, not because there is anything remarkable about the bridge but because of something that happened there. Katharine Mayo has told the story.[2]

On a December night it was raining, raining, raining. "Still the torrents descended, lashed by a screaming wind, and the song of rushing waters mingled with the cry of the gale." The call came to the State Constabulary at Greensburg for help at a foundry town on the Allegheny River, and a detail of troopers was sent out into the storm, First-Sergeant Price, riding his faithful steed, John G, leading the way. Both horse and rider had been on the force from its organization, and the horse was twenty-two years old.

Progress was rapid in spite of the storm, until they reached a portion of the road near Logan's Ferry that was under twenty feet of water from the overflowed river. So there was no way to cross the river unless the party should ride to Pittsburgh and up the other bank.

Did they turn back? Members of the Pennsylvania State Constabulary do not know how to turn back when duty calls them on.

Sergeant Price thought of a railroad bridge. The bridge was found. "But behold, its floor was of crossties only—of sleepers to carry the rails, laid with wide breaks between, gaping down into deep, dark space whose bed was the roaring river."

The leader had a plan. Two of the troopers were sent

---

[2] "The Standard Bearers."

to secure two planks from a railroad yard across the bridge. They soon returned with two 2 x 12 inch timbers, and with the word that no train was due until five o'clock in the morning. The planks were laid end to end across the first ties.

"Come along, John; it's all right, old man!" the sergeant spoke to his horse, at the same time caressing him. Then he led the animal to the first plank. Two men were detailed to walk on each side of him.

Delicately, nervously, John G set his feet, step by step, till he reached the center of the second plank.

There the sergeant talked to him quietly again, while two troopers picked up the board just quitted, to lay it in advance.

"And so, length by length, they made the passage, the horse moving with extremest caution, shivering with full appreciation of the unaccustomed danger, yet steadied by his master's presence and by the friend on either side.

"As they moved, the gale wreaked all its fury on them. It was growing colder now, and the rain, changed to sleet, stung their skins with its tiny, sharp-driven blades. The skeleton bridge held them high suspended in the very heart of the storm. Once and again a sudden more violent gust bid fair to sweep them off their feet. Yet, slowly progressing, they made their port unharmed."

One by one, in the same way, the other horses were led over the stream. Then the troopers moved on, did their work, and, responding to a hurry call from Greensburg, returned through the storm by the same route, meeting difficulties as before.

The story would be incomplete without an additional touch. When John G was in his stable at last, his master, after riding eighty-six miles within twenty-four hours, without rest, spent three hours rubbing him down. Only at midnight, when there was not a damp hair on the animal's body, was the weary horse-lover free to sleep.

Now does it seem strange that the Pennsylvania Mounted Constabulary is accomplishing what may seem to be impossibilities?

More than one hundred and sixty years before John G and his master braved the storm and crossed the swollen stream at the call of duty, and only a few miles below, George Washington, by night, crossed the Allegheny, then in flood, and filled with treacherous ice. He too, was responding to the call of duty. His sole companion was Christopher Gist. Though they had no tool but "one poor hatchet," together they made a raft and on this they embarked. Let the man who lived to become the Father of His Country tell the story of what followed:

"Before we were half way over, we were jammed in the ice in such a manner that we expected every moment our raft to sink and ourselves to perish. I put out my setting pole to try to stop the raft that the ice might pass by, when the rapidity of the stream threw it with so much violence against the pole that it jerked us out into ten feet of water. Notwithstanding all our efforts, we could not get to either shore, but were obliged, as we were near an island, to quit our raft and make to it. The cold was so extremely severe that Mr. Gist had all his fingers and some of his toes frozen, and the water was shut up so hard that we found no difficulty in getting off the island on the ice in the morning."

The island on which Washington and Gist sought refuge that awful night is now known as Washington Island. It is within the limits of Pittsburgh.

ROUTE VIII
THROUGH THE HEART OF THE BLACK FOREST
A ROUND TRIP TO THE NORTH OF ALTOONA ABOUT 350 MILES

Now the joys of the road are chiefly these:
A crimson touch on the hardwood trees;

A shadowy highway cool and brown,
Alluring up and enticing down.

And O the joy that is never won,
But follows and follows the journeying sun,

By marsh and tide, by meadow and stream,
A will-o'-the-wisp, a light o' dream,

Delusion afar, delight anear,
From morrow to morrow, from year to year,
—*Bliss Carman.*

It was a Scotch soldier in France who wrote home: "I hope when the war is over that I may be able to spend a month somewhere among the hills; I often think that if more people in the world had lived among such hills as we have in Scotland there would have been no world war."

The nature lover who sees the glory of the hills in the central Pennsylvania highlands will be able to sympathize with the Scotchman, for he knows well that there is nothing like intimate touch with hill and forest to bring and keep one in touch with Him who laid the foundations of the earth, who stretched forth the heavens like a curtain, who speaks from Nature's solitudes, "Be still, and know that I am God."

Altoona is the natural starting point for a tour of the country of north central Pennsylvania, where, as has been said by one who knows the state thoroughly, "the scenery is easily the finest in Pennsylvania." The best part of this wild region is included in the tour marked out in this chapter; at least that is what will be felt until there is intimate acquaintance with counties farther east like Lycoming and Sullivan. Then clamor will be heard that the palm should be reserved for these counties. The truth is, the whole region is so wonderfully satisfying that it is difficult to compare counties and sections.

The way from Altoona is by the beautiful Tuckahoe Valley to Tyrone, the picturesque Blair County town situated in a valley so narrow that at one point an immense flag has been hung on a cable stretched from one side to the other. On the left Tussey's Mountain lifts its head, while Bald Eagle Mountain looks down on the town from the right.

Bald Eagle Valley, beyond Tyrone, affords a passage for both railroad and highway. The railroad turns to the left within a few miles, and climbs rapidly about one thousand feet in a dozen miles. Engineering problems even greater than those beyond Altoona, on the main line of the Pennsylvania, confronted the engineers who surveyed the road this short distance. The greatest achievement was the building of the Mule Shoe Curve in Emigh's Gap, eight miles from Tyrone. Here the curve is far more abrupt than at Kittanning Point, and the scenery is much more startling. The

GAP IN BALD EAGLE MOUNTAIN, LOOKING NORTH FROM BELLEFONTE
Photo by the Mallory Studio

WHERE CLEARFIELD GETS HER DRINKING WATER
(Montgomery Dam, five miles up on the mountain)
Photo by C. W. Howard

summit is crossed five miles farther on at a point where the view to the north reaches far into the watershed of the West Branch of the Susquehanna.

There is a wagon road that keeps near the railroad across the summit, but if there is desire for a smooth surface and an easier trip it will be found better to keep on the main highway as far as Port Matilda, turning there on the Susquehanna and Waterford turnpike toward Philipsburg.

Philipsburg on the Moshannon is four hundred and forty-five feet above Tyrone. The town was once called Moshannon, the name of the Indian village located on the site. Later, however, the name was changed in honor of a pioneer settler who came at a time when the best means of communication with the outside world was a footpath to Bellefonte.

Between the Moshannon at Philipsburg and the Susquehanna at Clearfield there are numerous long-distance outlooks along this section of the Oil City route. From the heights above Clearfield a number of the bends of the Susquehanna are in sight—a stream so crooked that in the diagonal course through Clearfield County the distance from border to border is almost one hundred miles, though a straight line measures less than fifty miles. No wonder the Six Nations called the river Quenischa-chack-ki, "the stream with long reaches."

Clearfield, the county seat, once had a name as unusual as that of the creek, Chinklacamoose. This was the name of an Indian town on the site. The later title, Clearfield, was bestowed because here was a plateau where the trees were few compared with those on the surrounding mountains.

Originally Clearfield was in the midst of forests of white pine, but lumbering operations were carried on so lavishly and so furiously that by 1884 these had almost entirely disappeared. Then lumbering had to be confined largely to the forests of hemlock and oak. The town is now a center of operation for the State Department of Forestry. The water supply is secured from a watershed protected by the department; a small revenue accrues from this source.

Bilger's Rocks near Curwensville and Luthersburg Knob, two thousand feet high, near Luthersburg, are but two of the numberless attractions along the line of the highway from Clearfield to the western border of a county noted for its scenery. Luthersburg is in Brady township, named for Captain Samuel Brady, Indian fighter and hunter.

Near Luthersburg, in 1830, a traveler saw on a wayside inn a sign displaying a bit of doggerel on which the pioneers and those who came after them acted all too literally:

"It is God's will
The woods must yield
And the wildwood turn
To a fruitful field."

Most of the towns and villages in the county owe their origin and initial prosperity to the purpose to remove the trees as soon as possible. In some of them the chief industry is still the handling of trees from the forests, such as they are, or some closely allied activities like tanning.

A little north of Luthersburg is Dubois and the great Beaver Meadow, 1390 feet above the sea. This is a plain five miles long and half a mile or more wide, where there is a fall of but twenty-one feet in five miles. The Cornplanter or Seneca Indians used to enjoy camping on this "geological breakdown," as it has been called by scientists. The place is like the bowl of a saucer, surrounded as it is on all sides by high hills.

The highlands continue into Elk County. Just over the border, in Fox township, a great trough is formed by Boone's Mountain on the east and Shawmut Mountain on the west. Farther north Boot Jack, near Ridgeway, is 2166 feet high. The hills about the town range from three hundred to six hundred feet above the Clarion River, which sweeps past the town after a headlong course from the north.

It has been claimed—and the claim seems to be justified—that some of the finest mountain scenery in the state is in the Elk Mountain region, near Johnsonburg. The seven miles of the road from Johnsonburg to Wilcox, directly on the present route, are through the finest part of the Elk Mountains. Here "striking peaks, sharp and glittering as the Matterhorn, surround one on all sides." The highest point in the region is Jarrett Summit, 2245 feet.

To the left, in the next township, the Big Level Ridge has an elevation ranging above two thousand feet. On the summit, in Revolutionary days, a military road was placed, for this was the easiest passage through a difficult country.

Fortunately the pioneers were not discouraged by the prospect of facing the privations of this mountain region. Some came singly and some came in companies. At least two picturesque colonies located in this county. One of these came to New Flanders, near Johnsonburg. Although encouraged in their venture by the Belgian government, they soon grew weary of the situation and vanished one by one. To St. Mary's, east of Ridgway, came a second colony that persisted, some of them from Baltimore and some from Philadelphia. A committee of the Benedictines, commissioned to investigate the situation, preceded the company and bought twenty-five thousand dollars' worth of land at seventy-five cents an acre. On November 1, 1842, a Baltimore contingent set out on the journey to the chosen spot. They took railroad to Columbia, then canal to Freeport. From there the way led overland. It is interesting to read their list of expenses: Transport, $86.69; utensils, $13.46; groceries, $18.02; books, $2.75; cash, $80; miscellaneous, $14.20; or not much more than two hundred dollars for the fifteen persons in the group.

When the first residents of St. Mary's were clearing the forests game was still plentiful. The country was one of the last resorts in the state of the buffalo as well as of the elk. In the northern part of the county, along the Clarion River, there are many isolated rocks and ledges, each of them the scene of the last stand of some hounded elk; it is said to have been the custom of the elk to seek an eminence at the last.

While the elk have disappeared, there is still much game in the mountains. There are wild-cats and there are bears. A local sportsman who writes of a modern bear hunt in Elk County, began by saying:

"Pennsylvania is the greatest bear state in the Union —or the world, either, for that matter, possibly excepting Alaska, which is several times its size. People don't realize that, if they kill a dozen bears in Colorado or Wyoming in a season, it is heralded far and wide, and the following year a small army of Pennsylvanians and other big game hunters spend some thousands apiece out there trying to get a bear, while they might in one-tenth the time and with one-fifteenth the expense run up into Elk, or McKean, or Potter, or Cameron, or Clinton, or some other nearby Pennsylvania county, and

HIGHWAY BRIDGE ACROSS ELK CREEK, NEAR RIDGWAY
Photo by State Highway Department

OLD HIGHWAY BRIDGE, NEAR BRADFORD
Photo by State Highway Department

FIRST FORK OF SINNEMAHONING, NEAR COSTELLO
Photo by State Department of Forestry

THROUGH THE BLACK FOREST

get one of the five hundred or six hundred bears that are killed in Pennsylvania every year."

Among the valiant hunters of the old days was Ga-ni-o-de-uh, or Cornplanter, friend of the whites, who, for services rendered to Pennsylvania in the Indian wars, in 1790 was allowed to select six hundred and forty acres on the west bank of the Allegheny northeast of Warren in Warren County, in the northeast corner of the county. Here his descendants, in number about two hundred, live in peace and plenty. The town of Cornplanter is on the route between Warren and Bradford, not far from the Indian cemetery where is the impressive monument erected by Pennsylvania to Cornplanter in 1868. This notes that the chief was 108 years old when he died, an age reached also by Jesse Logan, son of Captain John Logan, who died in 1916. Edward Cornplanter, grandson of the Ga-ni-o-de-uh, died in 1918. He was known among his own people as Sosondowa, "great night." Cornplanter chose his land in a region where the Indians delighted to roam. One of their favorite camping grounds was near the site of Bradford, McKean County. On Mount Raub, above the old camping grounds, they were accustomed to light signal fires to warn friends of the approach of enemies, or to pass the word that friends were coming to them.

Bradford, beautifully situated in the valley of the Tuna, or Tunuanguant, "big bullfrog," was a small village until the oil excitement of the late seventies brought population and prosperity. In 1883, during the early days of the new regime, Colonel A. K. McClure, of Philadelphia, wrote in the paper whose editor he was:

"The houses as a rule are pitched together like a winter camp, with here and there a solid brick edifice to mock the makeshift structures around it. The oil exchange is a beautiful building, and looks as if it were expected that oil gambling would continue even after the day of doom, regardless of the shifting of oil center."

The year before Colonel McClure wrote there was built, south of Bradford, the famous Kinzua viaduct, over Kinzua Creek. At the time this was spoken of as one of the greatest pieces of bridge engineering in the world. The trains passed three hundred and one feet above the bed of the creek on a structure 2051 feet long. This consisted of twenty lower spans of thirty-eight feet each and twenty-one intermediate spans of sixty-one feet each. That the viaduct might be made practicable for the heaviest trains of the day, it was rebuilt in 1900, on the old foundations. The weight of the original structure was 3,105,000 pounds. The weight of the present structure is 6,705,000 pounds.

An earlier engineering marvel was the Peg Leg Railroad, from Bradford to Tarport. This road was given up long ago, but it was such a curious structure that its story should be told. Let this be done in the words of Eli Perkins, who traveled by the road:

"The cars run astride an elevated track on a single rail. This rail is nailed to a single wooden stringer which rests on the top of piles. So evenly balanced is the train that, passing over a pond or creek at the rate of 20 miles an hour, the water is hardly disturbed. The motive for building is economy, the price per mile being $3,000, and the price of a ten-ton locomotive $3,000. The locomotive is a queer-looking thing. An Irishman has compared it to a gigantic pair of boots swinging on a clothes line. The boiler is without a flue, the engine without a piston, and the driver without a crank."

On this short road ten double trips were made each day "and there was an accident nearly every

THROUGH THE BLACK FOREST

trip." The life of the monstrosity was a little over two years; then it was sold by the sheriff, and the rails were removed.

The stiff grades mounted by railroads in McKean County may be imagined from the fact that while Smethport, southeast of Bradford, is but 1488 feet high, Prospect Peak, only a little more than two miles east, is 2495 feet. The railroad has to climb 1007 feet in this distance.

Smethport is on Potato Creek, a stream so named because a pioneer lost some potatoes from a canoe in the water. It is not strange that some citizens of the town wish to restore the Indian name of the stream, Nun-un-dah.

The first settlers near Smethport came up Potato Creek in 1810, bringing their families and goods in canoes. They had no such roads as have since been provided in all directions through a country not the best for road-building. Perhaps the difficulties encountered by one road contractor would have been a good reason for calling the highway laid out in 1825 from Ceres through Smethport, and the southwest, the "serious road." Yet this was not the explanation. It was once referred to officially as New Series. Later others called it simply Series. Serious was the final step in the development of the name.

Annin Township, south of Ceres Township, in which the Serious Road had its beginning, furnshes another example of curious nomenclature. A village in the township is called Turtle Point, because in 1836, the workmen discovered a huge turtle buried in the mill race of the first saw-mill built.

Past Turtle Point flows the Allegheny River, northward, on the way to the New York Stateline, and the loop is completed when the stream decides to flow back into Pennsylvania and on toward the Gulf of Mexico instead of toward the Great Lakes.

South of Turtle Point, also on the river, is Port Allegany, once the Canoe Place of the Indians and early settlers. This Canoe Place is about eighty miles, in a direct line, northwest of the Canoe Place at Cherry Tree, Indiana County, near the source of the West Branch of the Susquehanna, where was an easy portage between that river and a branch of the Conemaugh.

It will be noticed by the student of the map that the course of the numerous streams of Central Pennsylvania has had much to do not only with the development of the section, but that the bounds of the counties have been determined by the courses of rivers and creeks. Odd shapes and broken lines separating the counties from their surroundings may be accounted for in this way. On the prairies of Illinois or Iowa it is quite possible and wise to cut the land into right-angled counties and townships, but not in Pennsylvania. The map of the state, cut on county lines, would make a splendid and profitable picture puzzle not merely for boys and girls but for those who are older.

There is no better example of the curiously contoured county line that makes the state look like a craftily contrived map of gerrymandered congressional districts than Cameron County, where the valleys of the Driftwood and the Sinnemahoning, as well as the mountain ridges, have guided those who fixed the relations of the county to the surrounding territory. That is, there is no better illustration of this interesting fact than that county of central Pennsylvania in which the traveler happens to be at the time—until he goes into the very next county. In this case the next county happens to be Clinton; an

THROUGH THE BLACK FOREST

examination of its configuration is startling, while a study of the apparent reason for each corner and angle is not difficult.

The tablelands and mountains along the creeks were once covered with pine and hemlock forests, but these have become a part of the past. During the third quarter of the nineteenth century the timber was marketed in a wholesale manner that made Driftwood and Sinnemahoning busy waters and that made Emporium, the center of activities, a stirring town. The name given to Emporium in those picturesque days shows the confidence of its promoters in the future and their ambition for the county seat. The town has always dominated the county, as the mountain near Emporium, with its 2112 feet, has looked down on adjacent summits.

The names given to some of Cameron's streams, townships and villages, speak eloquently of the past. Driftwood, Lumber, Beechwood, Grove—could names go farther in giving information as to the past of a lumber county?

There are other names that are a denial of the facetious and unfair words of one who has said of the county that the principal product in the past has been lumber, "but as that is about all gone, I would judge that for the next few years, at least, the principal product will be blackberries, black bears, and mountain trout." Let the name of the village, Rich Valley, near the headwater of Driftwood, be a part of the denial of such an unpleasant insinuation. Cameron County has a worthy future, as it has had a stirring past.

Here, again, the Department of Foresty is taking an active part in preparing for the future by the production and growth of timber that may in days to come not only renew lumbering activities, to a limited extent, but will protect the slopes above the streams and tend to prevent floods, so saving the land from erosion and insuring water in time of drouth. The Sizerville Forest, north of Emporium, and the Cameron and Lushbaugh Forests, north of Sinnemahoning, are maintained for this purpose.

There is still ample cover for game, and hunters find their way in numbers into the valleys of the creeks and to the ridges near by. Each season as they come they listen to old residents who tell tales handed down to them of departed game. One story often repeated tells of the coming of the elk to the Great Elk Lick in Shippen township, above Emporium. This was the resort of so many elk and deer that the neighborhood was actually cleared of brush by their tramping. One old hunter said that he had seen as many as thirty elk in the lick at one time.

About 1820 a "poem," composed by a local humorist, told of "A Sinnemahoning Deer Chase." The lines begin by telling of the coming of the first minister to the region, and the reason:

> "There is a place called Sinnemahone,
> Of which but little good is known;
> For sinning, ill must be its fame,
> Since Sin begins its very name.
> So well indeed its fame is known.
> That people think they should begin
> To drop the useless word Mahone,
> And call the country simply Sin."

The minister came and the people gathered in the log schoolhouse to hear him preach. The service began.

> "The singing o'er, the prayer was said,
> But scarcely had the text been read,
> When, panting with fatigue and fear,
> Rushed past the door a hunted deer.

Prayer, hymn and text, was all forgot—
And for the sermon mattered not.
Forth dashed the dogs, not one was mute—
Men, women, children, followed suit."

"Tis all in vain!" the preacher groaned. But Billy French, the only one of the congregation left behind (and he only because he was suffering from rheumatism), called out consolingly,

" 'Tis not in vain! . . .
When my good hound, old Never-fail,
Once gets his nose upon the trail,
There is not a spikebuck anywhere
Can get away from him, I'll swear."

Sinnemahoning Creek tumbles through a wild region. Mountains from 1200 to 1400 feet high border on either side the narrow valley whose width, at some points only three thousand feet, seem small when compared with the heights. Many little streams enter from both sides, through wild ravines and rocky gorges in the mountains. The courses of the tributaries are tortuous, owing to jutting peaks that turn the water as it rushes down to the valley.

A point of special interest along Sinnemahoning is Round Island, several miles east of the west border of Clinton County. Here is Altar Rock. This oddity, seventy feet high, is described as a spiral of rocks, standing on the north bank of the stream in full view of the Pennsylvania Railroad tracks, and thus within view of the highway also.

A few miles farther on the Sinnemahoning enters the West Branch. At this point it is nearly as wide as the larger stream. For this reason—and because the West Branch changes its direction at the point of junction, while the Sinnemahoning flows from the west—some of the pioneers who ascended the West Branch were puzzled whether to go on to the west, or to the southwest, to Chinklacamoose.

In ascending the West Branch pioneers were apt to pause at Renovo, whose situation in an oval-shaped valley, perhaps a mile and a half long, always attracts. Above the river on the south towers a mountain more than one thousand feet high, while on the north shore is a second mountain of little less altitude.

To the south of Renovo lies the interesting Hopkins Forest, on a good road. Another fairly good road runs north along Drury's Run, through mountain scenery that should not be missed. The road leads to Cross Fork, but on the way is Tamarack Swamp, of which Henry W. Shoemaker tells a pleasing story. He says that the discovery, in 1850, of fragments of bones was made here, which resembled moose or caribou bones. Yet no one had known of the presence of these animals in Pennsylvania. However, an Indian legend came to the rescue. This says that the northern animals whose bones were found were imported by Ko-wat-go-chee, to satisfy his homesick bride, Me-shon-ni-ta, who had come from the North, and pined for the scenery and surroundings of her old home. Her lover husband grubbed out the local trees and replaced them by trees brought from the North—tamarack, white spruce, firs, and cedars. The animals from her old haunts followed, and she was content.

Another Indian legend is told to account for the naming of Young Woman's Creek, the stream that enters the West Branch east of Renovo. An Indian killed a woman prisoner here, so the story goes, and ever afterward he avoided this desirable camping spot because he thought he saw her ghost. But the more prosaic

BEECH CREEK, CLINTON COUNTY
Photo by State Department of Forestry

ON THE BLACK MOSHANNON, CENTER COUNTY
Photo by State Department of Forestry

ON THE ROAD TO BRUSH VALLEY NARROWS, CENTER COUNTY
Photo by State Highway Department

PENN'S VALLEY, LOOKING TOWARD BOALSBURG
Photo by State Department of Forestry

account given by the pioneers is that in 1779 a young woman, while escaping from the Indians, was drowned in the waters of the creek.

The village at the mouth of the creek was once called Young Woman's Town, but the more descriptive name, North Bend, was given to it. From here to Hyner the river, after being kept by the mountains to the northeasterly course, prepares for its sudden turn to the southeast, taking advantage of a break in the mountains through which it can turn toward Chesapeake Bay.

To this glorious region near the Susquehanna a company of sportsmen come regularly to Otzinachson Park, a game park of three thousand acres, surrounded by wire fences thirteen feet high. The park is near Haneyville, five miles from Hyner.

The Susquehanna is at its best between Hyner and Lock Haven. Mountains rise from eight hundred to fourteen hundred feet above the water; sometimes the bases come down to the shore, again they are farther away. At Ferney they come so close that the river seems to cut its way through them, in gaps worthy to be named with others better known. Near Lock Haven the scenery becomes less rugged, but the quiet valley has attractions all its own.

Lock Haven has a well chosen site on a point between the West Branch and Bald Eagle Creek. The Muncy Hills or Bald Eagle Mountain supply variety to the prospect from Clinton's county seat, whose name tells of the locks in the canal at this point, as well as the basin in the river, built to supply water to the dam, and used for many years as a harbor for rafts.

The land on which Lock Haven was laid out was owned by Jerry Church, a character who desired to capitalize the completion of the West Branch Canal. How he did this can be told best in his own diverting words:

"I now undertook to divide the counties of Lycoming and Center, and make a new county to be called Clinton. I had petitions printed to that effect and sent them to Harrisburg . . . The people of the town of Williamsport, the county seat of Lycoming, and Bellefonte, the county seat of Center County, had to be up and doing something to prevent the division; and they commenced pouring in their remonstrances and praying aloud to the Legislature not to have any part of either county taken off, for it was nothing more than one of Jerry Church's Yankee notions. However, I did not despair. I still kept wishing every year, for three successive years, and attended the Legislature myself every winter. I then had a gentleman who had been a citizen of Lock Haven . . . who harped in with me. We entered into the division together. We had to state a great number of facts to the members of the Legislature, and perhaps something more, in order to obtain full justice. We continued on for nearly three years longer . . . and at last we received the law creating the county of Clinton."

"Eagle" was the name first selected for the county. But Jerry Church, noting that neither this name nor the project was in favor, changed the name to Clinton. It was said that many voted for the bill who had been opposed to the plan, not realizing that they were voting for the same bill as before.

When Jerry Church came to Lock Haven in 1833 the country back from the river was almost unbroken, and in 1839, when the new county was formed, there were few roads. But to-day there are roads everywhere, not only the highways provided by the state and the county, but the fire roads of the Department of Forestry that give access to the forests above and below Lock Haven

THROUGH THE BLACK FOREST

and, incidentially, make accessible numberless points of great interest.

At Lock Haven the mountains again prove too much for the West Branch, and it is compelled to yield its ambition to keep to the southeast. Bald Eagle Mountain, the great barrier, is for many miles the dominating feature of the landscape, though from different points of view the aspect of the rugged eminence is most varied.

From McElhattan the mountain shows a conspicuous bare place on its slope, a landmark for miles. A larger bare place, stretching from the summit nearly to the base, is visible from Castanea.

McElhattan has more than the river and the mountain to attract the traveler. There is the Indian monument on the site of the old Indian town of Pipsisseway, chief of the Susquehannocks. Then there are the Meadow Sweet Farms, a part of the dowry of Meadow Sweet, the Leni Lenape bride of Pipsisseway, and McElhattan Gap, with Mount Jura on the east and Mount Logan on the west.

The path which leads over the southeast slope of Mount Logan, on to Nittany Valley, was once a wolf path. A fit neighbor, to the east of Booneville, is the road of the Forestry Department which was once a good buffalo path, marked by tens of thousands of hoofs in the annual winter migration to Georgia. Those who know the road well say that they have found marks of the hoofs.

Booneville is named for a brother of Daniel Boone, who stopped here to make his home when Daniel and his family passed through these mountains on the way to Kentucky. The town is some miles south of the West Branch, just far enough to make the land journey back to Lock Haven, through valleys and past mountains, including Flat Rock Mountain, a side trip whose memories will abide.

From Lock Haven the road back to Altoona is on the bank of Bald Eagle Creek. Within a few miles of Lock Haven it passes into Center County, which reluctantly yielded a part of its territory to make Jerry Church's lands valuable.

Bellefonte, in the Nittany Valley, is the city of beautiful views, as well as the city of the beautiful spring. Lafayette, who visited the town in 1824, was greatly attracted by this spring, which supplies the town with water. But Bellefonte is not only beautiful in itself; it is a center for side trips to other beautiful and interesting spots.

To the northwest a trip may be taken up Moose Run to Snow Shoe. On the way is the "silent city" where are more than one thousand great ant hills.

Snow Shoe received its name in 1775 when a party of hunters were halted by lack of provisions on the mountain near Moshannon Creek. On snowshoes which they made hastily they pushed their way thirty miles to the nearest settlement. In more recent years the Snowshoe Company operated here, but to-day the timber is gone, and the settlement is deserted.

Not far west of Snow Shoe, near Peale, is the wonderful horseshoe curve of the Black Moshannon, three hundred feet below the tracks of the New York Central. The accurate dimensions of the curve were accounted for by the Indians, who said it was the hoof print left in the water by the great steed of Chet-ta-mic-co, a hero of the days of the world's creation.

State College, south of Bellefonte, is in the midst of so much that is superlatively beautiful that it is difficult to know which way to explore first. Perhaps the best

ALONG THE JUNIATA, HUNTINGDON COUNTY
Photo from Birmingham School

thing for the visitor to do is to take a look over the country from the tower of old College Hall, then take the road northeast toward the county's sharp point. The road leads through Boalsburg and the gateway to the Seven Mountains—a gorge with Bald Top on one side and Tussey Knob on the other, past beautiful Coburn, into Povalley, visited by Edgar Allan Poe in 1838, when he sought an inheritance from the Pohs, with whom he claimed relationship; into Pine Creek Hollow, near Woodward, where is a hundred acre tract of primeval white pine. "The great trees, rising to a height of nearly two hundred feet, and straight as gun barrels, are always sighing in the wind, and are weird and sad survivors of the grand forests which once covered the central Pennsylvania uplands."[1]

But perhaps the greatest natural wonder of this county of wonders is Penn's Cave, about halfway between Penn's Creek and Bellefonte, not far from Center Hall. This cavern was once owned by the Pohs. It seems strange that it is not better known, for it is in the midst of mountains, it has an unusual entrance, the passages and chambers are varied and curious, and the boat ride within has been said to be finer than anything of the sort provided by Mammoth Cave.

It is not necessary to return to Bellefonte before making the trip back to Tyrone and Altoona. There is a lower road to State College, then through the distinctive scenery of south Center County, over the line into Huntingdon, and north to Warrior's Mark where, until a few years ago, the tree was still pointed out that was used by the Indians as a target. This tree gave the name to the town.

All the way from Warrior's Mark to Altoona the

[1] Henry W. Shoemaker, in "Eldorado Found."

country speaks eloquently of the most lovable Indian of whom Pennsylvania history has record—Captain John Logan, whose sad but inspiring story should be familiar. The son of Shikellimy, he was as different as could be from his older brother James, a man whose evil fame has tarnished the name Logan. Thachnectoris, as John Logan was called, was the friend of the settlers, and he had the confidence of the provincial government to such an extent that he was nominated by the Penns to succeed his father as vicegerent of the Iroquois until the council at Onondaga should elect its chief. This the council refused to do, because he had lost an eye in a fight with Indian marauders.

For a time John Logan made his home in Logan Valley, in the heart of what is now Tyrone. Here he lived during the early days of the Revolution. More than once he helped the patriotic cause. His service as a spy attracted Washington's favorable notice.

After the war he was driven off his land by a white settler, because he had not proved title. So he went to Chinklacamoose (Clearfield). His bit of land there was lost in the same way, while he was absent in Ohio, pleading with his brother to give up his bad habits and be a friend instead of an enemy of the white people. Later, though the holder of the lands he had claimed at Chinklacamoose urged him to live with him to the end of his days, he went to his son, Tod-kah-dohs, who had married a daughter of Cornplanter. His last days were spent on the Cornplanter Indian Reservation, though every year he made a trip to Sunbury to see the graves of his wife and children, and to Lewisburg, for a hunt with an old friend.

Captain Logan died in 1820, in his one hundred and second year. For eighty years, ever since he had grown to manhood, he had been a friend of the white people, though he had been mistrusted by them many times. His was one of the noblest characters ever known among the Indians.

His monument is the great Black Forest where he roamed, and the historic Logan House, at Altoona, the hotel built by the Pennsylvania Railroad in 1855, six years after the founding of the town in the midst of the almost unbroken wilderness of the mountains. It stands not many miles from the Kittanning Trail, the pathway which Logan trod many times, as he probably trod nearly every portion of the way through the heart of the Black Forest, looking in wonder at the majestic mountains, following with delight the crystal rivers, and adoring the Great Spirit who spoke to him in the healing spring, in the tumbling cataract, in the fleecy clouds above his head, or in the secret places of the forest where he found the peace denied him by those to whom he gave the best he had.

And now he calls to those who live after him to follow him to the same mountain-girt forests, that they, too, may know peace amid turmoil, and may gain new strength for fighting life's battles.

BIBLIOGRAPHY

Along the Western Brandywine. Wilmer W. MacElree, West Chester, 1912.

Bull, Ole. Sarah C. Bull. Boston, 1883.

Coleridge, Samuel Taylor, Letters of. Edited by Ernest Hartley Coleridge. London, 1895.

Coleridge, Samuel Taylor, Life of. Hall Caine. London, 1887.

Conemaugh, Valley of the. Thomas J. Chapman. Altoona, 1865.

Continental Congress at York, Pennsylvania. George R. Browell. York, 1914.

Down the Eastern and up the Black Brandywine. Wilmer W. MacElree. West Chester, 1912.

Eldorado Found. Henry W. Shoemaker. Altoona, 1917.

Early Footprints of Developments and Improvements in North West Pennsylvania. Isaac B. Brown. Harrisburg, 1903.

Extempore on a Wagon. A Musical Narrative. George Henry Loskiel. Lancaster, 1887.

Foresters, The: A Poem. Alexander Wilson. Norristown, Pa., 1818.

Girard, Stephen, Life and Times of. McMaster. Philadelphia, 1918.

Gist, Christopher, Journal of. Edited by William W. Darlington. Pittsburg, 1893.

Highways and Byways of the Great Lakes. Clifton Johnson. New York, 1911.

Journal of a Tour in Unsettled Parts of North America. Francis Baily. London, 1806.

Justice to All: The Story of the Pennsylvania Mounted Police. Katherine Mayo. New York, 1917.

Lawrence, Uncle Jonas, Historical Letters of. Elmira, N. Y., 1886.

BIBLIOGRAPHY

Lehigh Valley Railroad, Guide Book to the. Philadelphia, 1872.

Little Rivers, Henry van Dyke. New York, 1914.

Logan, Captain, Blair County's Indian Chief. Henry W. Shoemaker. Altoona, 1915.

Lumber Industry of Pennsylvania, History of the. Defenbaugh, James Eliot. Chicago, 1907.

Maclay, Samuel, Journal of. Williamsport, 1857.

Making of Pennsylvania, The. Sydney George Fisher. Philadelphia, 1896.

National Road, The. Robert Bruce. Washington, D. C., 1916.

New Purchase, The. Robert Carleton. Princeton, 1916.

New Travels in the United States of America in 1788. J. P. Brissot de Warville. London, 1794.

Northwestern Pennsylvania, Pioneer Outline History of. W. J. McKnight, M.D., Philadelphia, 1905.

Oil Bubble, The. Samuel P. Irvin. Franklin, Pa., 1868.

Old Time Notes of Pennsylvania. A. K. McClure. Philadelphia, 1905.

Old Tioga Point and Early Athens. Louise Welles Murry. Athens, Pa., 1908.

Otzinachson. A History of the West Branch Valley of the Susquehannah. By J. F. Meginness. Williamsport, 1889.

Over the Alleghenies and across the Prairies in 1848. John Lewis Peyton. London, 1870.

Pennsylvania Mountain Stories. Henry W. Shoemaker. Reading, 1912.

Pennsylvania, History of the Commonwealth of. William H. Egle. Philadelphia, 1883.

Pennsylvania Railroad, The. William B. Sipes. Philadelphia, 1875.

Pen Pictures of America, Vols. 1 and 2. Joel Cook. Philadelphia, 1903.

Petrolia, or the Oil Regions of the United States. F. B. Wilkie. Chicago, 1865.

Pictorial Sketch Book of Pennsylvania. Eli Bowen. Philadelphia, 1852.

Picturesque Pennsylvania; a series of articles by George E. Mapes. Philadelphia Record of 1907-8.

Pike, the Old. Thomas A. Searight. Uniontown, Pa., 1894.

Pithole, History of. Charles C. Lenard. Pithole City, Pa., 1867.

Pleasant Peregrinations through the Prettiest Parts of Pennsylvania. Peregrine Prolix. Philadelphia, 1836.

Propagation of Forest Trees. George H. Wirt. Harrisburg, 1902.

Progressive Pennsylvania. J. M. Swank. Philadelphia, 1908.

Schuylkill Valley, Vignettes of the. Philadelphia, 1874.

Standard Bearers, The. Katherine Mayo. Boston, 1918.

St. Lawrence, The, to Virginia. Clifton Johnson. New York, 1913.

Susquehanna, Up the. Hile C. Pardoe. New York, 1895.

Tales of the Bald Eagle Mountain. Henry W. Shoemaker. Reading, 1912.

Travels in America, Performed in 1806. Thomas Ashe. New York, 1811.

Travels in North America in 1780, 1781 and 1782. Marquis de Chastellux. London, 1787.

Travels in Some Parts of North America in the years 1804, 1805 and 1806. Robert Sutcliffe. Philadelphia, 1812.

Travels in the United States of America, 1793 to 1797. William Priest. London, 1802.

Travels in the Confederation. Johan David Schœpf. Philadelphia, 1811.

Travels Through the Unknown Parts of America. Thomas Ambury. London, 1797.

Travels through the United States of North America, 1795, 1796, 1797. Duc de la Rochefoucauld-Liancourt. London, 1800.

Weiser, Conrad, Life of. C. Z. Weiser, D.D. Reading, 1876.

Wilderness Trail. Charles A. Hanna. New York, 1911.

INDEX

Adams County, 50
Adams, John, gives name to Adams County, 50
Adams, John, inspires Congress, 48
Adams, Samuel, inspires Congress, 48
Airbrakes, first test of, 288
Alden, Henry M., quoted, 303
Allegheny Mountains, extent, 18, 134
Allegheny River, 73, 193, 197, 289, 290, 296, 297, 311, 312, 323
Allen, Horatio, tests first locomotive in United States, 242
Allen's Valley, 60
Allentown, 256, 266
Altoona, 145, 316, 335
Amberson's Valley, 60
Ambury, Thomas, quoted, 31
Ambuscade feared, 176
Analomink Creek, 230
Antes Fort, 186
Anthracite, experiments in burning, 215
Antietam Creek, 52, 96
Antrim, 192
Ararat, Mount, 247
"Arbustum Americanum," 82
Arch Spring, 147
Ariel Lake, 245
Armstrong, Colonel, Indian fighter, 310
Armstrong County, 309
Asaph, 192
Ashe, Thomas, quoted, 90, 165, 285
Assunepachla, 148
Asylum, 202
Athens, 200
Auburn, 214
Audubon, John James, 23, 125, 284
Aughwick Creek, 60, 143
Aux Boeufs, River, 281

Bailey, Francis, quoted, 57, 66
Bald Eagle Creek, 332

Bald Eagle Mountain, 183, 316
Baltimore, Lord, and William Penn, 42
Bard, Richard, captured by Indians, 51, 143
Barns of Lancaster County, 31
Bartram, John, 81
Bear hunting, 320
Bedford, 68, 145
Bedford County, 65
Bedford Springs, 68
Beach Lake, 245
Bear Creek, 225
Bear Lake, 225
Beaver, 273
Beaver County, 271
Beaver Falls, 274
Beaver River, 272
Beaver Springs, 171
Bellefonte, 317, 332
Bennett, James Gordon, 195
Berkley, 267
Berks County, 129, 212
Berwick, 207
Bethania, 31
Bethlehem, 33, 257
Bethlehem Steel Works, 258
Beulah Road, 160
Bienville, Celeron de, 271, 277, 280, 291 297
Big Crossings, 102
Big Level Ridge, 299, 319
Big Pucketa Creek, 312
Birmingham, 147
Black Forest, 315, 335
Blaine, James G., 114
Blair's Gap, 154
Blairsville, 134, 163, 164
Blockhouse Road, 190
Bloody Run, 66
Blooming Grove Park, 240
Blossburg, 190, 191
Blue Bell Tavern, Philadelphia, 79, 81
Blue Hill, 177
Blue Knob, 69
Blue Mountains, 91, 127
Boalsburg, 333

INDEX

Boat-building activities, 86, 111, 269
Boiling Springs, 93
Boone, Daniel, 331
Booneville, 331
Boot Jack, 319
Boundary disputes, with Maryland, 35, 42, 78; with Virginia, 116; between Huntingdon and Mifflin Counties, 140
Bouquet, Colonel, 67, 71, 92, 271
Braddee, Dr. John F., robs the mail, 109
Braddock, General, grave of, 103
Braddock's defeat, 72
Braddock's Field, 73
Braddock Memorial Park Association, 104
Braddock's Road, 67, 100
Bradford, 321
Bradford County, 188, 247
Brady, Captain Samuel, 290, 318
Brady, Captain John, 179
Brady's Jump, 200
Brandywine Creek, 28, 82
Brandywine, Battle of, 83, 257
Brainerd, David, at Duncans Island, 91, 135; at Gnadenhütten, 254
Bridges: Wrightsville, 38; first chain suspension, 72; camelback at Harrisburg, 90; on National Road, 99; at Little Crossings, 101; at Big Crossings, 102; Turkey's Nest, 107; Brownsville, 113; S-bridge near Washington, 119; Rockville, 134; Juniata covered bridge, 136, 166; Portage railroad, 154; Port Trevorton, 173; Nicholson Viaduct, 249; John G.'s bridge, 312; Kinzua Viaduct, 322
Bridgewater, 274
Brier Hill, 111
Bristol, 262
Brokenstraw Creek, 297
Brookville, 304, 305
Brown, John, 52, 58
Brownsville, 110, 111, 112
Bruce Robert, quoted, 100
Brumbaugh, Ex-Governor, 139, 145
Bryant, William Cullen, quoted, 45, 167, 172

Buchanan James, birthplace of, 61
Buck Hill Falls, 228
Bucks County, 259, 265
Buffalo, last stand of, 168–70; adventure with, 285.
Buffalo Cross Roads, 170
Buffalo Valley, 169
Buhler, M. E., quoted, 224
Bulkheads, invention of, 161
Bull, Ole, and his colony, 193
Burd, Colonel James, 175
Burr, Aaron, 274
Bushkill, 236, 237
Butler, 289
Butler, Colonel Zebulon, 224
Butler County, 289

Caledonia, 52
Callensburg, 300
Cambria County, 155
Cambridge Springs, 281
Cameron County, 324, 325
Camp Crane, Allentown, 257
Camp Hill, 91
Campbell's Ledge, 220
Canal journey described, 137, 149
Canal visions of Robert Fulton, 88
Canals, 38, 127, 213, 242, 251, 262, 273, 276, 311
Canals, Washington's comprehensive plans for, 87
Cannon and ammunition for Revolution, 46, 128, 132, 264
Canoe Camp, 190
Canoe Place, 198, 310, 324
Capital of the United States, candidates for, 33, 34, 37, 47, 49
Carbon County, 219
Carbondale, 242, 246, 249
Carey Lake, 206
Carleton, Robert, 63
Carlisle, 93
Carman, Bliss, quoted, 315
Carnegie, Andrew, 294
Carnegie Museum, Pittsburgh, 154
Carondowana, 210
Carriage of George Washington damaged, 36
Castleman River, 101, 159
Catasauqua, 256
Catawissa Creek, 209

INDEX

Catfish Camp, 116
Caves, on Conodoguinet Creek, 93; Naginey, 142; Arch Spring, 147; Great Bear, 163; Oriole, 185; Sweden Valley Ice Mine, 197; Penn's, 333.
Cement, 256
Center County, 177, 332
Center Hall, 333
Center Road, 213, 216
Ceres, 198, 323
Chambers, Benjamin, 57
Chambers, Reuben, courtship of, 31
Chambersburg, 57
Chartiers Creek, 118
Chastellux, Marquis de, 258, 263
Chemung River, 201
Chester, 24, 78
Chestnut Ridge, 69, 71
Chickies Rock, 40
Chickies Valley, 41
Chikiswalungo, 41
Chillisquaque Creek, 177
Chinklacamoose, 317
Christiana, 43, 85
Church, Jerry, 329
Circle Line, 16, 116
Clarion, 300
Clarion County, 299
Clarion River, 300
Clark, George Rogers, 111
Clark's Knob, 56
Clay, Henry, 99, 113, 119, 120, 269
Claysville, 119
Clermont, Robert Fulton's steamboat, 44
Clearfield, 317
Clearfield County, 299, 302, 317
Clinton County, 324, 327, 330
Coal, 191, 215, 217, 242, 253, 303
Coatesville, 28, 29
Codorus, steamboat, 44
Coffee, introduced into Snyder County, 171
Coleridge, Samuel Taylor, 203
Columbia, 35, 37, 38, 320
Columbia County, 207
Columns from burned State Capitol, 90, 186
Colonizing experiments — Gallitzin, 157; Beulah Road, 160; Ole Bull, 193; Asylum, 202; Samuel

Taylor Coleridge, 203; Wyalusing, 204; Horace Greeley, 240; Economy, 272, 286; Harmony, 286; New Flanders, 319; St. Mary's, 319
Concord, 55
Conemaugh, 162
Conemaugh River, 134
Conestoga Creek, 32, 42
Conestoga Village, 42, 43
Conestoga wagon described, 77
Conewago Creek, 50, 86, 297
Confluence, 102
Conneaut, 275
Conneaut Lake, 275, 282, 283
Connecticut Claim to Wyoming Valley, 222
Connecticut Susquehanna Company, 200, 222
Conococheague Creek, 55, 60, 98
"Conocojig Settlement," 55
Conodoguinet Creek, 55, 60, 91
Conoquonessing Creek, 286
Conowingo Creek, 44
Coolbaugh, Judge John, 236
Cooper, Thomas, quoted, 63
Cooperstown, 289
Copper mine, at Gap, 30
Cornplanter, 297, 321, 334
Cornwall Furnace, 132
Cornwall ore banks, 132
Coudersport, 192, 196
Coudersport and Jersey Shore turnpike, 193, 196
Courtship, a strange, 31
Cove Valley, 62
Cowan's Gap, 60
Crawford County, 275, 276, 281
Cresap, Thomas, 36
Cresap's War, 36
Cresco, 228, 229
"Crossing the Isthmus" at Erie, 280
Cumberland Valley, 56
Curwensville, 302, 318
Cussewago Creek, 282

Dan's Rock, 100
Danville, 210
Declaration of independence of the "fair-play men," 182
Declaration, signers of, in Carlisle, 92
Delaware Indians, 262

341

INDEX

Delaware River, 22, 228, 229, 232-234, 236, 237, 239, 255, 261, 265
Delaware Water Gap, 228, 229, 232-34, 236, 239
Delmar, the story of the name, 192
Denison, Colonel Nathan, 224
Dial Rock, 220
Diahoga, 200
Dingman's Creek and Falls, 237, 238
Dingman's Ferry, 237
Dobbins, Captain Daniel, 278
Donegal Valley, 41
"Don't give up the ship," 278
Doubling Gap, 94
Dougherty, Captain John, 161
Douglas, General Ephraim, 108
Downingtown, 28
Doylestown, 263, 265
Drake, Colonel E. L., 292
Dream, Why Shikellimy regretted, 170
Driftwood Creek, 324
Drinker, Henry, 227, 229, 245
Dubois, 318
Duncannon, 135
Duncan's Island, 91, 135
Dundaff, 246
Durham, 264
Durham boats, 264
Dutoit, Anthony, 233

Eaglesmere, 179, 180
Early railway journey described, 124
Earth and Sky, The, quoted, 233
East Stroudsburg, 231
Easton, 261
Ebensburg, 160
Echo Lake, 237
Economy, 272
Eddystone, 80
Elizabethtown, 86
Elk, 170, 320, 326
Elk County, 319
Elk Mountains, 319
Ellett, Elizabeth F., quoted, 234
Emerson, Ralph Waldo, quoted, 131, 299
Emigh's Gap, 316
Emporium, 198, 325
Ephrata, 132
Erie, 280

Erie, Lake, 18, 273, 278
Esther, Queen, 210
Everett, 65, 66,

Fairmount Park, Philadelphia, 23, 24
"Fair-play men," 182
Fairview Summit, 222, 250
Falling Spring, 57
Falls Creek, 206
Farmington, 102
Fayette County, 104
Ferney, 329
Fisher, Sydney George, quoted, 219
Fitch, John, 23, 43, 266, 269
Fithian, Philip, 139
Forbes, General, 57, 60, 67, 71, 74
Forbes Road, 67
Forest County, 296, 298
Forestry, State department of, 52-54, 70, 82, 139, 184, 192, 207, 213, 228, 238, 318, 325, 330.
Forests, State—Mont Alto, 52; Loyalsock, 181, Bald Eagle, 184; Black, 187; Blackwell's, 192; Chatham, 192; Ole Bull, 196; Wyoming, 205; Sizerville, 326; Cameron, 326; Lushbaugh, 326; Hopkins, 328
Fort Allen, 254
Fort Augusta, 175, 178, 179
Fort Du Quesne, 33, 112, 268, 271
Fort Franklin, 292
Fort Freeland, 179
Fort Granville, 140
Fort Hamilton, 230
Fort Hendricks, 171
Fort Ligonier, 71
Fort Louthier, 92
Fort Muncy, 179
Fort Necessity, 102
Fort Penn, 230
Fort Pitt, 71, 74
Fort Shirley, 309
Fort Stanwix, treaty of, 141, 178, 204, 310
Forty Fort, 223
Foul Rift, 262
Fox hunting, 85
Foxburg, 300
Franklin, 290, 291
Franklin, Benjamin, 33, 254
Franklin, Colonel John, 201

342

INDEX

Franklin, William, 271
Frankstown Juniata, 145
Frazier, John, 73
Freemansburg, 261
French Creek, 281, 282, 283
Friedenshütten, 204
Fries, John, 266
Frolics on the Portage Railroad, 153
Fugitive slaves defended, 85
Fulton County, 64
Fulton, Robert, 44, 88, 269, 270

Galeton, 192
Gallitzin, 155
Gallitzin, Prince, story of, 156
Game, wild, 85, 141, 196, 240, 320, 326
Ganoga Lake, 181
Gap, 29
Gap gang, 30
Gap, nickel mine at, 30
Gaps in Kittatinny Range, 215
Garland, Hamlin, quoted, 244
Geology, 138, 232, 235, 251, 255, 262, 302, 318
Gettysburg, 50
Girard Estate, 218
Girard, Stephen, 217, 218
Gist, Christopher, 66, 101, 102, 271, 311
Glade road, 67
Glen Onoko, 252
Glen Summit, 250
Glen Thomas, 251
Gnadenhütten, 254
Gorusch, Edward, 85
Gosgoschunk, 296
Gouldsboro, 227
"Granary of America, The," 30
Grand View, 69
Gray, Zane, quoted, 241
Great Bend, 247
Great Cove Valley, 64
Great Meadows, 102
Great Swamp, 225, 226
Great Valley, 27
Greeley, Horace, 240, 280
Greencastle, 95, 96
Greensburg, 306
Greenwood Furnace, 146
Groome, Colonel John C., 307
Gulph road, 26
Gulph Rock, 26

Hagerstown, 97, 98
Hall, Abijah, 174, 253
Halleck, Fitz Greene, quoted, 219
Hancock, John, 36
Hanover, 50
Hanway, Castner, 85
Harmony, 286
Harris Ferry, 90
Harris, John, 89, 134, 143
Harris, Thaddeus Mason, quoted, 63
Harrisburg, 89, 134
Harrison, Benjamin, 62; William Henry, Jr., 62
Harvey Lake, 206
Hawley, 240, 242
Hazleton, 263
Heilprin, Anthony, quoted, 233
Henry, Patrick, 116
Henry, William, 43
Hershey, 133
Highway Department, 65, 146, 196, 208
Hog Island, 79
Holliday, Adam, 148
Hollidaysburg, 146
Hornaday, W. T., quoted, 168
Horsheshoe Curve, 155
Hunter's Lake, 181
Hunting wild game, 85, 141, 196, 240, 320, 326
Huntingdon, 145
Huntingdon County, 143
Huston, A. F., 29
Hyner, 329

Inclined plane railways, 150-152, 242, 244, 253
Indiana County, 163, 309, 324
Indian legends, 180, 265, 290, 328, 332
Indian Steps, the, 147
Indians — Susquehannocks, 42; Conestogas, 42; Leni Lenapes, 147, 259; Shawnees, 177; Cayugas, 204; Nanticokes, 202; Shawanese, 209; Six Nations, 222; Delawares, 262.
Indians, captured by, 51, 92, 140; driven from Fort Augusta, 175; massacre at Forty Fort, 223; sale of lands by, 28, 89, 148, 177, 235, 259; vacation ground of, 17.

INDEX

Invasion of Pennsylvania by Confederates, 38, 58, 59, 64, 91, 92, 97
Irvine, General James, 108
Irvine, Dr. William, 297
Irvineton, 297
Irwin, Archibald, 62; Elizabeth, 62; Jane, 62; General William, 278
Isle of Que, 170

Jack's Narrows, 143
Jacob's Creek, 72
Jarrett Summit, 319
Jefferson County, 301, 306
Jennerstown, 70
Jersey Shore, 182, 184, 186, 197
"John G.," the story of, 312
Johnsonburg, 319
Johnstown, 150, 162
Jordan, Phineas, 44, 49
Juniata, 98
Juniata River, 134
Jumonville, 107

Karoondinha, Gorge of, 177
Kelly, Colonel John, 170
Kaskaskunk, 274
Kenny James, quoted, 269
Kilmer, Joyce, poem on trees, 54
Kinzua Creek, 297
Kinzua Viaduct, 322
Kipling, Rudyard, quoted, 273
Kishacoquillas Valley, 141
Kiskiminetas River, 149, 163, 309
Kittanning, 309
Kittanning Point, 155
Kittanning trail, 155, 162, 335
Kittatinny Mountains, 56, 255
Kittatinny Park, 233
Kittatinny Valley, 91
Kyn, Joran, 80

Lackawanna River, 206
Lackawanna Valley, 221
Lackawanna Gap, 220
Lackawanna Creek, 239, 240, 241, 261
Lafayette College, 262
Lafayette, Marquis de, 120, 257, 266, 322
Lahaska, 265
Lake Erie, battle of, 274
Lancaster, 32-34

Lancaster County, 32
Lands purchased from Indians, 89, 148, 177, 235, 259
Landscape? Who owns the, 131
Lapackpicton, 209
La Porte, 181
Latrobe, 163
Laurel Hill, 70, 105, 107
Lawrence County, 274
Lawunukhannock, 297
Lebanon, 132
Le Boeuf, Fort, 281
Legends of Indians, 180, 265, 328, 332
Lehigh Coal and Navigation Company, 253
Lehigh Gap, 254, 255
Lehigh River, 219, 251, 256
Lehigh University, 262
Lenhartsville, 214
Leni Lenapes, 147, 259
Lewis, Albert, private forest reserve, 225
Lewis, David, 94,
Lewisburg, 178
Lewistown, 140
Lewistown Narrows, 139
Liberty Bell in Allentown, 257
Ligonier, 71
Lincoln's Gettysburg address quoted, 51
Lincoln Highway, 22
Lititz, 132
Little Crossings, 101
Little Juniata River, 134
Little Kettle Creek, 194
Little Mahoning Creek, 309
Little Schuylkill River, 219
Little Water Gap, 262
Livingston, Chancellor, 270
Lock Haven, 193, 195, 329, 331
Lodore, Lake, 245
Log-boom, the Williamsport, 183
Logan, Chief, 142, 176, 321, 334
Logan House, Altoona, 335
Logan, James, 30, 264
Logstown, 271
Long House of the Six Nations, 200
Lookout Mountain, 221
Loretto, 157
Loskiel, George Henry, quoted, 65, 204
Loudon, Fort, 59

344

INDEX

Loyalhanna Creek, 70, 72, 163
Loyalsock Creek, 181
Lumbering, 183, 188, 206, 297, 305, 318, 325
Luthersburg, 318
Luzerne County, 219
Lycoming County, 178, 188
Lycoming Creek, 182

McClure, Colonel A. K., quoted, 321
McConnellsburg, 62
McElhattan, 186, 331
McElhattan Gap, 331
McElree, W. W., 83
McKean County, 197, 299, 321, 323
Maguires, Molly, 218
Mahantango Creek, 167
Mahoning Creek, 306
Mahoning River, 274
Manheim, 132
"Manor of Mask," the, 51
Map of Pennsylvania, 15
Map, relief, of Pennsylvania, 17
Maple sugar experiment, why a failure, 245
Maps, school teaching without, 15
Marcus Hook, 80
Marienville, 299
Marietta, 41, 45
Marketing experiences of the pioneer, 115, 197, 302
Marshall, Edward, 260
Marshall, Humphrey, botanist, 81
Marshall's Falls, 236
Marshallton, 81
Marvel, Ik, 262
Mason and Dixon's Line, 96, 97
Mauch Chunk, 251, 252, 254, 261
Mayo, Katherine, quoted, 308, 312
Maxatawny, 267
Meadow Sweet, 331
Meadville, 281, 282
Media, 80, 81
Mercer, 285
Mercer County, 275, 281
Mercer, General Hugh, 61
Mercersburg, 61
Mercersburg's three representatives in the White House, 62
Meshoppen Creek, 248
Middleburg, 171
Middletown, 87

Mifflin, Lloyd, tribute to Robert Fulton, 44
Mifflintown, 139
Milford, 238
Millerstown, 136
Milton, 179
Milton, John, quoted, 212
Mine Hill, 29
Minesink, battle of, 240
Minisink (Delaware Water Gap), 232
Minnetunkee, 209
Molly Maguires, 308
Monaca, 272
Monongahela River, 73
Monroe County, 228
Mont Alto Park, 52
Montour, Andrew, 210
Montour County, 209
Montour, Madame, 210
Montour Ridge, 176
Montrose, 248
Moore, Augusta, quoted, 256
Moosic Mountains, 244, 246
Moraly, William, "Gent," quoted, 231
Moravians, 204, 254, 258
Mormons in Franklin County, 95
Morris, Robert, 189, 202, 217, 246, 289
Morris, Thomas, 200
Moshannon Creek, 184, 332
Mount Gretna, 132
Mount Penn, 212
Mount Pocono, 228, 232
Mount Union, 142
Mountain Top, 222, 250
Mounted police, 96, 306, 308, 312
Muhlenberg, Henry Melchior, 125, 131
Muir, John, 174
Muncy, 179
Muncy Creek, 181

Nanticoke, 207
National Road, 78, 119
Navigation of Ohio River, 269, 270
Nay Aug Valley, 249
Nazareth, 259
Nemacolin, 111
Nemacolin's Path, 272
Nescopeck Mountain, 219

345

INDEX

Neshaminy Creek, 260
Neshannock Falls, 275
Neversink Mountain, 212
New Berlin, 172
New Brighton, 274
New Castle, 274
New Hope, 265
New Orleans, the first steamer on the Ohio River, 270
New Wilmington, 275
Nicholson viaduct, 205
Nit-a-nee, 142
Nittany Mountain, 142
Nittany Valley, 331
Noailles, duc de, 202
Nockamixon Rocks, 265
Norristown, 26
North Bend, 329
Northampton County, 255
Northbrook, 81
Northumberland County, 174

Octoraro Creek, 43, 85
Oil, 196, 198, 292, 293
Oil City, 294
Oil City route, 301, 317
Oil Creek, 292
Ohio Country, prophecy concerning, 37
Old State Road to Erie, 301
Onojutta, 145
Onoko Falls, 252
Ontelaunee Creek, 214
Opposition to turnpike, 106; to railroads, 106.
Orwigsburg, 216
Otzinachson Park, 329
Outlook, David Lewis's, 69

Packer, Asa, 262
Palisades of the Delaware, 265
Panhandle of West Virginia, 17, 118
Pantisocracy, 203
Pardee, Ario, 262
Parkman, Francis, quoted, 73
Path Valley, 55
Peach Bottom, 46
Pechoquealin, 236, 264
Pedro, Dom, 311
Peg Leg Railroad, 322
Penn, John, 43, 89, 260
Penn, Thomas, 126, 127, 260

Penn, William: Statue of, 22; confidence of Indians in, 28; in Gap, 30; and Lord Baltimore, 42; and Maryland boundary, 78; leases Susquehanna Country, 89; at Reading, 126; buys real estate, 148; methods of land purchase, 259, 260
Pennamite War, 223
Penn, Mount, 127
Pennsylvania, Map of, 15
Pennsylvania Canal, 148
Pennsylvania Furnace, 147
Pennypacker, Governor, 307
Pequea Creek, 29, 46
Perkiomen Creek, 23
Perkins, James H., 183
Perry, Commodore Oliver Hazard, builds fleet at Presque Isle, 278
Perry County, 136
Petroleum Center, oil boom town, 295
Philadelphia, 22
Philipsburg, 317
Pickering, Colonel Timothy, 200
Picture Rocks, 179
Pike County, 228, 237, 238, 239
Pilgrimage of the Moravians, 204
Pinchot, Gifford, 238
Pine Creek, 182, 187, 197
Pipsisseway, 148, 331
Pithole City, oil boom town, 295
Pitt, Fort, 52, 269
Pittsburgh, 74-76, 123, 287
Pittston, 220, 247
Pocono Mountains, 223, 260
Pocono Plateau, 225, 229
Poe, Edgar Allan, 142, 333
Port Allegany, 197, 198, 234
Port Carbon, 213
Port Clinton, 215
Port Matilda, 317
Port Trevorton, 173
Portage Railway, 148
Porter, Col. Arthur, quoted, 279
Post, Christian Frederick, 271
Potter County, 192, 196
Pottstown, 126
Pottsville, 215, 216
Powder train route to Lake Erie, 281
Presque Isle, 273, 277, 278

INDEX

Priestley, Dr. Joseph, 176
Prisoners, escape of, from Lancaster, 33
Proctor, Colonel Thomas, 208
Prolix, Peregrine, describes canal journey, 149
Prophecy of Philip Fithian, 139; of Adam Holliday, 148.
Prospect Hill, 198
Prospect Rock, 221
Prospectus, an early promoter's, 30
Punxsutawney, 306
Putnam, General Rufus, 66, 111
Pymatuning Swamp, 277

Quaker Valley, 69
Quakers, why they favor the Poconos, 230
Quick, Thomas, Indian fighter, 239

Railroad journey, early, described, 38
Railroads: Philadelphia to Columbia, 38; Huntingdon and Broad Top, 69, 145; Wilmington and Northern, 83; "Tapeworm," 97; Mont Alto, 97; Waynesburg to Washington, 121; Reading to Pottsville, 128; Pennsylvania, 134, 265, 316; Portage, 150; Baltimore and Ohio, 160; Lykens Valley, 167; Middle Creek Valley, 173 Trevorton and Susquehanna, 173; Pine Creek and Jersey Shore, 187; Wellsboro to Antrim, 192; Sunbury and Erie, 194; Delaware, Lackawanna and Western, 205, 229; Catawissa, 209; Danville to Pottsville, 218; Erie, 229, 244, 247; Delaware and Cobb's Gap, 220, 230; Delaware Valley, 239; Honesdale and Carbondale, 242; Scranton to Hawley, 244; Lehigh Valley, 248, 250; Atlantic and Great Western, 283; Panhandle, 287; Peg Leg, 322; New York Central, 332.
Railroads, humorous descriptions of, 83, 122
Rapp, George, 286
Raub, Mount, 321

Rauchtown, 185
Ray's Hill, 64
Raystown Juniata, 66, 140, 145
Read, Thomas Buchanan, 29
Reading, 83, 126, 212, 267, 306
Rebellion of John Fries, 266
Red Bank Creek, 305
Redstone Old Fort, 111, 112, 113
Reed, James, 142
Reedsville, 141
Reno, oil town, 293
Renovo, 328
Repplier, Agnes, 18
Rhys, Morgan John, 160
Richmond Furnace, 60
Ridge Road, 216
"Road, the Great," from Sunbury to Reading, 176
Rochefoucauld - Liancourt, Duc de la, 208
Rockville Gap, 134
Rokeby Furnace, 29
Rose, Robert H., 248
Rose Tree Hunt, 85
Roosevelt, Nicholas J., 270
Roosevelt, Theodore, 238, 307
Ross, George, 92
Rouse, Henry R., legacy of, 298
Royall, Mrs. Annie, quoted, 90
"Runaway, the great," 178
Rush, Benjamin, 160
Ruskin, John, quoted, 23

Saegerstown, 282
Safe Harbor, 46
St. Clair, General Arthur, 71
St. John's Rock, 100
St. Mary's, 319
Salt wells, 71, 115, 104, 285, 311
Sandy Lick, 306
Sang Hollow, 163
Scenery Hill, 114
Schaefferstown, 131
Schellsburg, 69
Shoepf, Johan, quoted, 64, 226, 258
School teaching without maps, 15
Schooley's Gap, 221
Schuylkill County, 213
Schuylkill Gap, 215
Schuylkill Haven, 213, 215
Schuylkill River, 23, 267
Scotland, 95
Scranton, 206, 239, 249

347

INDEX

Searight, Thomas B., 110
Seitz, Don C., quoted, 54
Selin, Anthony, 170
Selinsgrove, 169, 170
Seneca Indians, 318
Seneca Oil, 292
"Serious road," 323
Shackamaxon, 175
Shade Gap, 143
Shades of Death, 225
Shamokin (Sunbury), 52
Shannopin's Town, 67
Sharon, 275
Sharp Mountain, 252
Shenango River, 270
"Shunpike," the, 281
Shawnee-on-Delaware, 225, 236
Sheshequin trail, 188, 190
Sheshequin, Vale of, 202
Shickshinny, 207
Shikellimy, 142, 170, 176, 177
Shipyards, 22, 23, 79
Shippensburg, 61, 92
Shippensville, 304
Shoemaker, Colonel George, 215
Shoemaker, Colonel Henry W., 147, 168, 328
Shohola Creek, 240, 241
Shohola Falls, 240
Sideling Hill, 64, 99, 145
Sigourney, L y d i a Huntley, quoted, 220
Silliman, Professor, geologist, 255
Sinking Creek, 147
Sinnemahoning Creek, 193, 324, 327
"Sinnemahoning Deer Chase," 326
Six Nations, 175, 262, 279, 317
Slatington, 256
Smethport, 198, 323
Smith, James, road adventures of, 67
Smith, Joseph, 286
Smith, Thomas, 92
Smith, Dr. William, 142
Snyder County, 170
Snyder, Simon, 171
Snow Shoe, 332
Somerset County, 70
Song that reunited mother and daughter, 93
Sosondowa, 321
South Fork dam, 162

South Mountain, 29, 51
South Mountain Hospital, 129
Spanish Hill, 199
Sparks, Jared, quoted, 101
Spaulding, Bishop, quoted, 274
Stage coach tales, 105, 107
Stage driver, invitation of, 263
Standing Stone: Huntingdon, 145; on the North Branch, 202
Starucca Creek, 247
State College, 332
Steam canal boat, first, 164
Steamboats, first, 43, 44, 112, 270, 310
Stevens, Thaddeus, 52, 97
Stoddartsville, 225
Stogies, origin of, 119
Stourbridge Lion, 242
Stowe, Harriet Beecher, 195
Stoyestown, 70
Strasburg, 31, 46
Stratagem, fort captured by Indian, 291
Straw paper, first made at Meadville, 282
Stroud, Colonel Jacob, 230
Stroudsburg, 222, 223, 230, 231
Sugar maple trees, avenue of, 236
Sullivan County, 180
Sullivan, General, 87, 202, 225
Sullivan's Trail, 229
Sunbury, 175, 176, 334
Susquehanna and Waterford turnpike, 301, 317
Susquehanna County, 246
Susquehanna Gap, 133
Susquehanna River, 133, 167, 201, 247, 329
Susquehannocks, 121, 147
Sutcliffe, Robert, quoted, 37
Swatara Creek, 87, 176
Swatara Gap, 133
Swiftwater Creek, 228

Tamanend, Story of, 266
Tamaqua, 219
Tamarack Swamp, 328
Tanacharison, Chief, 271
Tarachawagon (Conrad Weiser), 131, 170
Tarascon, Louis Anastasius, and navigation of Ohio River, 269

INDEX

Taverns of turnpike days, 104, 109, 110, 111, 119
Taylor, Bayard, quoted, 46, 82, 126; Mrs. Bayard Taylor, quoted, 84
Teedyuscung, 231, 262
Telegraph, primitive, 35
Thachnectoris, 334
Thanksgiving proclamation, first, 48
Thomson, Alexander, letter of, 95
Thomson, Charles, quoted, 235
Three Mountain Road, 94
Tiadaghton Creek, 187
Timrod, Henry, quoted, 250
Tinicum Island, 79
Tivoli, 180
Tioga County, 188
Tioga Point, 189, 190
Tioga Valley, 188
Tionesta, 296
Tionesta Creek, 297, 298
Titusville, 292
Toll house at Addison, 102
Towanda, 202
Transportation, progress in, 124
"Treatise on the Improvement of Canal Navigation," Fulton's, 88
Trees at Braddock's grave, 103
Triangle, story of the, 16, 279
Troxelville, 169
Tucquan Lake, 46
Tuckahoe Valley, 316
Tulpehocken, 130
Tulpehocken Creek, 127
Tunnels, early, 155, 161, 214
Tunkhannock, 205, 248, 249
Turkey Foot, 67
Turtle Creek, 72
Tuscarawas Trail, 272
Tuscarora Creek, 55, 138
Tuscarora Gap, 136
Tuscarora Mountains, 55, 57, 64
Tuscarora Summit, 63, 64
Tussey Mountain, 147
Tyrone, 316, 334

Underground railway adventures, 85, 86
Union County, 168
Uniontown, 104, 108
Upland, 80
Upper Strasburg, 56

Valley Forge, 23, 26, 27
Van Dyke, Henry, quoted, 211, 227
Van Horn, Cornelius, 283
Venango County, 290, 293
Venango, Fort, 281

Walking Purchase, the, 234, 259, 265
Wallace, John, 96
Wallenpaupack Creek, 228, 229, 239, 240
Wallpack Bend, 237
Wapwallopen, 207, 250
Warren, 298
Warren County, 297, 321
Warrior's Gap, 66, 67, 99
Warrior's Mark, 333
Warville, J. P. Brissot de, quoted, 43
Washington, 114
Washington and Jefferson College, 115
Washington Borough, 42
Washington Island, 314
Washington, George: in Montgomery County, 23; damage to carriage of, 36; at Ligonier, 71; with Braddock, 73; on the Chester road, 78; plans for canals, 87; on the " great road," 91; at Carlisle, 92; adventures on Youghiogheny, 101; at Great Meadows, 102; on Laurel Ridge, 107; at Brownsville, 111; owner of land at Washington, 115; lands in Washington County, 118; on Neshaminy, 266; at Logstown, 271; in Beaver County, 273; on French Creek, 281; at Franklin, 291; in the Alleghenies, 314; uses Logan as a spy, 334.
Washington Springs, 107
Water Gap, 263
Water Street, 147
Waterford, 281
Waugh-wau-wame, 219
Wayne County, 237, 239, 244, 245
Wayne, General Anthony, 96, 121, 278
Waynesboro, 96, 97
Waynesburg, 120
Weikert, 169

349

INDEX

Weiser, Conrad, 130, 143, 170, 210, 271
Weissport, 254
Wellsboro, 192
Welsh Mountains, 28
Wernersville, 130
West Alexander, 119
West Chester, 28, 180
Westinghouse, George, 287
Westmoreland, 223
Westmoreland County, 70
Western Pennsylvania boundary dispute with Virginia, 117
Western Pennsylvania lands of George Washington, 103, 118, 123
Westsylvania, petition for organization of province of, 117
Weygadt Mountain, 262, 263
Whiskey Insurrection, 63, 73, 91, 92, 112
Whitehall, 256
White Haven Junction, 257
Whittier, John G., quoted, 86
Wiconisco Creek, 168
Wilkes-Barre, 206, 219, 249
Wilkes-Barre Mountain, 221
William Penn Highway, 124
Williams, Charles, 189
Williamson Road, story of the, 189
Williamsport, 179, 183, 188
Willis, N. P., quoted, 137, 201, 238
Wills Creek, 100
Wills Mountain, 99
Wilmot, David 202
Wilson, Alexander, quoted, 133, 200, 235, 264
Wilson, James, 92
Wind Gap, 225, 234, 259, 260, 263
Winola, Lake, 206, 249
Wissahickon Creek, 25
Womelsdorf, 130
Wright, Samuel, 35
Wright's Ferry, 35, 37
Wrightstown, 260
Wrightsville, 35
Wyalusing, 204
Wyoming, 201, 224, 306
Wyoming County, 205
Wyoming Massacre, 176
Wyoming Path, 225
Wyoming Valley, 140, 206, 219, 222, 223, 230, 250
Wysox Valley, 202

Yellow Breeches Creek, 91
York, 33, 49
York County, 47
"York," railway locomotive of 1831, 49
Youghiogheny River, 72, 102
Young Woman's Creek, 328

Zeisberger David, 274, 296, 297, 306
Zelienople, 286